DISJUNCTIVISM

Matthew Soteriou

LONDON AND NEW YORK

First published 2016
by Routledge
2 Park Square, Milton Park, Abingdon, Oxon OX14 4RN

Simultaneously published in the USA and Canada
by Routledge
711 Third Avenue, New York, NY 10017

Routledge is an imprint of the Taylor & Francis Group, an informa business

© 2016 Matthew Soteriou

The right of Matthew Soteriou to be identified as the author of this work has been asserted by him in accordance with sections 77 and 78 of the Copyright, Designs and Patents Act 1988.

All rights reserved. No part of this book may be reprinted or reproduced or utilised in any form or by any electronic, mechanical, or other means, now known or hereafter invented, including photocopying and recording, or in any information storage or retrieval system, without permission in writing from the publishers.

Trademark notice: Product or corporate names may be trademarks or registered trademarks, and are used only for identification and explanation without intent to infringe.

British Library Cataloguing in Publication Data
A catalogue record for this book is available from the British Library

Library of Congress Cataloging in Publication Data
Sherman, Jon Foley, 1972-
A strange proximity : stage presence, failure, and the ethics of attention / Jon Foley Sherman.
pages cm
Includes bibliographical references and index.
ISBN 978-1-138-90776-8 (hardback) — ISBN 978-1-138-90777-5 (pbk.) — ISBN 978-1-315-69490-0 (ebook) 1. Acting—Psychological aspects. 2. Stage presence. I. Title.
PN2058.S53 2016
792.02′8019—dc23
2015036214

ISBN13: 978-0-415-68621-1 (hbk)
ISBN13: 978-0-415-68622-8 (pbk)
ISBN13: 978-1-315-63683-2 (ebk)

Typeset in Joanna
by Swales & Willis Ltd, Exeter, Devon, UK
Printed and bound in Great Britain by
Ashford Colour Press Ltd, Gosport, Hampshire

DISJUNCTIVISM

It is commonly held that the experiences involved in cases of perception, illusion and hallucination all have the same nature. Disjunctivists deny this. They maintain that the kind of experience you have when you perceive the world isn't one you could be having if you were hallucinating. A number of important debates in the philosophy of mind and epistemology turn on the question of whether this disjunctivist view is tenable.

This is the first book-length introduction to this contested issue. Matthew Soteriou explains the accounts of perception that disjunctivists seek to defend, such as naïve realism, and the accounts to which they are opposed, such as sense-datum theories and representationalist theories. He goes on to introduce and assess key questions that arise in these debates:

- Is disjunctivism consistent with what has been established by the science of perception?
- Does introspective reflection support naïve realism?
- Can disjunctivism be motivated by appeal to the role that perception plays in enabling us to think demonstratively about mind-independent objects and qualities in our environment?
- Does disjunctivism offer the best account of perceptual knowledge?
- What can disjunctivists say about the nature of hallucination and illusion?

Including chapter summaries, annotated further reading and a glossary, this book is an ideal starting point for anyone studying disjunctivism for the first time, as well as for more advanced students and researchers.

Matthew Soteriou is a professor of Philosophy at the University of Warwick, UK. He is the author of *The Mind's Construction: The Ontology of Mind and Mental Action* (2013), and co-editor (with Lucy O'Brien) of *Mental Actions* (2009).

NEW PROBLEMS OF PHILOSOPHY
Series Editor: José Luis Bermúdez

'Routledge's *New Problems of Philosophy* series has a most impressive line-up of topical volumes aimed at upper-level undergraduate and graduate students in philosophy and at others with interests in cutting edge philosophical work. The authors are influential figures in their respective fields and notably adept at synthesizing and explaining intricate topics fairly and comprehensively.'

– *John Heil, Monash University, Australia, and Washington University, St Louis, USA*

'This is an outstanding collection of volumes. The topics are well chosen and the authors are outstanding. They will be fine texts in a wide range of courses.'

– *Stephen Stich, Rutgers University, USA*

The *New Problems of Philosophy* series provides accessible and engaging surveys of the most important problems in contemporary philosophy. Each book examines a topic or theme that has either emerged on the philosophical landscape in recent years, or a longstanding problem refreshed in light of recent work in philosophy and related disciplines. Clearly explaining the nature of the problem at hand and assessing attempts to answer it, books in the series are excellent starting-points for undergraduate and graduate students wishing to study a single topic in depth. They will also be essential reading for professional philosophers. Additional features include chapter summaries, further reading and a glossary of technical terms.

Also available:

Analyticity
Cory Juhl and Eric Loomis

Fiction and Fictionalism
Mark Sainsbury

Physicalism
Daniel Stoljar

Noncognitivism in Ethics
Mark Schroeder

Moral Epistemology
Aaron Zimmerman

Embodied Cognition
Lawrence Shapiro

Self-Knowledge
Brie Gertler

Semantic Externalism
Jesper Kallestrup

Consequentialism
Julia Driver

Images
John V. Kulvicki

Attention
Wayne Wu

Egalitarianism
Iwao Hirose

Cognitive Phenomenology
Elijah Chudnoff

Forthcoming:

Metaphysics of Identity
André Gallois

Perception
Adam Pautz

Modal Epistemology
Otávio Bueno and Scott Shalkowski

Consciousness
Rocco J. Gennaro

Abstract Entities
Sam Cowling

Cognitive Architecture
Philip Robbins

Properties
David Robb

Innateness and Cognition
Mark Cain

Relativism
Maria Baghramian and Annalisa Coliva

Imagination
Fabian Dorsch

Social Metaphysics
Amie L. Thomasson

CONTENTS

Acknowledgements		x
Introduction		1
1	**Sense-datum theories and the argument from hallucination**	5
	1.1 The relational assumption	6
	1.2 Arguments from hallucination	16
	1.3 Chapter summary	26
	Notes	28
	Further reading	28
	References	28
2	**Representational content, the science of perception, and disjunctivism about conscious character**	30
	2.1 Representational content and the science of perception	32
	2.2 Disjunctivism about conscious character	39
	2.3 Hinton's disjunctivist commitments	48
	2.4 Chapter summary	52
	Notes	53
	Further reading	54
	References	54

3 Does introspective reflection support naïve realism? 56
3.1 Relationalist and representationalist accounts of the phenomenology of perceptual experience 58
3.2 Martin's phenomenological argument for naïve realism 65
3.3 Objections to Martin's argument 74
3.4 Chapter summary 80
Notes 81
Further reading 81
References 82

4 Naïve realism, perceptual acquaintance, and perceptually based thought 83
4.1 The explanatory role of the phenomenal character of perception 84
4.2 Qualia and phenomenal concepts 89
4.3 Campbell on the explanatory role of conscious perception 93
4.4 Objections to Campbell's proposal 101
4.5 Chapter summary 111
Notes 113
Further reading 114
References 114

5 Epistemological disjunctivism 117
5.1 Epistemic asymmetries between 'good' and 'bad' cases 120
5.2 McDowell's epistemological disjunctivism 127
5.3 Objections to McDowell's epistemological disjunctivism 136
5.4 Epistemological disjunctivism and scepticism 145
5.5 Chapter summary 151
Notes 153
Further reading 153
References 154

6 Disjunctivist accounts of hallucination and illusion 157
6.1 A causal argument against naïve realism 158
6.2 Martin's negative epistemic account of causally matching hallucination 169
6.3 Perceptual illusion 184
6.4 Chapter summary 191
Notes 193
Further reading 194
References 195

7	**Varieties of disjunctivism**	**197**
	7.1 Fundamental kinds and psychological difference	198
	7.2 Disjunctivism and common element claims	203
	7.3 Epistemological disjunctivism and its metaphysical commitments	206
	7.4 Disjunctivism in Snowdon's argument against the causal theory of perception	208
	7.5 Conclusion	211
	7.6 Chapter summary	211
	Notes	213
	Further reading	213
	References	214
	Glossary	217
	Index	225

ACKNOWLEDGEMENTS

I owe thanks to colleagues and students at the Philosophy Department at Warwick University for helpful discussions of this work. To Hemdat Lerman and Guy Longworth I owe special thanks for providing me with extremely useful written comments on a draft of the book. I am grateful to Tony Bruce and Adam Johnson of Routledge for their encouragement and patience, and I thank Susanna Siegel and two anonymous referees for their very helpful comments and advice.

My deepest thanks go to my wife, Sandra, who has helped me in more ways than I could ever hope to express, and to whom I dedicate this book with all my love.

INTRODUCTION

Perceptual experiences are often divided into three broad categories: veridical perceptions, illusions, and hallucinations. A common way of distinguishing these three categories is as follows. In the case of a veridical perception you perceive an object in your environment as it really is – for example, you see a red object in your environment and you really do see its red colour. In the case of an illusion, you succeed in perceiving some object in your environment, but the object you perceive isn't the way it perceptually seems to you to be – for example, you see a green object in your environment, but the object looks red to you. And in the case of hallucination, you fail to perceive any object in your environment – for example, you have an experience as of a red object, but you fail to perceive any object in your environment. Many maintain that the same account should be given of the nature of the conscious experience that occurs in each of these three cases. Those who hold a disjunctive theory of perception deny this. And they reject the claim that the same kind of experience is common to all three cases because they hold views about the nature of veridical perception that are inconsistent with it.

So at the heart of the disputes between disjunctivists and their opponents is a disagreement over the answer that should be given to the following question: to what extent, and in what ways, should the existence of illusion and hallucination impose constraints on the account we give of our perception of the world? Roughly speaking, the disjunctivist seeks to defend a view of our conscious perception of the world that would be untenable if there were in place the constraints that her opponent claims there are. Not all disjunctivists defend exactly the same view of perception, and one finds widely diverging views of perception among those who oppose disjunctivism. But nonetheless, there is a common pattern of argumentation in the to and fro of the debates between disjunctivists and their opponents. The opponent of disjunctivism argues that reflection on the existence of illusion and hallucination can show that the disjunctivist's favoured view of perception is not a viable option, and the disjunctivist, in turn, attempts to identify and undermine assumptions upon which such arguments are based. Disjunctivism can therefore be thought of as a defensive strategy that is adopted in defence of some positive view of perception, in the face of considerations that are invoked to challenge and undermine that positive view of perception (where the considerations in question centre on claims about what is common to cases of veridical perception, illusion, and hallucination).

A number of substantive and important philosophical debates turn on the question of whether this form of disjunctive, defensive strategy is successful: debates about the metaphysics and phenomenal character of perceptual consciousness, debates about the relation between – and differences between – thought and sensory experience, debates about the role played by conscious perception in grounding our concepts of the objects and features in the environment that we perceive, debates about the warranting role played by perception in grounding our acquisition of propositional knowledge about our surroundings, debates about self-knowledge, debates about our concept of perception, and debates about the metaphysical status of our manifest view of the world. The aim of this book is to introduce the reader to these debates by providing a survey of the various motivations and arguments for a disjunctive approach to perception, and by outlining and assessing the various objections that have been raised against it.

We'll start, in Chapter 1, by considering the argument from hallucination for a sense-datum theory of perception. The sense-datum theory is one that disjunctivists reject. Many opponents of disjunctivism also reject sense-datum theories. But there are disjunctivists who disagree with their opponents about where the argument from hallucination goes wrong. So an examination of the argument, and the possible responses to it, will help to illuminate the nature of some of the core debates between disjunctivists and their opponents. Our discussion of sense-datum theories of perception will also be used to introduce an assumption about the metaphysical structure of conscious perceptual experience that a number of disjunctivists wish to endorse and defend. This is the assumption that the conscious perceptual experience that one has when one genuinely perceives the world is a *relational* phenomenon. Clarification of the assumption will turn out to be important to an understanding of some of the core commitments of these disjunctivists.

Chapter 2 will introduce the *non*-relational views of perceptual experience that are endorsed by the majority of those who reject sense-datum theories of perception. It will also introduce the relational, naïve realist accounts of veridical perception to which such non-relational accounts are opposed. In this chapter we will discuss whether these naïve realist accounts of conscious perception are inconsistent with what has been established by the science of perception, and we will outline how naïve realists have appealed to a form of disjunctivism about the phenomenal character of perceptual experience in defence of their account of veridical perception. Here the reader will be introduced to the disjunctive, defensive strategy first proposed by J. M. Hinton.

In Chapter 3 we will consider whether introspective reflection supports the naïve realist's account of the phenomenal character of veridical perception. In particular, we'll outline and assess an argument that M. G. F. Martin has presented in support of the claim that it does. In Chapter 4 we will outline and critically evaluate further arguments that have been appealed to in support of the naïve realist, relationalist view of the phenomenal character of conscious perception. These arguments, which are principally due to John Campbell, purport to show that we need to adopt the relational, naïve realist view if we are to accommodate adequately the distinctive role that conscious perception plays in enabling one to think about the mind-independent objects and qualities one perceives. Campbell's contention is that only a naïve realist account of phenomenal character can accommodate an epistemic role that conscious perception plays in grounding the *concepts* we possess of the mind-independent objects and qualities we perceive.

In Chapter 5 we will continue to examine epistemological motivations for disjunctivism, but we will move on from debates about the putative role played by the phenomenal character of perception in grounding our possession of *concepts* of the items we perceive, and we will instead focus on forms of disjunctivism that are adopted in defence of the role played by perception in providing us with *propositional* knowledge about our surroundings: knowledge *that* things are thus and so in our environment. Here we will focus primarily on the form of epistemological disjunctivism that has been advocated by John McDowell, and we will discuss whether those espousing McDowell's epistemological disjunctivism need commit themselves to a form of metaphysical disjunctivism.

In Chapter 6 we will consider what disjunctivists can and should say about hallucination and illusion. Here we will discuss the difficulties faced by the naïve realist in providing an adequate account of so-called 'causally matching' hallucination, i.e. a hallucination that involves the same kind of proximate cause and brain state as a veridical perception. We will also discuss whether it is right to assume that there is a uniform account to be given of the experiences that are involved in all cases of illusion and hallucination; we will consider debates and disagreements over which experiences it is appropriate to count as 'illusory'; and we will consider how such debates impact on the options that are open to disjunctivists when it comes to providing accounts of the kinds of experiences that are involved in different cases of illusion and hallucination.

And finally, having considered some of the central concerns and arguments of some of the main protagonists in debates about disjunctivism, in Chapter 7 we will review and note some of the differences between the views of perception that fall under the disjunctivist label, and we will consider and clarify some of the discussions about different varieties, and formulations of, disjunctivism that one finds in the literature.

1

SENSE-DATUM THEORIES AND THE ARGUMENT FROM HALLUCINATION

This chapter will introduce an argument that purports to show that the fact that we can hallucinate should lead us to recognise, and accommodate, the following significant constraint on an account of perception: whenever one has a conscious perceptual experience one is perceptually aware of entities – sense-data – that are not the mind-independent material objects that we ordinarily take ourselves to perceive. This form of argument from hallucination threatens to undermine the intuitive thought that perception provides one with direct and immediate access to one's environment, for it threatens to show that we can at best be perceptually aware of objects in our environment, and their properties, in an 'indirect way', through being *directly* aware of these *sense-data* and *their* properties. The task of responding to that challenge, by showing what is wrong with such arguments for 'sense-datum' theories of perception, is sometimes labelled 'the problem of perception'.

Disjunctivists reject sense-datum theories, and they claim to have an adequate solution to the problem of perception. However, so too do many opponents of disjunctivism. Thus it would be a mistake to think that the disjunctive theory of perception is distinguished by its rejection of sense-datum theories of perception. But although disjunctivists and many of their opponents are united in their rejection of sense-datum theories, they nonetheless disagree on where the argument from hallucination goes wrong. So an examination of the argument, and the possible responses to it, will help to illuminate the nature of some of the core debates between disjunctivists and their opponents, including those opponents who reject sense-datum theories.

More positively, consideration of the argument from hallucination for sense-datum theories can also be helpful when it comes to understanding the metaphysical commitments of some of those adopting a disjunctive account of perception, as there are disjunctivists who think that there is a background metaphysical assumption implicit in the sense-datum approach that should be made explicit and given serious consideration. This is the assumption that conscious perceptual experience is a *relational* phenomenon. As we shall see, a number of disjunctivists advocate a metaphysical claim that is very close to the 'relational' view of experience that seems to be assumed by sense-datum theorists; so, clarification of the assumption will turn out to be important to an understanding of some of the core commitments of these disjunctivists. In section 1.1 I shall introduce and clarify the sense-datum theorist's background metaphysical assumption that conscious perceptual experience is a relational phenomenon, and I shall mention some initial grounds for thinking that the assumption has some warrant. In section 1.2 we shall see how the assumption can be deployed by the sense-datum theorist in an argument from hallucination.

1.1 The relational assumption

Let's start with an example of a psychological phenomenon that I think it should not be controversial to regard as relational: the activity of looking at something. A relation obtains only if its relata exist, i.e. the entities that stand in that relation. In the case of *looking at*, one of the terms of the relation is the subject doing the looking, and the other term of the relation is the thing being looked at by that subject. So we have an instance of looking *at* only if the following relata of the relation exist: the subject doing the looking, and the thing she is looking at. While it is possible for a subject to be looking *for* something that doesn't exist, she can't be looking *at* something that doesn't exist. It may seem to a subject as though she is looking at something when she isn't, but then this wouldn't be a genuine case of looking at. Note that the activity of looking isn't itself one of the relata of the relation of looking at. That is to say, the activity of looking at something isn't itself looked at by the subject who is doing the looking. However, when a subject is looking at something she may be aware that she is looking at something, as well as being aware of what she is looking at.

With these points in mind, let's now turn to the proposal that conscious perceptual experience is a relational phenomenon. According to those who advocate this view, when you have a conscious perceptual experience it seems, from the inside, as though you are *perceptually aware* of various entities, and this is to be explained by the fact that when you have a conscious perceptual experience you *are* perceptually aware of various entities. A distinctive kind of conscious, perceptual *relation* obtains between you, as subject of the experience, and various entities that you are perceptually aware of in having that experience. This relation of conscious perceptual awareness only obtains if its relata exist, and in this case one of the terms of the relation is the subject having the conscious perceptual experience, and the other terms of the relation are the entities the subject is perceptually aware of in virtue of having the experience. The conscious perceptual experience is not itself one of the relata of this perceptual relation. (Just as in the case of looking at, the activity of looking isn't itself one of the relata of the relation of looking at.) Nonetheless, the obtaining of this conscious perceptual relation is something you can be aware of in having that experience. When you reflect on the conscious perceptual experience you are having at any given time, you may be aware of a conscious perceptual relation that obtains, as well as the entities you are thereby perceptually related to. For example, I now believe that I am consciously, perceptually aware of a blue, round thing. I am not *perceptually* aware of that perceptual relation. But my belief that the relation obtains is not groundless. The relationalist will claim that my belief is grounded in the phenomenology of the experience I am having. That is to say, it is grounded in reflection on what it is like for me to have that experience. In reflecting on what it is like for me to have the experience, I am aware of the obtaining of the relation.

When one has a conscious perceptual experience, one is perceptually aware of various entities and one is in a position to be aware of being perceptually aware of those entities. (Again, compare here the thought that in the case of looking at, you can be aware that you are looking at something, as well as being aware of what you are looking at.)

Those who advocate this relational view of conscious perceptual experience suggest that given that conscious perceptual experience has this relational structure, in providing an account of conscious perceptual experience one should at least aim to address the following key questions:

(i) What is distinctive of the kind of conscious perceptual *relation* that obtains when you have a conscious perceptual experience?
(ii) What kind of entities are you perceptually aware of when that relation obtains?[1]

To help clarify this relational view of conscious perceptual experience, let's compare it with a couple of alternatives. According to one alternative, to have a conscious perceptual experience is to undergo a certain kind of mental *event*. The occurrence of this kind of event does not in itself involve the obtaining of a relation of conscious perceptual awareness, for one can undergo an event of this kind without being perceptually aware of anything. On this view, in providing an account of conscious perceptual experience one's aim should be to provide an account of the nature of this sort of event and its distinctive properties, and this doesn't require characterising a distinctive kind of conscious perceptual relation that obtains whenever the event occurs.

According to another alternative, to have a conscious perceptual experience is to be in a certain kind of mental *state*.[2] We might think of this mental state as a psychological property of the subject having the experience. The obtaining of this kind of mental state does not in itself involve the obtaining of a relation of conscious perceptual awareness, for one can be in a perceptual state of this kind without being perceptually aware of anything. From this perspective, in providing an account of conscious perceptual experience, one's aim should be to provide an account of the nature of this kind of mental state, and its distinctive properties, and this doesn't require characterising a distinctive kind of conscious perceptual relation that obtains whenever the state obtains.

So far I have mentioned three different categories that one might appeal to in providing an account of conscious perceptual experience: relation, event, and state. It could be held that we need to appeal to all three of these categories. In one such view, in providing an account of conscious perceptual experience one will need to appeal to the occurrence of psychological events, and the obtaining of psychological states, *as well as* the obtaining of a conscious perceptual relation. This is consistent with the relational approach as I am construing it here. Someone adopting the relational view of conscious perceptual experience need not deny that perceptual events occur, and perceptual states obtain, when one has a conscious perceptual experience, just as someone who holds that *looking at* is a relational phenomenon need not deny that perceptual events occur, and perceptual states obtain, whenever a subject is looking at something. What is distinctive of the relational approach to conscious perceptual experience, is the claim that an appeal to the obtaining of a relation of conscious perceptual awareness is *essential* to an account of conscious perceptual experience. So, while advocates of this view may agree that when one has a conscious perceptual experience psychological events do occur and perceptual states do obtain, they deny that your conscious perceptual experience is just some psychological event or state, or some combination of both, that can occur and/or obtain, whether or not a relation of conscious perceptual awareness obtains.

In later chapters I shall be looking in detail at some specific arguments for a relational view. At this point I just want to introduce some initial considerations that might be thought to lend support to the view. In particular, I shall briefly introduce, in outline, the suggestion that there is positive introspective support for the view, and an absence of introspective support for the alternative, non-relational views.

Let's start with some of the less controversial claims that are often taken to be common ground in these discussions. As a self-conscious subject, when you have a conscious perceptual experience, you are typically in a position to know that you are having a conscious perceptual experience, and you are typically in a position to know something about the kind of conscious perceptual experience that you are having. Moreover, there is something it is like for you to be having that conscious perceptual experience, and as a self-conscious subject you are typically in a position to reflect on what it is like for you to be having that experience, and know what it is like for you to have that experience. Such knowledge doesn't depend on the testimony of others, but is, rather, acquired via the distinctive mode of access that you have to your own mental states/events, by virtue of being the subject of those mental states/events. This distinctive mode of access that one has to one's own mental states/events, by virtue of being the subject of those mental states/events, is often referred to as 'introspection'.

With these background assumptions in mind, one thing a relationalist may be keen to highlight is the following. When you attempt to introspect those qualities of your experience that determine what it is like for you to be having it, you find yourself attending to qualities that are neither qualities of some psychological event you are undergoing, nor qualities of some psychological state that you are in. For example, as I now introspectively reflect on what it is like for me to be having my current experience I find myself attending to a blue, round thing. But I don't think I am thereby attending to a blue, round psychological event that I am undergoing, or a blue, round psychological state that I am in. And on the assumption that these qualities – blue and round – are not properties of my experience, they can't be the what-it-is-like properties of *my experience*. We find something like this line of thought expressed by the sense-datum theorist G. E. Moore (1903). He notes that when one introspectively reflects on a 'sensation of blue', the quality that one seems to be in a position to attend to directly is the colour blue, and this is a quality that it is unlikely that the sensation itself actually possesses.

From this it doesn't follow that I'm not, after all, introspectively aware of the conscious perceptual experience I am now having, and it doesn't follow that it is not possible for me to reflect introspectively on what it is like for me to have the experience I am now having. What does seem true, though, is that the qualities that I seem to be attending to when I attend introspectively to my experience (blueness, roundness) appear to play an important role in determining what it is like for me to be having this experience, even if those qualities are not themselves what-it-is-like properties of my experience. So, for example, if when introspectively attending to my experience I found myself attending to different qualities – for example greenness and squareness – then what it would be like for me to be having the experience would be different.

The relationalist is in a position to offer the following explanation of these observations. Your conscious perceptual experience involves the obtaining of a conscious perceptual relation. Introspective reflection on your experience involves being aware of what you are related to. There is something it is like for you to have a conscious perceptual experience insofar as there is something it is like for you to be the subject of the conscious perceptual relation that obtains when you have that experience, and this is determined, at least in part, by what you are related to. So the quality of blueness, what *that* quality is like, while not a quality of experience itself, nonetheless determines, at least in part, what it is like for you to be consciously, perceptually aware of it.

We find something of this idea, I think, in the positive proposal that G. E. Moore endorses:

> To be aware of the sensation of blue is not to be aware of a ... 'thing' of which 'blue' and some other element are constituent parts in the same sense in which blue and glass are constituents of a blue bead. It is to be aware of an awareness of blue ...
>
> When we know that the sensation of blue exists, the fact we know is that there exists an awareness of blue. And this awareness is not merely ... itself something distinct and unique, utterly different from blue: it also has a perfectly distinct and unique relation to blue.
>
> (1903: 40)

We've so far looked at the suggestion that there is positive introspective support for the relational view. Let's now turn to the suggestion that there is also an absence of introspective support for the alternative approaches. According to these alternative approaches, your conscious perceptual experience is some psychological event that you undergo, and/or some psychological state that obtains, and the occurrence and obtaining of these psychological events and states are not in themselves sufficient for the obtaining of a relation of conscious perceptual awareness. They can occur and obtain without you being perceptually aware of anything. A negative claim that the relationalist may want to push here is the following: when you have a conscious perceptual experience and you reflect introspectively on the experience you are having, it doesn't seem to you as though you are in a position to focus introspectively in on, and discern, some conscious psychological element that is insufficient for perceptual contact with something. That is to say, introspective reflection does not appear to reveal something meeting the following description: some conscious element of your current situation – for example some conscious event or state – that isn't in itself enough to make you perceptually aware of something, which isn't in itself sufficient for the obtaining of that conscious perceptual relation, for attending to the conscious experience seems to involve attending to an object of which you are perceptually aware. It seems, from the inside, so to speak, as though one cannot focus introspectively on one's conscious perceptual experience *without* attending to some object one is perceptually aware of in having that experience. My attempt to now shift my attention from that blue, round object and its properties to some psychological event or state and its properties – a conscious event or state that isn't in itself enough to put me in perceptual contact with that object – seems to fail.

I think we also find this line of thought in Moore in the following passage:

> Although I know for certain both that I have had many experiences, and that I have had experiences of many different kinds, I feel very doubtful whether to say the first is the same thing as to say that there have been many *events*, each of which was an experience and an experience of mine ... The proposition that I have had experiences does not necessarily entail the proposition that there have been many *events* which *were* experiences; and I cannot satisfy myself that I am acquainted with any events of the supposed kind [my emphasis].
>
> (1925: 123)

From the point of view of the relationalist, the obvious diagnosis to be given of the failure of my attempt to shift my introspective attention from the object I am perceptually aware of to some psychological event I am undergoing is the following. My conscious perceptual experience is not some event/state that is insufficient for the obtaining of a relation of conscious perceptual awareness. The conscious perceptual element of my current situation is *sufficient* for the obtaining of that relation. That is why I cannot focus on my conscious perceptual experience without attending to the entities that are constituents of the conscious perceptual relation that obtains when I have a conscious perceptual experience.

The relationalist might concede that perhaps there are psychological events that I am undergoing when I have my conscious perceptual experience that are not sufficient for the obtaining of the relation of conscious perceptual awareness. But she is likely to maintain that such events are not introspectively discernible (as Moore puts it, 'I cannot satisfy myself that I am acquainted with any events of the supposed kind'), whereas my conscious perceptual experience *is* introspectively discernible. Moreover, the relationalist might also perhaps concede that when I have a conscious perceptual experience I am thereby in a mental state that plays a certain kind of functional role, one that plays a causal role in producing other mental states and behaviour. And perhaps it is possible for a state of this functionally specified kind to obtain when the relation of conscious perceptual awareness does not obtain. Perhaps it is even possible for me to be in a state with this specified functional role when I am not having a *conscious* perceptual experience at all. But then in that case, the relationalist will say, my conscious perceptual experience is not to be identified with this functionally specified psychological state, and this functionally specified psychological state is not to be identified with what I am introspectively aware of when I introspectively reflect on my conscious perceptual experience. When I have a conscious perceptual experience, what is introspectively discernible is the conscious perceptual relation that obtains, rather than some functionally specified psychological state that can obtain whether or not that conscious perceptual relation obtains.

The relationalist may then argue that her view accommodates, and provides the best account of, what it is like to have a conscious perceptual experience, and also what it is like to introspect that experience. Introspecting your experience seems to involve looking at entities of which you are perceptually aware. There is something odd in the following request: introspect the experience you are having now while making sure that you don't look at anything. Indeed, the activity of introspecting your experience seems itself to be a relational phenomenon in the same way that the activity of looking at something is. It seems to be an activity that depends on the obtaining of the same kind of conscious perceptual relation that looking at something depends on. And this would make sense if the conscious perceptual experience essentially involves the obtaining of a conscious perceptual relation.

I suggested that according to this relationalist view of conscious perceptual experience introspective reflection on such experience involves being aware of what one is consciously related to, and the manner in which one is consciously related to it. If this is correct, then such introspective evidence may play a role in helping one to answer the two questions that I earlier suggested the relationalists think one should aim to address in providing an account of conscious perceptual experience:

(i) What is distinctive of the kind of conscious perceptual *relation* that obtains when you have a conscious perceptual experience?
(ii) What kind of entities are you perceptually aware of when that relation obtains?

In the following passage Moore notes a difficulty that seems to be involved in introspectively fixing on, and articulating the nature of, the conscious relation itself, as opposed to what we are related to.

> when we refer to introspection and try to discover what the sensation of blue is, it is very easy to suppose that we have before us only a single term. The term 'blue' is easy enough to distinguish, but the other element which I have called 'consciousness' – that which sensation of blue has in common with sensation of green – is extremely difficult to fix. . . . in general, that which makes the sensation of blue a mental fact seems to escape us: it seems, if I may use a metaphor, to be transparent – we look through it and see nothing but the blue; we may be convinced that there *is something* but what it is no philosopher, I think, has yet clearly recognised.
>
> The moment we try to fix our attention upon consciousness and to see *what*, distinctly, it is, it seems to vanish: it seems as if we had before us a mere emptiness. When we try to introspect the sensation of blue, all we can see is the blue: the other element is as if it were diaphanous.
>
> (1903: 41)

However, when Moore says that the conscious element of the sensation of blue seems to one to be diaphanous, he adds, 'Yet it *can* be distinguished if we look attentively enough, and if we know that there is something to look for' (1903: 42). And we do find some of the sense-datum theorists who endorse this relational view trying to articulate what is distinctive of the kind of conscious relation that obtains when one has a conscious perceptual experience, and appealing to introspection in doing so. Indeed, this relational approach invites the notion that there may be a division of phenomenological labour to be uncovered. While certain aspects of a conscious experience, and what it is like for one to have that experience, are to be explained in terms of the nature of the entities one is consciously related to when one has the experience, other aspects of the conscious experience, and what it is like for one to have the experience, are to be explained in terms of the distinctive nature of the relation: the manner in which one is related to them. As it happens, the particular stance taken by most sense-datum theorists on this issue of the division of phenomenological labour is one that assigns the vast majority of the explanatory work to the nature of the entities to which one is consciously related, and one might question whether their stance on this issue is the one best supported by introspection. But for now we will focus on what they say about the nature of the entities we are consciously related to.

The term 'sense-data' is introduced to refer to these entities, and the term is often introduced by these philosophers in a way that is supposed to be relatively neutral on the question of the nature of the entities to which it refers, for example whether or not such entities are mind-dependent. Introspection is supposed to make it obvious that conscious perceptual experience has a relational structure, and hence it is introspection that is supposed to make it obvious that 'sense-data' exist, i.e. those entities one is consciously related to when one has a conscious perceptual experience. Hence we have Price (1932) making the following claim when he introduces the term:

> It is impossible from the nature of the case to prove that there are sense-data . . . The utmost we can do is to remove misunderstandings which prevent people from searching for them and acknowledging them when found. After that, we can only appeal to every man's own consciousness.
> (1932: 6)

Introspective reflection is also supposed to make obvious the truth of certain claims about the qualities possessed by sense-data, for example the claim that in the case of visual experience these entities have colours and shapes. For all that has been said so far, these sense-data may be material objects – or parts, or surfaces, of material objects – in one's environment. However, it is subsequently suggested that further theoretical reflection on the existence of perceptual illusion and hallucination rules this out.

So, to summarise, the line of thought here is the following. The notion that conscious perceptual experience has a relational structure is a commitment that is supposed to be motivated by introspective reflection, prior to, and independently of, a consideration of cases of illusion and hallucination. Hence the existence of 'sense-data' – entities we are consciously related to when we have a conscious perceptual experience – is supposed to be assured prior to, and independently of, a consideration of cases of illusion and hallucination. Further theoretical reflection on the existence of illusion and hallucination does not undermine the independently motivated claim that experience has a relational structure. But it does reveal something surprising about the nature of the entities we are consciously related to whenever we have a conscious perceptual experience. For it undermines the idea that these sense-data are the material objects that we ordinarily take ourselves to be aware of when we consciously perceive. In the next section we will consider arguments that are supposed to lead us to this conclusion.

1.2 Arguments from hallucination

Sense-datum theorists often appeal to cases of perceptual illusion when they argue in support of their thesis that sense-data are not the mind-independent material objects that we ordinarily take ourselves to perceive. As I shall be discussing in Chapter 6, the question of which experiences it is appropriate to classify as illusory is not entirely uncontroversial. And indeed some of the cases of 'illusion' that some of the sense-datum theorists cite are ones that we would not usually regard as in any way misleading. At this stage, in order to simplify things, and to postpone addressing these debates about illusion, I shall be focusing on arguments for sense-datum theories that appeal to cases of complete hallucination. In particular, I shall be focusing on cases of complete hallucination that are subjectively indistinguishable from cases of genuine perception. When a subject has this kind of experience there is no suitable mind-independent material object in her environment to serve as a candidate object of perceptual awareness, even though she is having an experience that is subjectively indistinguishable from a genuine perception of the world.

Sense-datum theorists hold that the fact that such experiences are subjectively indistinguishable from cases of genuine perception should lead us to accept that they have a relational structure. The thought here is that any introspective evidence that you now have for the claim that your current experience has a relational structure would equally be present in the case of a subjectively indistinguishable hallucination. So, if you think that your current introspective evidence is sufficient to warrant the claim that the experience you are having now has a relational structure, you should hold that the same conclusion is warranted in the case of a subjectively indistinguishable hallucination. In the case of a complete hallucination, the perceived relata of the conscious perceptual relation that obtains cannot be the mind-independent material objects that we ordinarily take ourselves to be consciously aware of when we perceive. So, we have reason to think that the subject of a complete visual hallucination is consciously aware of entities that have sensory qualities such as shape and colour, but which are not to be identified with any of the mind-independent material objects in her environment. The sense-datum theorist then proceeds to argue that in order to accommodate adequately what a genuine perception and a subjectively indistinguishable hallucination have in common, we should accept that even in the case of genuine perception the sense-data we are consciously aware of are not to be identified with the mind-independent material objects that we ordinarily take ourselves to perceive.

It is sometimes suggested that the mere fact that a complete hallucination can be subjectively indistinguishable from a genuine perception should lead us to accept that the sense-data that the subject of experience is consciously aware of in each case must be entities of the same kind. Presumably the thought here is that if such experiences really are genuinely subjectively indistinguishable, then the sense-data that the subject is consciously aware of in each case must be perceptually indistinguishable, i.e. entities that one cannot distinguish on the basis of perception alone; and the fact that the relevant sense-data are perceptually indistinguishable is best explained by the proposal that they are entities of the same kind. So since the sense-data that are objects of conscious awareness in the case of hallucination are not mind-independent material objects in the subject's environment, we have reason to deny that the sense-data that are objects of conscious awareness in the case of genuine perception are mind-independent material objects in the subject's environment.

J. L. Austin (1962) introduced an objection to this form of argument. He suggested that even if we make the prior admission that we are aware of sense-data in the case of hallucination, and even if we accept that the entities we are consciously aware of in the case of genuine perception are perceptually indistinguishable from these sense-data, all that would follow is that the entities we are consciously aware of in each case are qualitatively alike. And from the mere fact that two entities are qualitatively alike, it doesn't follow that they are 'generically' alike, for example it doesn't follow that they have the same metaphysical status.

Austin claims that it is a 'pretty gratuitous idea' to think that 'things "generically" different could not be qualitatively alike' (1962: 54). He writes,

> If I am told that a lemon is generically different from a piece of soap, do I 'expect' that no piece of soap could look just like a lemon? Why should I?
> (50)
> why on earth should it *not* be the case that, in some few instances, perceiving one sort of thing is exactly like perceiving another?
> (52)

In effect, Austin is arguing here that a mere appeal to the subjective indistinguishability of a genuine perception and a hallucination would not be enough to rule out as untenable a view according to which (a) the entities we are consciously aware of in the case of hallucination are not mind-independent material objects in our environment, but (b) the entities we are consciously aware of in the case of genuine perception are the very mind-independent material objects that we ordinarily take ourselves to perceive. In what remains of this section I shall be looking at arguments that purport to undermine the tenability of a view that commits to the conjunction of (a) and (b). These arguments do not merely appeal to the subjective indistinguishability of genuine perception and certain cases of complete hallucination. They also invoke certain claims about the causal origin of the experiences we have in cases of genuine perception.

Here is a first attempt to spell out one such argument. Consider a case in which a subject, S, visually perceives in her environment a mind-independent material object, for example a lemon. The conscious perceptual relation that obtains between S and the lemon depends on the occurrence of some psychological effect, E, that the lemon has on S. In particular, the relevant perceptual relation doesn't begin to obtain (i.e. S doesn't begin to see the lemon) until the lemon has produced in S some appropriate psychological effect, E. In the causal chain of events leading to that psychological effect E we can mark distinctions between the more proximate causes of E, and the more distal causes of E. The events in that causal chain that are the more distal causes are those that are temporally prior to the events in the causal chain that are the more proximate causes. So, for example, the events in that causal chain that involve light being reflected from the lemon are the more distal causes of E, relative to the event of S's optic nerves being suitably stimulated by the light that reaches her eyes, which is the more proximate cause of E. In what follows I shall use the letter 'D' to denote the former, more distal cause of E, the letter 'P' to denote the latter, more proximate cause of E, I shall use 'O' to denote the lemon, and I shall use the letter 'T' to denote S's total physical and psychological condition immediately prior to her perception of O. The significance of the appeal to T will emerge in due course. The argument proceeds as follows.

1   When S perceives O, the proximate cause P of psychological effect E on S is preceded by, and caused by, the distal cause D. But that is not the only way in which an event of kind P can occur. An event of kind P can in principle occur in the absence of O, and in the absence of any mind-independent material objects that are qualitatively similar to O (i.e. in the absence of objects that could be candidate objects of perception for S when she is having an experience subjectively indistinguishable from a genuine perception of O).
2   Condition T can also, in principle, obtain in the absence of O and in the absence of mind-independent material objects that are qualitatively similar to O. Indeed, we can envisage a situation in which T obtains *and* P occurs even though no suitable mind-independent O-like material object is present.
3   In any such situation, the occurrence of P won't be causally sufficient for S to be perceptually aware of a mind-independent material object in her environment.
4   In any two situations in which both T obtains and P occurs, the immediate psychological effect, E, on S will be the same.
5   We have said that we can envisage a situation in which T obtains and P occurs where the immediate psychological effect E on S isn't sufficient for S to be perceptually aware of a mind-independent material object in her environment. So if we accept (4), then we should accept that even if the distal cause of P involves O, the immediate psychological effect, E, that P has on S won't be sufficient for S to be perceptually aware of a mind-independent material object in her environment.
6   In the case of a genuine perception of O, the immediate psychological effect E of the proximate cause P is a conscious perceptual experience.
7   Therefore, the conscious perceptual experience involved in genuine perception is not sufficient for S to be perceptually aware of a mind-independent material object in her environment (given (5)).

8   On the assumption that conscious perceptual experience, E, is a relational phenomenon, then, the relevant relation must be one that obtains between S and some entity O*, which doesn't entail that S is perceptually aware of a mind-independent material object in her environment.
9   Therefore, when S perceives O, S is perceptually aware of some entity O* that is not identical with any mind-independent material object in her environment.

Does this argument succeed in undermining the tenability of a view according to which (a) the sense-data we are consciously aware of in the case of hallucination are not mind-independent material objects in our environment, but (b) the sense-data we are consciously aware of in the case of genuine perception are the very mind-independent material objects that we ordinarily take ourselves to perceive? The argument invokes a number of assumptions, and while many of these assumptions seem plausible, there is one in particular that the defender of the conjunction of (a) and (b) is likely to want to challenge. That is premise (4) of the argument.

According to premise (4), in any situation in which T obtains and P occurs the immediate effect of P on S will be the same, irrespective of variations in the distal cause of P. One might think of this as an application of the principle that the same kind of cause invariably produces the same kind of immediate effect. Note, however, that premise (4) does not commit to the claim that *whenever* P occurs, the effect of P on S will be the same. The commitment to the claim that the same effect will occur is confined to those situations in which T obtains. This qualification is designed to accommodate the idea that what effect the occurrence of an event has at a time may depend on what background conditions obtain at that time. The assumption behind premise (4), then, is that in any two situations in which it is true both that P occurs and T obtains, the effect of P will be the same, because the obtaining of T in both of those situations ensures that the causally relevant background conditions are the same. This is to assume that the presence or absence of O in S's environment, and the occurrence of distal cause D, prior to P, are not to be thought of as a causally relevant background conditions when it comes to the question of the psychological effect produced in S by the occurrence of P.

But why assume that what happens prior to P (e.g. the causal history the events leading to P) is not a causally relevant background condition when it comes to the question of the psychological effects produced in S by P? It is perhaps plausible to think that the effect that P has on the *intrinsic* qualities of S won't be affected by what happens prior to P. But why should we make the further assumption that the psychological effects that P has on S must be solely determined by the intrinsic qualities of S? Recall that a background assumption of the argument is that conscious perceptual experience is a *relational* phenomenon. So if one accepts this assumption, and one also accepts that P has the psychological effect of producing in S a conscious perceptual experience (premise (6) of the argument), then one is committed to the claim that a psychological effect of P on S is the obtaining of a conscious perceptual relation: a relation that obtains between S and something else, i.e. the entity S is perceptually aware of. It is not obvious that the obtaining of this relation must depend solely on the intrinsic qualities of S, and so it is not obvious that the obtaining of this relation cannot depend on what happens prior to P.

It is an assumption of the argument that the conscious perceptual relation that obtains when S has a conscious perceptual experience doesn't begin to obtain until the proximate cause P occurs. Now suppose we accept that assumption. Does it follow that the obtaining of that relation cannot depend on anything that happens prior to P? The obtaining of certain relations may constitutively depend on what happens prior to the moment at which they begin to obtain. Indeed, a number of sense-datum theorists will want to accept the idea that there are certain kinds of perceptual relation that constitutively depend for their obtaining on what happens prior to the moment at which they begin to obtain. Although sense-datum theorists hold that whenever we have a conscious perceptual experience we are consciously aware of sense-data that are distinct from material objects and their properties, they do think that there are differences to be identified between cases of genuine perception on the one hand, and cases of complete hallucination on the other. And a number of these sense-datum theorists hold that in the case of genuine perception although we are only *directly* aware of sense-data that are not to be identified with mind-independent material objects in our environment, we are thereby *indirectly* perceptually aware of material objects in our environment. Some hold that the obtaining of this relation of indirect perceptual awareness – a relation that obtains between the subject of experience and material objects in her environment – is determined by the causal origin of the experience that the subject has.

So the obtaining of that particular perceptual relation *does* depend on what happens prior to the moment at which it begins to obtain. In consequence it is not clear that this sort of sense-datum theorist can simply help herself to premise (4) in arguing for the claim that whenever we have a perceptual experience we are perceptually aware of sense-data that are distinct from material objects and their properties.

There are, however, other causal arguments for sense-datum theories that don't depend on premise (4). One such argument repeats the first three premises of the first version of the causal argument and then proceeds as follows:[3]

(4)* If T obtains and O is absent (and there are no other suitable O-like mind-independent material objects in S's environment to serve as candidate objects of perceptual awareness), then proximate cause P is sufficient to produce in S an experience of the kind that occurs when one has a hallucination that is subjectively indistinguishable from a genuine perception of an O.

(5)* When S has this kind of experience S is consciously aware of an entity O* that is not to be identified with any mind-independent material object in her environment.

(6)* The presence of O (and the fact that O is involved in an event D that is a distal cause of P) does not prevent the proximate cause P from producing the same kind of effect, i.e. the effect of producing in S a conscious perceptual awareness of O*, where O* is not to be identified with any mind-independent material object in the subject's environment.

(7)* Therefore, when S has a genuine perception of an O, S is consciously aware of some sense-datum O*, such that O* is not identical to O.

This argument assumes that when P occurs and T obtains and there are no suitable O-like mind-independent material objects in S's environment to serve as candidate objects of perceptual awareness, then S will have a hallucination subjectively indistinguishable from a genuine perception of O. It assumes that for any case of genuine perception it is possible, in principle at least, for there to be a corresponding 'causally matching' hallucination that is subjectively indistinguishable from that genuine perception – i.e. a hallucination that is subjectively indistinguishable from a veridical perception and which involves the same kind of proximate cause and brain state as that involved in the veridical perception. The argument further assumes that in such a case the conscious perceptual experience thereby produced is a conscious awareness of some sense-datum O*, which is not to be identified with any mind-independent material object in the subject's environment. If we grant these assumptions then the argument begins to look persuasive. For if we grant these assumptions we can ask the following question. Are the relevant background causal conditions that are necessary for P to produce the effect of making S consciously aware of O* *absent* in the case of genuine perception? It seems implausible to think so. Why should we think that the absence of a distal cause involving O is necessary to produce that kind of effect? Does this sort of distal cause somehow manage to prevent the proximate cause P from generating a conscious perceptual experience that is a conscious awareness of O*? That seems unlikely.

There is an important difference between this second version of the causal argument for a sense-datum theory and the previous causal argument I outlined. An assumption of the first causal argument is that in the case of genuine perception the occurrence of P produces in S *only* those psychological effects that P would produce in S if O were absent and S were having a causally matching hallucination. The second version of the causal argument doesn't commit to this claim. It commits to the weaker assumption that in the case of genuine perception there is *a* psychological effect produced in S by P which is the kind of effect that P would produce in S if O were absent and S were having a causally matching hallucination. So while the first argument commits to the idea that there are no differences between the psychological effects produced in S in cases of genuine perception and in cases of causally matching hallucination, the second argument commits to the weaker claim that there is a common psychological effect produced in cases of genuine perception and cases of causally matching hallucination (i.e. it commits to the claim that whatever psychological effect is produced in the case of hallucination is also produced in the case of genuine perception).

The common psychological effect cannot be a conscious perceptual experience that is sufficient for perceptual awareness of mind-independent material objects. So if we hold that the common effect is a conscious perceptual experience and we also hold, as the sense-datum theorist maintains, that all of our conscious perceptual experiences are relational phenomena, then we are led to the conclusion that the psychological effect that is common to cases of genuine perception and cases of hallucination is the obtaining of a conscious perceptual relation that the subject of experience bears to entities (i.e. sense-data) that are not mind-independent material objects. So whenever one has a conscious perceptual experience one is consciously aware of sense-data that are not the mind-independent material objects that we ordinarily take ourselves to perceive.

Let us review the options one might take if one wanted to reject the conclusion of this argument for a sense-datum theory. One option would be to reject premise (4)* – i.e. to reject the empirical assumption that when T obtains and O is absent, proximate cause P is sufficient to produce in S a hallucination that is subjectively indistinguishable from a genuine perception of O. An alternative response is to reject premise (6)*, i.e. to maintain that in the case of genuine perception the presence of O, and in particular the fact that O is involved in an event D that is a distal cause of P, *does* prevent P from producing the kind of psychological effect that P would bring about in the case of a causally matching hallucination, i.e. a conscious awareness of non-material sense-data. But the most popular sort of response to this sort of causal argument for a sense-datum theory, is the rejection of premise (5)*, i.e. the rejection of the claim that in the case of hallucination the subject of experience is consciously aware of some sense-datum O* that is not identical with any mind-independent material object in the subject's environment.

Those who reject premise (5)* are in effect rejecting the claim that the conscious experience produced in the case of a hallucination is a relational phenomenon. According to those who reject premise (5)*, when a subject has a complete hallucination, the subject of experience is not perceptually aware of any entities, even though it may seem to her as though she is. The conscious perceptual experience that a subject has in the case of complete hallucination just is some psychological event or state, or some combination of both, the occurrence and/or obtaining of which does not suffice for the obtaining of a relation of conscious perceptual awareness. Those who reject (5)* can still accept the following: the kind of psychological effect that is produced by P in the case of causally matching hallucination, is also produced by P in the case of genuine perception. But they will hold that the relevant psychological effect, common to genuine perception and causally matching hallucination, is a non-relational phenomenon.

Many of those who respond to the argument from hallucination in this way suggest that this should lead us to accept that the conscious perceptual experience that a subject has in the case of genuine perception is a *non*-relational phenomenon. In such a view, the conscious character of the conscious perceptual experience you have when you consciously perceive the world is to be explained by the occurrence/obtaining of an event/state that can occur/obtain whether or not you are perceptually aware of anything. If adopting such a position is the only reasonable way of rejecting (5)*, that would suggest that a consideration of the argument from hallucination brings to light the following constraint on an account of our conscious perceptual awareness of the world: If we are to reject the idea that we are consciously aware of non-material entities – sense-data – whenever we consciously perceive the world, then we must give up the claim that the conscious perceptual experience that we have when we genuinely perceive the world is a relational phenomenon.

This in turn would suggest that a consideration of the argument from hallucination shows that we can rule out as untenable a view according to which the conscious perceptual experience a subject has when she consciously perceives the world is sufficient to put her in perceptual contact with her environment. Either we endorse a relational view of such experience and accept that the relevant relation of conscious awareness is one that obtains between the subject of experience and non-material sense-data (rather than the mind-independent environment), or we accept a non-relational account of the conscious experience that a subject has when she perceives the world. In either case, the conscious character of the experience a subject has when she perceives the world is not to be explained by appeal to a relation of conscious perceptual awareness that obtains between the subject of experience and aspects of her environment.

Some disjunctivists wish to defend the view of conscious perception that this assessment of the argument from hallucination would suggest is untenable, a view according to which the conscious character of the experience a subject has when she perceives the world *is* to be explained by appeal to a relation of conscious perceptual awareness that obtains between the subject of experience and aspects of her environment. These disjunctivists reject premise (5)* of the argument from hallucination that I outlined, i.e. they reject the claim that that in the case of hallucination the subject of experience is consciously aware of some sense-datum O* that is not identical with any mind-independent material object in the subject's environment. So they are committed to denying that the conscious experience produced in the case of a hallucination is a relational phenomenon. However, they insist that this denial is consistent with accepting that the conscious perceptual experience that a subject has in the case of genuine perception *is* a relational phenomenon. In the next chapter we shall see how they attempt to defend that proposal. But before we get to their response, I shall introduce, in more detail, the non-relational view of perceptual experience that is endorsed by the majority of those who reject sense-datum theories of perception.

1.3 Chapter summary

In this chapter we considered arguments that purport to establish that the fact that we can hallucinate should lead us to recognise, and accommodate, the following significant constraint on an account of conscious perception: whenever one has a conscious perceptual experience one is perceptually aware of entities – sense-data – that are not the mind-independent material objects that we ordinarily take ourselves to perceive.

First of all we introduced a background metaphysical assumption that is implicit in these arguments for sense-datum theories, the assumption that conscious perceptual experience is a *relational* phenomenon. We contrasted this relational view of conscious perceptual experience with some non-relational alternatives, and we introduced some considerations that might be thought to lend support to the relational view of conscious perceptual experience. In particular, we considered the suggestion that there is positive introspective support for the relational view, and an absence of introspective support for the alternative non-relational views. In outlining these phenomenological considerations, we compared some remarks that were made by the sense-datum theorist G. E. Moore on what it is like to introspectively reflect on the 'sensation of blue'.

We noted that for some of these sense-datum theorists, the notion that conscious perceptual experience has a relational structure is supposed to be motivated by introspective reflection prior to, and independently of, a consideration of cases of illusion and hallucination. Hence the existence of 'sense-data' – entities we are consciously related to when we have a conscious perceptual experience – is supposed to be assured prior to, and independently of, a consideration of cases of illusion and hallucination. Further theoretical reflection on the existence of illusion and hallucination is then supposed to reveal something surprising about the nature of the entities we are consciously related to whenever we have a conscious perceptual experience, for it is supposed to undermine the idea that these sense-data are the material objects that we ordinarily take ourselves to be aware of when we consciously perceive.

We considered three attempts to reach that conclusion. The first simply appealed to the idea that a complete hallucination can be subjectively indistinguishable from a veridical perception. We examined an objection that J. L. Austin raised against that form of argument. This was the objection that, from the fact that two entities are qualitatively alike, it doesn't follow that they are 'generically' alike, for example it doesn't follow that they have the same metaphysical status.

We then considered two different causal arguments from hallucination that purport to show that the 'sense-data' of which we are directly aware in the case of veridical perception are not the material mind-independent objects in our environment that we ordinarily take ourselves to perceive. The first causal argument sought to establish that in the case of veridical perception the proximate cause of the subject's experience produces in that subject only those psychological effects that such a proximate cause would produce in the subject if she were having a causally matching hallucination. This form of argument relied on the assumption that the same kind of cause invariably produces the same kind of effect, and we considered how an opponent of sense-datum theories might try to resist that assumption. The second causal argument sought to establish the weaker claim that in the case of veridical perception there is a psychological effect produced in the subject by the proximate cause of her experience which is the kind of effect that such a proximate would produce in the subject if she were having a causally matching hallucination.

We noted that a common way of responding to this argument for a sense-datum theory is to reject the assumption that the conscious experience produced in the case of a hallucination is a relational phenomenon, and we noted that many of those who respond to the argument from hallucination in this way suggest that this should lead us to accept that the conscious perceptual experience that a subject has in the case of genuine perception is a non-relational phenomenon.

Notes

1 This isn't to suggest that only those who endorse a relational view are interested in questions about the kinds of entities we can be perceptually aware of. But as we shall see, in case of those who endorse the relational view, the existence of perceptual illusion and hallucination make such questions pressing in a distinctive way.
2 While mental events are to be thought of as aspects of mind that *happen*, *occur*, or *unfold* over time, mental states, by contrast, are to be thought of as aspects of mind that *obtain* over intervals of time.
3 This version of the causal argument is a modified version of a causal argument that M. G. F. Martin introduces and considers in his 2004. We will be considering a version of the causal argument from hallucination that is closer to the one Martin discusses in Chapter 6.

Further reading

For an introduction to sense-datum theories of perception, see Fish 2010, Ch. 2. For a useful overview of sense-datum theories and the arguments from illusion and hallucination, see Crane 2015. For a history of the sense-datum theory, see Crane 2000.

For a defence of the sense-datum theory, see Robinson 1994. Robinson's version of a causal argument from hallucination for a sense-datum theory can be found in his 1994, Ch. 6. Relevant selections from Robinson 1994 can be found in the Byrne and Logue 2009 collection. Selections from A. D. Smith 2002 that are relevant to causal arguments for sense-datum theories can also be found in Byrne and Logue 2009.

G. E. Moore's famous discussion of the 'sensation of blue' can be found in his 1903. For J. L. Austin's critique of sense-datum theories, see his 1962.

References

Austin, J. L., 1962, *Sense and Sensibilia*. Oxford: Oxford University Press.
Byrne, Alex and Logue, Heather (eds), 2009, *Disjunctivism: contemporary readings*. Cambridge, MA: MIT Press.
Crane, Timothy, 2000, 'The origins of qualia', in T. Crane and S. Patterson (eds), *The History of the Mind-Body Problem*. London: Routledge.

——, 2015, 'The Problem of perception', *The Stanford Encyclopedia of Philosophy* (Summer 2015 Edition), Edward N. Zalta (ed.). <http://plato.stanford.edu/archives/sum2015/entries/perception-problem/>.

Fish, William C., 2009, *Perception, Hallucination, and Illusion*. Oxford: Oxford University Press.

Martin, M. G. F., 2004, 'The limits of self-awareness', *Philosophical Studies*, 120: 37–89.

Moore, G. E., 1903, 'The refutation of idealism', *Mind*, Vol. 12.

——, 1925, 'A defence of common sense', *Contemporary British Philosophy* (2nd Series) ed. J. H. Muirhead. London: Allen and Unwin.

Price, H. H., 1934, *Perception*. London: Methuen and Co. Ltd.

Robinson, Howard, 1994, *Perception*. London: Routledge.

Smith, A. D., 2002, *The Problem of Perception*. Cambridge, MA: Harvard University Press.

2

REPRESENTATIONAL CONTENT, THE SCIENCE OF PERCEPTION, AND DISJUNCTIVISM ABOUT CONSCIOUS CHARACTER

The discussion of the argument from hallucination in the previous chapter suggested the following constraint on an account of our conscious perceptual awareness of the world. If we are to reject the idea that we are directly aware of sense-data when we consciously perceive the world, then we must reject the assumption that the conscious perceptual experience that we have when we genuinely perceive the world is a relational phenomenon. This means adopting a view according to which the conscious perceptual experience that you have when you consciously perceive the world is not in itself sufficient to put you in perceptual contact with your environment; and in this view, the conscious character of the conscious perceptual experience you have when you consciously perceive the world is explained by the occurrence/obtaining of an event/state that can occur/obtain whether or not you are perceptually aware of anything, rather than by the obtaining of a relation of conscious perceptual awareness.

Someone adopting this position needn't deny that in the case of genuine perception the subject of experience is perceptually aware of mind-independent material objects in her environment. They may claim that although the psychological effect that is common to genuine perception and causally matching hallucination isn't sufficient for the obtaining of a relation of perceptual awareness, there are further conditions that obtain in the case of genuine perception, which are absent in the case of hallucination, and which together with the common psychological effect, suffice for the obtaining of a relation of perceptual awareness, a relation that obtains between the subject of experience and mind-independent material objects in her environment.

In the previous chapter I suggested that those who advocate a relational view of conscious perceptual experience maintain that in providing an account of conscious perceptual experience one should at least aim to address the following key questions:

(i) What is distinctive of the kind of conscious perceptual *relation* that obtains when you have a conscious perceptual experience?
(ii) What kind of entities are you perceptually aware of when that relation obtains?

Under the non-relational approach, the focus of inquiry shifts from questions concerned with a conscious perceptual relation, to questions concerned with properties of a mental state or event, a mental state or event that can obtain or occur independently of the obtaining of a relation of perceptual awareness.

What should an account of the relevant mental state/event seek to explain? The discussion of the relationalist view of conscious perceptual experience in the previous chapter focused primarily on the conscious character of perceptual experience: what it is like for one to have such experience, and in particular, what introspective reflection suggests about such matters. However, while introspection may serve as a source of evidence when it comes to theorising about conscious perceptual experience, it isn't clear that we should restrict ourselves to the deliverances of introspection alone when it comes to assessing the relative merits of competing accounts of sense perception, for example, when assessing which account best accommodates and explains the *various* effects, both psychological and behavioural, that our conscious perceptual experiences have on us. I shall be returning to the issue of what introspective reflection suggests about the conscious character of perceptual experience in due course. For now I want to focus on the question of how best to accommodate what is often thought to be a further basic desideratum of any adequate account of conscious perceptual experience: to provide an adequate explanation of the role that conscious perceptual experience plays in enabling the subject of experience to acquire information about her immediate environment.

2.1 Representational content and the science of perception

On the assumption that conscious perceptual experience is a non-relational phenomenon, what would best accommodate and account for the role that conscious perceptual experience plays in enabling the subject of experience to acquire information about her immediate environment? Here I have in mind the role that conscious perceptual experience plays in guiding and supporting action (e.g. in enabling the subject of experience to interact with and navigate her immediate environment) as well as the role that such experience plays in the generation of a subject's perceptual beliefs about her immediate environment (e.g. beliefs about what and where things are).

The most popular answer to this question is that a subject's conscious perceptual experience is a *representational* mental state/event that is directed on her environment. According to accounts of this kind, a subject's perceptual experience is a psychological state/event with a representational content, a content that represents her environment to be a certain way. The representational content of a subject's experience is specified in terms of its veridicality conditions. These are the environmental states of affairs that have to obtain if the environment is to be the way the subject's experience represents it to be. Proponents of this sort of approach can maintain that it is the representational content of experience, specified in terms of its veridicality conditions, which provides the subject of experience with a source of information about her environment, information that supports and guides action, and which provides its subject with a source of knowledge about her environment.

On this view the representational content of experience can be inaccurate as well as accurate, just as the content of a subject's belief – what the subject believes to be the case – can be false as well as true. In the case of illusion or hallucination the representational content of experience is inaccurate – its veridicality conditions are not satisfied, and it thereby misrepresents the environment – so illusion and hallucination can be seen as akin to false belief in certain important respects. A hallucinatory experience may fail to provide its subject with accurate information about her environment, but by attributing to it a representational content that misrepresents the environment, we can explain what the subject is thereby disposed to believe about her immediate environment, and how she is disposed to behave.[1]

This way of accounting for the role that conscious perceptual experience plays in enabling the subject of experience to acquire information about her immediate environment has a number of virtues. It is generally accepted that the notion of a non-relational mental state with a representational content is one which we will in any case need to invoke in an account of other psychological states, such as belief. So this approach avoids the additional ontological commitment of the sense-datum theory: the positing of non-material entities, sense-data, that a subject is consciously aware of whenever she has a conscious perceptual experience. The thought here is that there is no need to invoke non-material sense-data that the subject of experience is consciously aware of in cases of hallucination, just as there is no need to invoke sense-data that a subject is cognitively related to in order to account for the phenomenon of false belief. Since there is no need to posit such non-material sense-data in the case of hallucination, there is also no need to posit such entities in the case of veridical perception. In that respect, such theories accommodate the idea that when all goes well, a subject's perceptual access to her environment is unmediated. There are no intervening entities – sense-data – that get in the way of a subject's direct perceptual access to the world. On such a view one can maintain that although the psychological effect common to cases of genuine perception and causally matching hallucination is not sufficient for the obtaining of a relation of perceptual awareness, when this common psychological effect accurately represents the environment, and when it is appropriately caused by what it represents, the subject of experience is directly perceptually aware of her environment.

A further virtue of this sort of account is that it provides a helpful framework within which scientific theorising about sense perception can be fruitfully pursued. On the assumption that sensory perception has the function of *representing* the world in the service of action and cognition, a central task of an empirical investigation of the senses becomes that of determining and explaining the processes by which perceptual systems generate perceptual states with specific veridicality conditions from specific types of stimulation of the subject's sensory receptors. The explanatory paradigm is one according to which our perceptual systems generate perceptual states *with representational content* by responding to information available in the stimulation of our sense organs.

In the case of vision, for example, although detectors in the retina are sensitive to arrays of light frequencies, the information available in these registrations of light arrays is relatively impoverished, insofar as such information significantly underdetermines what the environmental, distal causes of such effects on the retina are. On the assumption that visual perception plays a crucial role in enabling the sighted to acquire information about the immediate environment, the problem to be resolved by an empirical investigation of vision becomes the following: how is the information that is contained in such effects on the retina extracted, processed, and converted in a way that generates perceptual states that represent the environmental causes of such effects? The generation of perceptual states with representational content – specified in terms of veridicality conditions – is a fruitful way of thinking of what is to be explained here. The dominant model of explanation is one which attempts to identify 'biases' in the operation of the visual system which result in it systematically neglecting those aspects of the underdetermining proximal sensory stimulation that are *not* likely to correlate with environmental causes, in favour of those aspects of the underdetermining proximal sensory stimulation that *are* likely to correlate with environmental causes. The proposal is that the underdetermining proximal stimulation of the sensory receptors automatically triggers processes that operate under such biasing principles, thereby generating representations of the distal environment.[2]

In the scientific study of sense perception introspection is sometimes used as a source of evidence; for example, in perceptual and cognitive psychology the perceived qualities of objects, and the effects of experimental manipulation on experience, are sometimes investigated by techniques that rely on subjects' introspectively mediated responses to what they experience, and this can be used as a source of evidence in investigating the underlying psychological processes involved in sense perception. However, we cannot discern through introspection the way in which information about the environment is extracted and processed by the visual system, and we cannot introspectively discern the biasing principles under which the visual system operates. In this science the postulation of specific informational processes operating under specific biasing principles that mediate between sensory stimulation and our perceptual awareness of the environment does not ultimately derive from introspective reflection. The postulation of such processes is, rather, justified by their explanatory power.

I said earlier that while introspection may serve as a source of evidence when it comes to theorising about conscious perceptual experience, it isn't clear that we should restrict ourselves to the deliverances of introspection alone when it comes to assessing the relative merits of competing accounts of sense perception. If our concern is with the role that conscious perceptual experience plays in enabling the subject of experience to acquire information about her immediate environment, then, one might think, we should look to the science of perception for the best answer to the question of how it is that perception performs that role. And if the notion of perceptual states with representational contents, specified in terms of their veridicality conditions, is essential to this explanatory model in the science of perception, then the postulation of such representational states is also justified by its explanatory power.

This line of thought has been forcefully defended by Tyler Burge. As Burge puts it, 'Human perceptual states are to be classified as the science classifies them' (2011: 66), and Burge argues that the science of vision 'operates on an explanatory paradigm that makes attribution of perceptual states, with specific representational contents and veridicality conditions, fundamental to its explanations' (2010: 307). 'The central mode of explanation in this science takes representational content and transformations that produce representational states to be the central explanatory notions' (2010: 298). Ultimately, it is the success of the explanations offered by the science that justifies the attribution of the kinds of perceptual states it posits, and, as Burge puts it, the science offers 'numerous empirically supported, mathematically rigorous, powerful explanations of particular problems that the visual system solves in yielding perceptual representations' (2005: 12).

Burge has also argued that there is a principle implicit in the causal explanations offered by this science which should lead us to accept that perceptual states of the same fundamental kind can be generated in cases of successful perception, illusion, and hallucination. He labels this principle the 'proximality principle'. Discussion of this principle is important, for as we shall see, Burge has suggested that it shows that disjunctive theories of perception are incompatible with the science of perception.

What is the proximality principle, and what line of thought can be offered in support of it? Well, assume that the aim of the science is to identify processes and principles by means of which the perceptual (e.g. visual) system extracts, converts, and processes information contained in proximal stimulation, in order to generate perceptual states that represent the environment. In achieving this aim the science uncovers psychological laws under which the perceptual system operates when proximal sensory stimulation triggers its activity. The laws in question concern the way in which certain kinds of perceptual representational states are generated from nothing more than proximal stimulation, together with other antecedent psychological states of the subject. So the laws identified by the science predict that the same kinds of representational perceptual states will be generated by the perceptual system as long as the proximate causes, and antecedent psychological states of the subject, are kept constant, assuming that there is no malfunction in (or interference with) the relevant perceptual system. Given that proximal stimulation can be specified in a way that does not assume any particular environmental distal causes, the same kinds of representational perceptual states can be generated in cases of genuine perception, illusion, or hallucination. So as Burge puts it, 'Whether a given object is seen, or a duplicate object is seen, or a contextually indiscernible perceptual illusion is undergone, the transformations from the registration of the light array to the perceptual representation are, for psychological purposes, type identical' (2005: 46). This suggests that the following principle – the 'proximality principle' – is implicit in the causal explanations offered by the science of perception: 'On any given occasion, given the total antecedent psychological state of the individual and system, the total proximal input into the system suffices to produce a given type of perceptual state, assuming no malfunction or interference' (2005: 22).

Burge has argued that such considerations should lead us to accept that if one is to offer an account of perceptual experience that is compatible with the science of perception, then one's account will need to accommodate the following empirically supported claims:

(i) In cases of genuine perception and certain cases of hallucination (e.g. causally matching hallucination) there occurs a common *psychological* effect, and not merely a common physiological effect.
(ii) The common psychological effect includes a *non*-relational, representational perceptual state-kind that is attributable to the perceiver. That is to say, although the common psychological effect may include *sub*-personal informational processing that is not appropriately thought of as activity that the perceiving subject engages in, and so which is not attributable to the perceiving agent herself, processing of this kind generates, as common psychological effect, a non-relational, representational perceptual state-kind that *is* attributable to the perceiving subject. Moreover:
(iii) such non-relational, representational perceptual state-kinds, common to genuine perception and hallucination, play a *fundamental* explanatory role in the science of perception, and this explanatory classification of perceptual state-kinds should be accommodated by any adequate account of perceptual experience.

Suppose that we accept that if we are to provide an account of perceptual experience that is compatible with the science of perception, we should accept each of the above claims, (i)–(iii). Are we thereby committed to the claim that the nature of conscious perceptual experience is exhaustively accounted for, and explained by, the representational perceptual state-kinds postulated by the science? A widely contested issue in the philosophy of perception is whether it is possible to account for the conscious character of conscious perceptual experience simply in terms of the postulation of psychological states with representational content. Some argue that one can adequately accommodate the conscious character of perceptual experience by simply postulating the right combination of representational states, with the right kinds of representational contents, playing the right kinds of functional roles. Others deny this. They argue that we shan't be able to accommodate certain aspects of the phenomenology of conscious perceptual experience if we restrict ourselves to the postulation of such representational and functional features of our perceptual states. To properly and fully accommodate what it is like for one to have such experience, they contend, we will also need to appeal to *non*-representational phenomenal properties of experience, sometimes called 'sensational' properties, or 'qualia'.[3] It is generally thought that the science of perception has not yet established who is right about this. This assessment of the progress of the science of perception is reflected in the following quote from Burge:

> Perceptual psychology as it now stands does not attempt to give a complete theory of the essence of all perceptual states. For example, it is possible that consciousness is an aspect of the essence of perceptual states . . . The psychological theories that I have discussed do not attempt to explain consciousness. There is, currently, no scientific theory of consciousness.
> (2005: 46–47)

So note that if one were to concur with Burge's assessment of the science of perception one could endorse claims (i)–(iii) above, without being committed to the claim that the nature of conscious perceptual experience is exhaustively accounted for, and explained by, the representational perceptual state-kinds postulated by the science. One might hold that the postulated representational perceptual state-kinds do not suffice to fix and account for the conscious character of our conscious perceptual experiences.

If one adopts this position, then what options are available to one? Well, the second causal argument from hallucination that was discussed in the previous chapter puts pressure on the idea that one can accept both of the following claims:

(a) in the case of a causally matching hallucination one is aware of non-material sense-data;
(b) in the case of genuine perception one isn't aware of such sense-data.

This might prompt the following line of thought. Those who deny that we are aware of non-material sense-data in the case of genuine perception should deny that we are aware of such sense-data in the case of causally matching hallucination, in which case they should deny that we need to appeal to the obtaining of a relation of conscious perceptual awareness when accounting for the conscious character of the perceptual experience that a subject has when she hallucinates. And if they deny that we need to appeal to the obtaining of a relation of conscious perceptual awareness when accounting for the conscious character of the perceptual experience that a subject has when she hallucinates, then they also ought to deny that we need to appeal to the obtaining of a relation of conscious perceptual awareness when accounting for the conscious character of the perceptual experience that a subject has when she genuinely perceives the world, for the conscious character of the perceptual experience that you have when you genuinely perceive the world is *the same as* the conscious character of the experience that you would have in the case of a causally matching hallucination.

The above line of thought suggests the following: one should not appeal to the obtaining of a relation of conscious perceptual awareness when accounting for the conscious character of conscious perceptual experience, unless one is prepared to endorse a sense-datum theory of perception. This in turn suggests that if you reject a sense-datum theory of perception, and you also deny that one can adequately accommodate the conscious character of perceptual experience by simply postulating the right combination of representational states, then the only plausible option available to you is to endorse the following sort of view: a conscious perceptual experience is a non-relational psychological state/event whose conscious character is to be explained, at least in part, by its possession of *non*-representational phenomenal properties – qualia – where these are properties that an experience can possess whether or not the subject of experience is perceptually aware of anything.

If this assessment of the plausible options open to us is correct, we rule out, as ultimately untenable, a view according to which the conscious character of the experience a subject has when she genuinely perceives the world is to be explained, at least in part, by appeal to a relation of conscious perceptual awareness that obtains between the subject of experience and aspects of her environment. As I mentioned at the end of the previous chapter, this is a view of conscious perception that some disjunctivists wish to defend. In the next section we will look at how they respond to arguments that suggest that their view of conscious perception is not a viable option.

2.2 Disjunctivism about conscious character

As I mentioned at the outset, not all disjunctivists share exactly the same view of conscious perception. If we think of disjunctivism as a defensive strategy, adopted in defence of some positive view of conscious perception, then given that not all disjunctivists share exactly the same positive view of conscious perception, we should expect to find that some disjunctivists may be happy to concede some points that other disjunctivists may need to resist. The disjunctivists that I am concerned with at this stage are those who will need to resist the following set of claims if their account of conscious perception is to be defensible.

The conscious perceptual experience that you have when you genuinely perceive the world is not in itself sufficient to put you in perceptual contact with aspects of your environment. If we reject sense-datum theories of perception, then we should accept that the conscious perceptual experience that you have when you consciously perceive the world is some psychological state/event that can obtain/occur whether or not you are perceptually aware of anything. The conscious character of the perceptual experience that you have in such cases is solely determined by properties possessed by this non-relational psychological state/event – properties that the relevant psychological state/event can possess whether or not you are perceptually aware of anything. So the conscious character of the experience that you have when you consciously perceive the world is not to be explained by appeal to a relation of conscious perceptual awareness that obtains between you, as subject of experience, and aspects of your mind-independent environment. When you introspectively attend to the perceptual experience that you have when you consciously perceive the world, what you are thereby introspectively aware of just is some psychological state/event that can obtain whether or not you are perceptually aware of anything; and when you introspectively attend to the conscious character of the perceptual experience that you have when you consciously perceive the world, you are merely introspectively attending to properties of this psychological state/event, properties that it can possess whether or not you are perceptually aware of anything.

The disjunctivists I am concerned with – the 'naïve realists' – will need to resist the above set of claims, for they are committed to the following view of conscious perception. The conscious perceptual experience that you have when you consciously perceive the world *is* in itself sufficient to put you in perceptual contact with aspects of your mind-independent environment. When you introspectively attend to the experience you have when you consciously perceive the world, what you are thereby introspectively attending to is sufficient for the obtaining of a relation of conscious perceptual awareness, a relation that obtains between you, as subject of experience, and aspects of your mind-independent environment. The conscious character of the experience that you have when you consciously perceive the world is to be explained, at least in part, by the obtaining of this relation. When you introspectively attend to the conscious character of the experience that you have when you consciously perceive the world, you are thereby introspectively aware of a conscious perceptual relation that obtains between you, as subject of experience, and aspects of your mind-independent environment. You are not merely introspectively aware of some psychological state/event that can obtain whether or not you are perceptually aware of anything. You are not merely introspectively attending to properties of this psychological state/event that it can possess whether or not you are perceptually aware of anything. You are, rather, introspectively aware of the obtaining of a conscious perceptual relation, and aspects of your environment to which it relates you.

In what follows we'll consider what this disjunctivist can say in response to two lines of argument that purport to show that her favoured view of conscious perception is ultimately untenable. The first line of argument appeals to introspection, and in particular the idea that hallucinations can be introspectively indistinguishable from genuine perceptions; and the second line of argument appeals to the claim that the disjunctivist view is incompatible with the science of perception, and in particular, the proximality principle.

The argument from introspective indistinguishability proceeds as follows. Assume that a genuine perception and some causally matching hallucination are introspectively indiscriminable. From the subject's point of view, there is no introspectively discernible difference between the conscious perceptual experience that she has when she perceives the world, and the conscious perceptual experience she has when she hallucinates. If the subject is introspectively aware of some feature of her experience in the case of genuine perception, which she isn't introspectively aware of in the case of hallucination, then there will be an introspectively discernible difference between the cases. So if the subject of experience is introspectively aware of a conscious perceptual relation that obtains in the case of genuine perception, then she must also be introspectively aware of a conscious perceptual relation that obtains in the case of hallucination. Otherwise there will be an introspectibly discernible difference between the cases. If we accept that the subject of experience is introspectively aware of a relation of conscious perceptual awareness that obtains in the case of hallucination, then we are led, through the argument from hallucination, to a sense-datum theory of perception, according to which the subject of experience is consciously aware of non-material sense-data in the case of genuine perception; and this is inconsistent with the disjunctivist's favoured view of perception. If one is to avoid a sense-datum theory, one will need to deny that when a subject consciously perceives the world she can be introspectively aware of a conscious perceptual relation that obtains between her, as subject of experience, and aspects of her environment; and this is also inconsistent with the disjunctivist's favoured view of perception.

The key claim in this argument that the disjunctivist will try to resist is the following: if the subject of experience is introspectively aware of some feature of her experience in the case of genuine perception, which she isn't introspectively aware of in the case of hallucination, then there will be an introspectively discernible difference between the cases. The disjunctivist claims, in response, that if the causally matching hallucination really is introspectively indiscriminable from the conscious perceptual experience that the subject has in the case of genuine perception, then when she hallucinates it will *seem* to the subject as though she is introspectively aware of a conscious perceptual relation that obtains. But if we agree that we should reject a sense-datum account of hallucination, and deny that such a perceptual relation really does obtain in the case of hallucination, then the correct conclusion to draw is that the hallucinatory experience lacks a feature that it introspectively seems to have. If the hallucination seems, but only seems, to have the same introspectible features as genuine perception, this would suffice to explain the respect in which they are introspectively indiscriminable. One is not obliged to commit to the further claim that the genuine perception lacks the features that it introspectively seems to have. So one is not obliged to commit to the claim that the subject of experience is not introspectively aware of a conscious perceptual relation that obtains in the case of genuine perception.

So the dialectical position, as far as this disjunctivist is concerned, is the following. If one accepts that:

(a) in the case of genuine perception it seems to one as though one is introspectively aware of a conscious perceptual relation that obtains, then one should also accept that
(b) in the case of an introspectively indiscriminable hallucination it will also seem to one as though one is introspectively aware of a conscious

perceptual relation that obtains. If one accepts (a), but one denies that any such conscious perceptual relation obtains in the case of hallucination, then one thereby allows that

(c) a conscious perceptual experience can fail to be the way it introspectively seems to be.

And if one accepts (c), then from the claim that two experiences are introspectively indiscriminable, it doesn't automatically follow that those two experiences have the same introspectible features. For if one accepts (c) then one leaves open the possibility that while one of the experiences may actually have some introspectible feature F, the other experience may lack feature F, and only seem to possess it.

An analogy may help here. Let's assume that it is possible for a perceived object to lack some quality that it perceptually seems to have, for example let us assume that it is possible for there to be cases in which one is perceiving an object that looks red, but isn't. This is our analogue of claim (c): a conscious perceptual experience can fail to be the way it introspectively seems to be. In such circumstances, let us assume, one is not in a position to perceptually discriminate the object that one is perceiving from a red object. From this it doesn't follow that when one perceives what is in fact a red object, one isn't perceptually aware of that object's red colour. So from the fact that two objects are perceptually indiscriminable on a particular occasion, it doesn't automatically follow that those two objects share the same perceptible features. If we allow that it is possible for a perceived object to lack some quality that it perceptually seems to have, we leave open the possibility that while one of the perceived objects may have some perceptible feature – redness – the other object may lack this feature, and only seem to possess it.

Now a sense-datum theorist will want to maintain that if it perceptually seems to one as though one is aware of a red object, then there must be a red object that one is perceptually aware of; namely, a red sense-datum. But those who reject sense-datum theories will want to deny this. They will want to hold that it is possible for there to be cases in which the object one is perceptually aware of seems red, but isn't; and they will want to maintain that this isn't to be explained by the fact that one is aware of some other red object: a sense-datum. The disjunctivists we are considering here want to make an analogous claim about our *introspective* awareness of our conscious perceptual experiences. They want to maintain that it is possible for there to be cases – for example hallucination – in which the conscious perceptual experience one is having introspectively seems to be a way that it isn't.

We find this disjunctivist stance in J. M. Hinton's work.[4] Hinton's disjunctive defensive strategy against the argument from introspective indistinguishability isn't quite the same as the defensive manoeuvre deployed by Austin that I outlined in the previous chapter. The idea behind the Austinian defensive strategy is the following. One can maintain that genuine perception and hallucination are introspectively indistinguishable and yet metaphysically, and perhaps psychologically, different, because from the mere fact that two things are *qualitatively* alike, it doesn't follow that they are *generically* alike. And things that are not generically alike may be metaphysically, and perhaps psychologically, different. To adopt this strategy is to leave open the proposal that genuine perception and hallucination are introspectively indistinguishable because they are qualitatively alike – for example because they share the same phenomenal properties. By contrast, Hinton's defensive strategy is to question an assumption that goes unchallenged in the Austinian move. That is the assumption that genuine perception and introspectively indistinguishable hallucination are *qualitatively* alike.

Hinton remarks that in the case of perceptible objects, we don't assume that two objects have to have some property in common in order for the one to be mistaken for the other. (Compare here the example given above: the red object, and the object that merely looks red but isn't.) So why, he asks, should we assume that our *experiences* have to have properties in common in order for them to be mistaken for one another? 'Why should it not just seem as if they had properties in common?' (1967: 225). Those who reject sense-datum theories grant that from the fact that it perceptually seems to you as if there is a red object, it doesn't automatically follow that there is a red object that you are perceptually aware of. So why should we not also grant that from the fact that it introspectively seems to you as though you are having an experience with a certain feature, it doesn't automatically follow that you are introspectively aware of an experience that has that feature?

Hinton's argumentative strategy is, in effect, to press his opponents to justify what he takes to be the hitherto unjustified commitments of their view. His opponents assume that the conscious perceptual experience that one has in the case of genuine perception, and the conscious perceptual experience one has in the case of an introspectively indiscriminable hallucination, must have the same introspectible properties in common (the same 'worn-on-the-sleeve' properties in common, as he puts it (1967: 225)). But what justifies this claim? Is the claim supported by the introspective evidence?

Assume for now that you are genuinely perceiving the world. Can you be sure that the conscious perceptual experience that you are now having is not sufficient to put you in perceptual contact with the items you perceive? As you introspectively attend to your experience, can you be sure that you are not introspectively aware of a conscious perceptual relation that obtains between you and the items in your environment you now perceive – a conscious perceptual relation the obtaining of which contributes to the conscious character of your experience? Does it seem to you as though you are in a position to introspectively focus in on, and discern, some conscious psychological element of your current situation that is insufficient for perceptual contact with those items in your environment? If it doesn't seem that way to you, then how can you be sure that what you are introspectively aware of now just is what you would be introspectively aware of if you were having a causally matching hallucination?

Here one might respond as follows. Even if I was unsure whether or not I was genuinely perceiving the world, I could still be sure about the kind of experience I am now having. I could still be sure of its conscious character. So doesn't that show that my experience could have the same conscious character whether or not I was genuinely perceiving the world? And doesn't that suffice to show that what I am introspectively aware of now just is what I would be introspectively aware of if I were having a causally matching hallucination?

Hinton's response is to question whether you really can be sure about the kind of experience you are now having, if you can't be sure whether or not you are genuinely perceiving the world. Your uncertainty as to whether or not you are perceiving the world doesn't put you in a position to be certain about whether or not you are introspectively aware of a conscious perceptual relation that obtains between you and aspects of your environment. The fact that you are unsure whether or not you are genuinely perceiving the world, doesn't entail that you are now in a position to rule out the possibility that you are introspectively aware of a conscious perceptual relation that obtains between you and aspects of your environment, a conscious perceptual relation the obtaining of which contributes to the conscious character of your experience. If you are unsure whether or not you are hallucinating, you may be in a position to be sure of the following *disjunctive* claim: either I am introspectively aware of a conscious perceptual relation that obtains between me and particular features of my environment, or it merely seems to me as if I am. The challenge that Hinton issues to his opponents is to show that the introspective evidence entitles one to anything stronger and more committal than this sort of disjunctive claim. And if the introspective evidence doesn't entitle one to anything stronger and more committal than this sort of disjunctive claim, then the introspective evidence doesn't establish that what you are introspectively aware of now just is what you would be introspectively aware of if you were hallucinating.

Let us now return to Burge's discussion of the 'proximality principle', and consider whether an argument from science can establish that the disjunctivist's view of perception is ultimately untenable. Recall that Burge suggests that this principle, which is implicit in the causal explanations offered by the science of perception, shows that disjunctive theories of perception are incompatible with the science of perception. According to the proximality principle, 'On any given occasion, given the total antecedent psychological state of the individual and system, the total proximal input into the system suffices to produce a given type of perceptual state, assuming no malfunction or interference' (2005: 22). Is this something that the disjunctivist with whom we are currently concerned needs to reject?

The disjunctivist will need to reject this principle if the sort of perceptual state to which it refers is to be identified with the introspectible conscious perceptual experience that a subject has when she consciously perceives the world. For the kind of perceptual state referred to in the proximality principle is a *non*-relational, representational perceptual state. Recall that in Chapter 1, when I was introducing the relational assumption about the metaphysics of conscious perceptual experience advocated by the sense-datum theorist, I said that someone adopting that relational view may agree that when one has a conscious perceptual experience psychological events do occur and perceptual states do obtain. What is denied by the relationalist is that one's conscious perceptual experience *just is* some psychological event or state, or some combination of both, that can occur and obtain whether or not a relation of conscious perceptual awareness obtains. The disjunctivist we are concerned with here may make a similar claim. She may agree that perceptual states referred to in the proximality principle do obtain when one consciously perceives the world, where the relevant perceptual states are ones that are attributable to the perceiving subject and that can obtain whether or not one is perceptually aware of anything. What she will deny is that the conscious perceptual experience one has when one consciously perceives the world *just is* the relevant perceptual state. So the challenge that the disjunctivist will press at this point is the following: what justifies the claim that the kind of perceptual state referred in the proximality principle is identical to the introspectible conscious perceptual experience that a subject has when she consciously perceives the world, as opposed to a perceptual state that obtains when a subject consciously perceives the world?

Compare here the following remarks from Hinton:

> It would be absurd not to posit, not to hypothesize, similar going-on in me when I see a flash of light and when I have that illusion. It is then easy to confuse these goings-on with the subjective events that our *esprit faux* prompts us to introduce.
>
> It prompts us strongly when, say, we see a flash of light while reflecting on the fact that there must be something similar going on in us to what goes on when we get a phosphene. 'Not only must there be, but there is, and this is it' – is then our thought. 'This' however, is whatever it happens to be: if we are in fact seeing a flash of light it is our seeing a flash of light and not something that happens when we see a flash of light.
>
> (1967: 226)

The challenge that Hinton's remarks pose for the opponent of disjunctivism is the following. Assume that the science of perception does indeed establish that there are perceptual state-kinds that are common to cases of genuine perception and hallucination and that are attributable to the perceiving subject. This won't in itself be enough to establish that what you are introspectively aware of in the case of genuine perception *just is* what you would be introspectively aware of in the case of hallucination. For in order to establish that claim one would also need to establish that what you are introspectively aware of in the case of genuine perception *just is* the perceptual state kind postulated by the science. And neither the science nor introspection has established that.

If one isn't justified in claiming that the nature of conscious perceptual experience is exhaustively accounted for – and explained – by the representational perceptual state-kinds postulated by the science of perception, then one isn't justified in claiming that the kind of perceptual state that is referred to in the proximity principle is identical to the introspectible conscious perceptual experience that a subject has when she consciously perceives the world (as opposed to a perceptual state that obtains when she has such an experience). So the disjunctivist position isn't incompatible with the science of perception given that the science of perception hasn't established that the representational perceptual state-kinds that it postulates suffice to fix – and account for – the conscious character of our conscious perceptual experiences.

In the final section of the chapter we'll review and clarify what one would, and wouldn't, be committed to in adopting Hinton's disjunctivist stance.

2.3 Hinton's disjunctivist commitments

Someone endorsing Hinton's disjunctivism need not deny that there is some common effect that occurs both in cases of genuine perception and causally matching hallucination. The view that Hinton is targeting is one that takes a particular stance on what that common effect will be. According to Hinton, we may be justified in asserting that there is some common effect that occurs both when one genuinely perceives an O, and when one hallucinates an O. He says, 'It would be absurd not to posit that happening, but there is no reason to identify it with, or marry it to, a chimera' (1967: 220). So what is the 'chimera' that we have no reason to identify this common effect with, according to Hinton?

The particular view that Hinton seems to want to target is one that commits to the following. There is some conscious experiential event that occurs both when one genuinely perceives an O and when one hallucinates an O, *which has exactly the same introspectible properties*: the same 'worn-on-the-sleeve' properties. On this view, the conscious character of the perceptual experience that one has when one genuinely perceives an O is solely determined by introspectible properties – phenomenal properties – that this experiential event can possess whether or not one is perceptually aware of an O. So on this view, the conscious character of the experience that a subject has when she consciously perceives an O isn't determined by the obtaining of a *relation* of conscious perceptual awareness, a relation that obtains between the subject and the object, O, that she is perceiving.

According to the target view, given that a conscious perceptual experience is an event whose conscious character is solely determined by its possession of phenomenal properties that it can possess whether or not the subject of experience is perceptually aware of anything, when a subject has a conscious perceptual experience she is thereby in a position to establish conclusively what kind of phenomenal event she is undergoing, simply through introspection, while remaining *neutral* on the question of whether or not she is genuinely perceiving anything.[5]

Hinton takes that target view to be unwarranted. For according to Hinton, when a subject consciously perceives an O, she is not in a position to conclusively establish through introspection that the conscious character of her experience is *not* determined by the obtaining of a *relation* of conscious perceptual awareness, a relation that obtains between her and the object, O, that she is perceiving. So if a subject is consciously perceiving an O, and she is uncertain as to whether or not she is genuinely perceiving an O, then she won't be in a position to conclusively establish through introspection alone that her experience is some event the conscious character of which is solely determined by its possession of phenomenal properties that that event can possess whether or not she is perceiving an O. From Hinton's point of view, then, those who endorse the target view are making an unwarranted assumption about what can be established through introspection.

Hinton isn't saying that if one is uncertain as to whether or not one is perceiving an O, then one can't know *anything* through introspection about the conscious experience one is having. For Hinton notes that one can establish through introspection that *either* one is seeing an O, *or* one is having an illusion of so doing. But the challenge that Hinton issues to his opponents is to show that the introspective evidence entitles one to anything stronger and more committal than what is captured by disjunctive claims of this form, hence the 'disjunctivist' label that has been attached to this approach to perception. One may be able to express one's neutral report of what one can establish through introspection in non-disjunctive form. For example, if one is unsure whether or not one is genuinely perceiving an O, one may be in a position to know, through introspection alone, that one seems to see an O. 'I seem to see an O' is not a disjunctive statement. But Hinton argues that that doesn't in itself show that one has thereby established anything stronger than what is captured by the disjunctive statement. According to Hinton, you may be justified in thinking that you seem to see an O both when you see an O and when you hallucinate an O. But you should not assume that an event of the same kind justifies your thinking that in each case. You may not be in a position to know what kind of conscious perceptual experience is justifying you in thinking that you seem to see an O – the kind you have when you see an O, or the kind you have when you hallucinate and merely seem to see an O.[6]

So Hinton's view appears to be the following. Although we may be justified in asserting that there is something that happens both when one genuinely perceives an O, and when one hallucinates an O, the 'chimera' with which one has no reason to identify that common effect, is some conscious experiential event that occurs both when one genuinely perceives an O, and when one hallucinates an O, and which has exactly the same introspectible phenomenal properties in each case. In adopting Hinton's disjunctivist stance one doesn't thereby rule out the possibility that there is a common *psychological* effect that occurs both in cases of genuine perception and cases of causally matching hallucination. Moreover, one doesn't thereby rule out that there may be a common psychological effect that plays an important explanatory role in the science of perception. So it seems that someone's adopting Hinton's disjunctivist stance need not deny the claims that I listed earlier when discussing Burge's assessment of what the science of perception has established:

(i) in cases of genuine perception and certain cases of hallucination (e.g. causally matching hallucination) there occurs a common *psychological* effect, and not merely a common physiological effect;
(ii) the common psychological effect includes a non-relational, representational perceptual state-kind that is attributable to the perceiver;
(iii) such non-relational, representational perceptual state-kinds, common to genuine perception and hallucination, play a fundamental explanatory role in the science of perception.

What someone adopting Hinton's disjunctivist stance will need to deny is the following: the proximate cause of the conscious perceptual experience that a subject has in a case of genuine perception produces in that subject *only* those psychological effects that the relevant proximate cause would produce in the subject if she were having a causally matching hallucination. But an advocate of Hinton's disjunctivism isn't obliged to deny the following, weaker claim:

in the case of genuine perception there is a psychological effect produced in the subject of experience by the proximate cause of her experience which is the kind of effect that such a proximate cause would produce in her if she were having a causally matching hallucination.

In this disjunctivist view, although there may be a common psychological effect produced both in cases of genuine perception and hallucination, there is, nonetheless, a psychological *difference* between these cases. The genuine perception actually has the conscious character that the causally matching hallucination merely seems to have. If the disjunctivist is right in thinking that there really is this psychological difference between the cases, then one might wonder what explanatory role, if any, should be assigned to the difference. A related but more general question one might ask is the following: if we assume that the representational perceptual state-kind that is postulated by the science of perception can explain the role played by experience in enabling the subject of experience to acquire information about her environment, and if we further assume that this representational perceptual state-kind does not suffice to fix the conscious character of experience, then what additional explanatory role, if any, is played by the conscious character of experience? These are questions we shall be addressing in Chapter 4.

There are further important questions to be asked of the sort of disjunctivist position that I have sketched so far. As we've seen, a crucial feature of this form of disjunctivism about conscious character is the claim that in the case of hallucination the subject's conscious perceptual experience seems to possess an introspectible feature that it in fact lacks. Hinton appears to think that this claim should be no more problematic than the claim that a perceived object can lack some feature that it perceptually seems to have. But is this really so? We shall discuss whether there may be reason to think otherwise in Chapter 6. As we'll also discuss in Chapter 6, if the disjunctivist's view of conscious perception is to be tenable, she'll need to provide an adequate response to a modified version of the sort of causal argument from hallucination that I outlined in Chapter 1.

First though, we shall be examining in more detail whether there really is any positive reason to think that the disjunctivist's view of conscious perception is correct. So far we have looked at ways in which the disjunctivist may attempt to block certain arguments that purport to show that her favoured view of conscious perception is untenable. But the success of that defensive manoeuvre wouldn't in itself show that the disjunctivist's favoured view of conscious perception was sufficiently motivated. In the next chapter we will be looking in more detail at some of the competing proposals that have been made about the conscious character of conscious perceptual experience, and examining an argument that purports to show that there are considerations that tell in favour of the disjunctivist's proposal.

2.4 Chapter summary

In this chapter we introduced a *non*-relational view of perceptual experience that is endorsed by the majority of those who reject sense-datum theories of perception. According to this view a subject's conscious perceptual experience is a *representational* mental state/event that is directed on her environment. Those who endorse this view hold that our perceptual experiences have representational contents that are specified in terms of their veridicality conditions.

We noted that this representationalist approach to perceptual experience offers a way of accounting for the role that conscious perception plays in enabling the subject of experience to acquire information about her immediate environment – for example in enabling the subject of experience to interact with and navigate her immediate environment – as well as the role that such experience plays in in the generation of a subject's perceptual beliefs about her immediate environment, for example beliefs about what and where things are. A further virtue of the representationalist approach is that it appears to provide a helpful framework within which scientific theorising about sense perception can be fruitfully pursued. On the assumption that sensory perception has the function of *representing* the world in the service of action and cognition, a central task of an empirical investigation of the senses becomes that of determining and explaining the processes by which perceptual systems generate perceptual states with specific veridicality conditions from specific types of stimulation of the subject's sensory receptors.

We considered the case that Burge makes for this approach, and his argument for the claim that there is a principle implicit in the causal explanations offered by the science of perception which should lead us to accept that perceptual states of the same fundamental kind can be generated in cases of successful perception, illusion, and hallucination. This is the 'proximality principle'.

We then introduced a relational, naïve realist account of veridical perception. We considered whether these naïve realist accounts of conscious perception are inconsistent with what has been established by the science of perception, and we outlined how naïve realists have appealed to a form of disjunctivism about the phenomenal character of perceptual experience in defence of their account of veridical perception.

Here we introduced the disjunctivist strategy that was first proposed by J. M. Hinton. Hinton's disjunctivism questions the assumption that introspectively indistinguishable experiences must have the same introspectible properties in common. We compared and contrasted Hinton's defensive disjunctive strategy with the defensive manoeuvre deployed by J. L. Austin (1962), which was introduced in Chapter 1. We considered how Hinton's disjunctivist strategy can be deployed by the naïve realist in response to two lines of argument that purport to establish that her favoured view of veridical perception is untenable. The first line of argument appeals to introspection, and in particular the idea that hallucinations can be introspectively indistinguishable from genuine perceptions; and the second line of argument appeals to the claim that the disjunctivist view is incompatible with the science of perception, and in particular, the proximality principle.

We ended the chapter by reviewing what one would and wouldn't be committed to in adopting Hinton's disjunctivist stance.

Notes

1 Those who endorse the idea that perceptual experiences have representational contents with veridicality conditions include Evans 1982, Searle 1983, Harman 1990, Peacocke 1992, Burge 1993 and 2010, Tye 1992 and 1995, Pautz 2010, and Siegel 2010.
2 For a summary and further discussion of this approach, see Burge 2005 and 2010.
3 See for example Peacocke 1983: Ch. 1, Block 2003, or Chalmers 1996.
4 See Hinton 1967, 1973, and 1980.
5 Hence we have Hinton saying, when addressing his opponent, 'You want a predicate whose applicability to what is happening in or to me is made clear to me by the very fact of that thing's happening' (1967: 225).
6 See Hinton 1967: 223.

Further reading

The following are among those who endorse the idea that perceptual experiences have representational contents with veridicality conditions: Evans 1982, Searle 1983, Harman 1990, Peacocke 1992, Burge 1991 and 2010, Tye 1992 and 1995, Dretske 1995, Byrne 2001, and Siegel 2010. For an overview of different appeals to the representational content of perceptual experience, see Siegel 2015.

For Burge's defence of the 'proximality principle', and his critique of disjunctivist views of perception, see his 2005, 2010, and 2011. For an excellent general introduction to the science of vision, see Palmer 1999. For a disjunctivist response to Burge, see Campbell 2010. See also Travis 2011, which is also collected in his 2013.

For a Hinton's disjunctivism see his 1967, 1973, and 1980. Hinton's 1967, and selections from his 1973, can also be found in Byrne and Logue 2009. For discussion of the historical significance of Hinton, see Snowdon 2008. For a discussion of the question of whether introspective indistinguishability entails sameness of phenomenal character, see Martin 1997, which also appears in Byrne and Logue 2009.

References

Austin, J. L., 1962, *Sense and Sensibilia*. Oxford: Oxford University Press.
Block, N., 2003, 'Mental paint', in M. Hahn and B. Ramberg (eds), *Reflections and Replies: essays on the philosophy of Tyler Burge*. Cambridge, MA: MIT Press.
Burge, Tyler, 2005, 'Disjunctivism and perceptual psychology', *Philosophical Topics*, 33: 1–78.
——, 2007, *Foundations of Mind*. Oxford: Oxford University Press.
——, 2010, *Origins of Objectivity*. Oxford: Oxford University Press.
——, 2011, 'Disjunctivism again', *Philosophical Explorations*, 14 (1): 43–80.
Byrne, Alex and Logue, Heather (eds), 2009, *Disjunctivism: contemporary readings*. Cambridge, MA: MIT Press.
Campbell, John, 2010, 'Demonstrative reference, the relational view of experience and the proximality principle', in Robin Jeshion (ed.), *New Essays on Singular Thought*. Oxford: Oxford University Press, pp. 193–212.
Chalmers, D. J., 1996, *The Conscious Mind: in search of a fundamental theory*. New York: Oxford University Press.

Dretske, Fred, 1995, *Naturalizing the Mind*. Cambridge, MA: MIT Press.
Evans, Gareth, 1982, *The Varieties of Reference*. Oxford: Clarendon Press.
Harman, Gilbert, 1990, 'The intrinsic quality of experience', in J. Tomberlin (ed.), *Philosophical Perspectives*, 4. Atascadero, CA: Ridgeview, pp. 31–52.
Hinton, J. M., 1967, 'Visual experiences', *Mind*, 76 (April): 217–227.
——, 1973, *Experiences: an inquiry into some ambiguities*. Oxford: Clarendon Press.
——, 1980, 'Phenomenological specimenism', *Analysis*, 40 (January): 37–41.
Martin, M. G. F., 1997, 'The reality of appearances', in M. Sainsbury (ed.), *Thought and Ontology*. Milan: Franco Angeli, pp. 77–96.
Palmer, Stephen, 1999, *Vision Science: photons to phenomenology*. Cambridge, MA: MIT Press.
Pautz, Adam, 2010, 'Why explain visual experience in terms of content?', in B. Nanay (ed.), *Perceiving the World*. Oxford: Oxford University Press, pp. 254–310.
Peacocke, Christopher, 1983, *Sense and Content: experience, thought and their relations*. Oxford: Oxford University Press.
——, 1992, *A Study of Concepts*. Cambridge, MA: MIT Press.
Searle, John, 1983, *Intentionality*. Cambridge: Cambridge University Press.
Siegel, Susanna, 2010, *The Contents of Visual Experience*. Oxford: Oxford University Press.
——, 2015, 'The contents of perception', Edward N. Zalta (ed.), *The Stanford Encyclopedia of Philosophy* (Spring 2015 Edition). <http://plato.stanford.edu/archives/spr2015/entries/perception-contents/>.
Snowdon, P. F., 2008, 'Hinton and the origins of disjunctivism', in Fiona Macpherson and Adrian Haddock (eds), *Disjunctivism: perception, action, knowledge*. Oxford: Oxford University Press, pp. 35–56.
Travis, Charles, 2004, 'The silence of the senses', *Mind*, 113 (449): 57–94.
——, 2011, 'Desperately seeking Ψ', *Philosophical Issues* 21 (1): 505–557.
——, 2013, *Perception: essays after Frege*. Oxford: Oxford University Press.
Tye, M., 1992, 'Visual qualia and visual content', in Tim Crane (ed.), *The Contents of Experience*. Cambridge: Cambridge University Press, pp. 158–176.
——, 1995, *Ten Problems of Consciousness*. Cambridge, MA: MIT Press.

3

DOES INTROSPECTIVE REFLECTION SUPPORT NAÏVE REALISM?

When I introduced the sense-datum theory in Chapter 1, I mentioned some considerations that might be appealed to by those wishing to defend the claim that conscious perceptual experience is a relational phenomenon. In particular, I briefly summarised a case that might be made for thinking that there is positive introspective support for the view, and an absence of introspective support for the alternative non-relational views. Those who adopt the disjunctivist view of the conscious character of perceptual experience that I introduced in Chapter 2 agree that there is introspective support for the claim that conscious perceptual experience is a relational phenomenon. Although they reject sense-datum theories, they nonetheless maintain that when you genuinely perceive the world, the conscious perceptual experience that you have is relational: they hold that the conscious character of the experience that you have when you consciously perceive the world is to be explained, at least in part, by the obtaining of a relation of conscious perceptual awareness, a relation that obtains between you, as subject of experience, and aspects of your mind-independent environment.

If these disjunctivists are right in thinking that introspective reflection really does support their commitments with regard to the conscious character of the perceptual experience involved in genuine perception, then this has the potential to weaken significantly the dialectical position of those defending a non-relational account of the conscious character of perceptual experience. Those defending such non-relational views would have to concede that none of our conscious perceptual experiences actually have the sort of conscious character that they introspectively seem to have. In making this concession they obviously thereby allow that it is possible for a conscious perceptual experience to lack the conscious character that it introspectively seems to have. As we saw in the previous chapter, once that point is conceded, the disjunctivist can argue that the fact that a hallucination can be introspectively indiscriminable from a genuine perception should not in itself oblige us to provide the same account of the conscious character of each; for we can instead adopt a view according to which the genuine perceptions actually have the conscious character that they introspectively seem to have, while the introspectively indiscriminable hallucinations merely seem to have that conscious character. The disjunctivist may then argue that it is better to adopt a view on which at least some of our conscious perceptual experiences – the genuine perceptions – have the sort of conscious character that they introspectively seem to have, rather than sticking to a view that has as a consequence a commitment that is more drastically at odds with the deliverances of introspection, namely a view according to which *none* of our perceptual experiences has the sort of conscious character that they introspectively seem to have.

In this chapter we'll be looking in more detail at whether there really are phenomenological considerations that tell in favour of the disjunctivist's account of the conscious character of genuine perception. We'll begin by reviewing some of the phenomenological considerations that were sketched out in Chapter 1. We'll consider ways in which one may be able to accommodate the deliverances of introspective reflection without committing to a relational account of perceptual experience, and without committing to the claim that hallucinations lack the conscious character that they introspectively seem to have. We'll then consider an argument put forward by M. G. F. Martin (2002) that purports to identify a problem for the non-relationalist's attempt to accommodate the conscious character of perceptual experience. As we'll see, with this argument Martin attempts to show that introspective reflection on the phenomenology of sensory imagination can provide a way of revealing shortcomings in the non-relationalist's attempt to accommodate certain aspects of the phenomenology of conscious perceptual experience.

3.1 Relationalist and representationalist accounts of the phenomenology of perceptual experience

Let's now reconsider in more detail some of the phenomenological claims that I suggested a relationalist might appeal to in support of their view of the conscious character of experience. In Chapter 1 I suggested that the relationalist might offer the following description of what it is like to attend introspectively to an experience of a blue, round object. Claim 1:

> As I attempt to introspect those qualities of my experience that determine what it is like for me to be having the experience, it seems as though I am thereby attending to a blue, round thing. The qualities that I seem to be attending to as I introspect my experience (blueness, roundness) are neither qualities of some psychological event I am undergoing, nor qualities of some psychological state that I am in, so it doesn't seem as if those qualities can be what-it-is-like properties of my experience. However, those qualities (blueness, roundness) nonetheless appear to play an important role in determining what it is like for me to be having the experience. So, for example, if when introspectively attending to my experience I found myself attending to different qualities – for example greenness and squareness – then what it would be like for me to be having the experience would be different.

I suggested that the relationalist is in a position to offer the following explanation of this aspect of the phenomenology.

> Your conscious perceptual experience involves the obtaining of a conscious perceptual relation. Introspective reflection on your experience involves being aware of what you are related to and the manner in which you are related to it. There is something it is like for you to have a conscious perceptual experience insofar as there is something it is like for you to be the subject of the conscious perceptual relation that obtains

when you have that experience, and this is determined, at least in part, by what you are related to. So the quality of blueness, what *that* quality is like, while not a quality of experience itself, nonetheless determines, at least in part, what it is like for you to be consciously, perceptually aware of it.

According to the alternative, non-relationalist accounts, one's conscious perceptual experience is some psychological state/event that can obtain/occur whether or not you are perceptually aware of anything. The conscious character of the perceptual experience that you have in such cases is solely determined by properties possessed by this non-relational psychological state/event, properties that the relevant psychological state/event can possess whether or not you are perceptually aware of anything. So the conscious character of the experience that you have when you consciously perceive a blue round object is not to be explained by appeal to a relation of conscious perceptual awareness that obtains between you, as subject of experience, and the blue round object you perceive. Against this claim I suggested the relationalist may make the following phenomenological observation. Claim 2:

> When you have a conscious perceptual experience and you introspectively reflect on the experience you are having, it doesn't seem to you as though you are in a position to introspectively focus in on, and discern, some conscious psychological element that is *in*sufficient for perceptual contact with something. It seems, from the inside, so to speak, as though one cannot focus introspectively on one's conscious perceptual experience *without* attending to some object one is perceptually aware of in having that experience. I cannot now introspectively discern some conscious psychological element of my current situation that seems to be *in*sufficient for the presence of the blue, round object. My attempt to now shift my attention from that blue, round object and its properties to some psychological event or state and its properties – a conscious event or state that isn't in itself sufficient for the presence of that object blue round object – seems to fail.

The relationalist will offer the following explanation of this aspect of the phenomenology.

> Your conscious perceptual experience is not some event/state that is insufficient for the obtaining of a relation of conscious perceptual awareness. When you introspectively attend to the conscious character of your

experience you are not merely introspectively aware of some psychological state/event that can obtain whether or not you are perceptually aware of anything. The conscious perceptual element of your current situation is *sufficient* for the obtaining of that relation. That is why you cannot focus on your conscious perceptual experience without attending to the entities that are constituents of the conscious perceptual relation that obtains when you have a conscious perceptual experience.

Now let us consider what a non-relationalist may say in response to these phenomenological claims. The non-relationalist can accept that when you consciously perceive something, a perceptual relation obtains between you, as subject of experience, and the entities that you perceive. However, she will maintain that the conscious character of the experience that you have when you perceive an object is solely determined by properties that the experience can possesses whether or not that perceptual relation obtains. Given that constraint, what sort of properties of experience might the non-relationalist cite in an attempt to accommodate the deliverances of introspection?

As we saw in the previous chapter, the non-relationalist may cite representational properties that the experience possesses in virtue of being a state/event with a representational content that has veridicality conditions. It should be noted that those adopting this view may hold that there are important differences between the content of thought and the representational content of experience, and they may maintain that such differences play an important role in accommodating what is phenomenologically distinctive of conscious perceptual experience, in contrast to thought. For example, they may hold that the representational content of perceptual experience, in contrast to thought, is non-conceptual, they may hold that such experiential contents are more replete with informational detail than the content of thought, and they may maintain that such experiential contents are analogue in character.[1] As I noted in Chapter 2, there is a debate among non-relationalists as to whether one can adequately accommodate certain aspects of the conscious character of perceptual experience by simply postulating the right combination of representational states, with the right kinds of representational contents. Some non-relationalists contend that to accommodate fully what it is like for one to have such experience, we should also appeal to *non*-representational phenomenal properties of experience – sometimes called 'sensational' properties, or 'qualia'. I shall be considering that proposal in Chapter 4, but for now I want to put aside that particular debate, and focus instead on a further feature of perceptual experience that plays a key role in the non-relationalist's attempt to accommodate the deliverances of introspective reflection.

The non-relationalist who appeals to the representational content of experience in attempting to accommodate the conscious character of perceptual experience has reason to accept the following. The representational properties that a psychological state possesses simply in virtue of having a representational content with veridicality conditions won't in themselves suffice to fix the kind of impact that the relevant psychological state has on the mental life of its subject. To see why, consider, for example, the difference between a belief that p and a mere supposition that p (e.g. the kind of supposition in play when one merely supposes that p for the sake of argument). Although both aspects of mind have exactly the same propositional content, and in that sense have the same representational properties, the causal and rational roles that each play in one's mental economy are very different. This is because the individuation of a psychological state as a *belief* that p, as opposed to say a mere supposition that p, crucially depends not merely on the content of the state, but also on the distinctive attitude taken to that content; and we need to appeal to this distinctive attitude if we are to accommodate the distinctive sort of causal and rational role that such a psychological state plays in one's mental economy.

The relevance of this point to our concern with the non-relationalist's account of the conscious character of perceptual experience is the following. When we consider the resources that are available to the non-relationalist in accommodating the deliverances of introspective reflection, we need to bear in mind that she may appeal not only to the representational content of the psychological state one is in when one has a conscious perceptual experience, but also to the distinctive causal/functional and rational role of that psychological state. An account of the distinctive causal/functional and rational role of the kind of psychological state that one is in when one has a conscious perceptual experience is likely to focus in particular on the way in which such experience will tend, in the normal case, to fix and rationalise one's beliefs about one's immediate environment. So, for example, if the content of the psychological state one is in when one has a conscious perceptual experience represents a blue round object before one, then one will, in the normal case, believe that there is such an object there; and one will, in the normal case, be justified in so believing. Specification of the causal/functional role of the relevant psychological state need not commit to the claim that such states will inevitably fix one's beliefs about one's immediate environment come what may. For example, a subject may fail to believe that there is a blue round object before her even though she has an experience that represents one, if there are countervailing considerations that give her reason to distrust her senses on that occasion. However, even if the subject distrusts her senses (e.g. even if she has reason to believe she is hallucinating) there is a respect in which the experience itself will still be committal on the question of whether there is a blue round object before her. (That is why we would regard such an experience as misleading.) And this, the non-relationalist will claim, is a reflection of the causal/functional role of the kind of psychological state one is in when one has such an experience.

With these points in mind, let's turn to what a non-relationalist may say in response to the phenomenological claims outlined above – i.e. those phenomenological claims that were supposed to lend support to the relationalist view. With respect to Claim 1, the non-relationalist may respond in the following way.

> When you have a conscious perceptual experience as of a blue, round object you will be in a psychological state with a content that represents a blue round object. Moreover, given the causal/functional role of the psychological state you are thereby in, it will seem to you as if (and in the normal case you will believe that) there is a blue round object before you for you to attend to. The qualities that you thereby seem to be in a position to attend to – blueness and roundness – are not themselves properties of your experience, and so they are not what-it-is-like properties of your experience. They are, rather, properties *represented* by the psychological state you are in. However, the representational properties of your experience contribute to determining what it is like for you to have the experience. So if the content of your experience represented different qualities – for example if it represented a green and square object – you would thereby seem to be in a position to attend to a green square object, rather than a blue round object, and what it would be like for you to have that experience would be different.

With this form of response, the non-relationalist can maintain that one can adequately accommodate those aspects of the phenomenology of conscious perceptual experience upon which Claim 1 is based, without having to appeal to the actual obtaining of a relation of conscious perceptual awareness. One can adequately accommodate the phenomenology by citing instead the representational content of the psychological state you are in when you have a conscious perceptual experience, as well as the causal/functional role of that psychological state.

In response to the second phenomenological claim – Claim 2 – the non-relationalist may say the following.

> When you have an experience as of a blue round object, the apparent presence before you of that object is to be explained by the representational content of the psychological state you are in and the causal/functional role that a state of that kind plays in your mental economy. The conscious perceptual experience that you have is not in itself sufficient for the presence of the blue object, but the experience is itself nonetheless committal on the question of whether there is such an object there. The respect in which the experience is committal and non-neutral is a reflection of the distinctive causal/functional role of the psychological state you are in, and the distinctive causal/functional role of the state is not altered or neutralised when you attend introspectively to your experience. When you introspectively attend to your experience you are still in a psychological state that is committal about the presence of a blue round object, and so it will still seem to you as if (and in the normal case you will believe that) there is such an object there for you to attend to.

Note here that the relationalist and the non-relationalist can both assent to the general claim that there is a respect in which conscious perceptual experience is *committal* with respect to the question of whether the object of experience is actually present; and they can both agree that this remains the case when one attempts to shift one's introspective focus to the experience itself. But they offer rather different accounts of this committal aspect of the phenomenology. According to the non-relationalist, the relationalist misdescribes, or at least overdescribes, this aspect of the phenomenology. The relationalist claims that it introspectively seems to one as if the experience itself is *sufficient* for the actual presence of the object of experience, for she claims that it introspectively seems to one as though the experience itself suffices for the obtaining of a relation of perceptual awareness – a relation that obtains between the subject of experience, and the object she seems to perceive. Hence the relationalist's claim that if the apparent object of experience is not present, then one's experience doesn't have the sort of conscious character that it introspectively seems to have. The non-relationalist, on the other hand, denies that introspective reflection supports the claim that the experience itself suffices for the actual presence of the object. According to the non-relationalist, the committal aspect of the phenomenology of perceptual experience is, rather, to be explained by the causal/functional role of the psychological state one is in when one has a conscious perceptual experience. And this feature of the psychological state doesn't depend on the obtaining of a relation of perceptual awareness. In virtue of the fact that one is in a psychological state with that distinctive causal/functional role, it will perceptually seem to one as though the object of experience is present, and that will remain true when one introspects one's experience. If the object of experience is not present, then things will be misleading, in so far as one's environment won't be the way that it perceptually seems to one to be. But introspective reflection doesn't support the further claim that in such a case one's *experience* isn't the way it seems to be, for it doesn't introspectively seem to one as though the experience itself *suffices* for the actual presence of the object of experience.

At the beginning of this chapter I said that those who adopt a disjunctivist view of the conscious character of perceptual experience maintain that there is introspective support for the claim that conscious perceptual experience is a relational phenomenon. Although they reject sense-datum theories, they nonetheless hold that the conscious perceptual experience that you have when you genuinely perceive the world is relational. They hold that the conscious character of the experience that you have when you consciously perceive the world is to be explained, at least in part, by the obtaining of a relation of conscious perceptual awareness; a relation that obtains between you, as subject of experience, and aspects of your mind-independent environment. These disjunctivists agree that there is introspective support for the relationalist account of the committal phenomenology of conscious perceptual experience. They agree that if the apparent object of experience is not present, then one's experience doesn't have the sort of conscious character that it introspectively seems to have.

Since they reject sense-datum theories of perception, and so deny that the conscious experience had in the case of complete hallucination is a relational phenomenon, they hold that such hallucinations don't have the conscious character that they introspectively seem to have. So a key point of dispute between this sort of disjunctivist and her non-relationalist opponents centres on a disagreement over the appropriate characterisation of what I have been calling the committal phenomenology of conscious perceptual experience.

If the disjunctivist's characterisation of the committal aspect of the phenomenology of perceptual experience is correct, then it introspectively seems to one as if one's experience itself suffices for the actual presence of the object of experience; and if the apparent object of experience is not present, then one's experience doesn't have the sort of conscious character that it introspectively seems to have. On the other hand, if the non-relationalist's characterisation of the committal phenomenology of perceptual experience is correct, introspective reflection does not support the claim that one's experience itself suffices for the actual presence of the object of experience. According to the non-relationalist, if the object of experience is not present, then things will be misleading in so far as one's environment won't be the way that it perceptually seems to one to be. But introspective reflection doesn't support the further claim that in such a case one's *experience* isn't the way it seems to be.

In the next section we'll examine an argument introduced by M. G. F Martin (2002) that purports to show that there is reason to favour the disjunctivist's characterisation of the committal phenomenology of conscious perceptual experience.

3.2 Martin's phenomenological argument for naïve realism

The argument presented by Martin is offered in support of naïve realism. According to this view, when one genuinely perceives one's environment, the phenomenal, conscious character of one's experience is constituted, at least in part, by the mind-independent aspects of one's environment that one perceives: the concrete mind-independent individuals, their properties, and the events they partake in. In this view, the conscious perceptual experience you have when you perceive the world is relational. The mind-independent entities you perceive are constituents of that relation, and hence constituents of your experience. The conscious character of the experience you have is to be explained, at least in part, in terms of the actual obtaining of that conscious perceptual relation, hence the mind-independent constituents of that relation (e.g. the mind-independent objects and properties you perceive) contribute to determining what it is like for you to be having the experience. Those advocating this naïve realist view endorse the relationalist characterisation of the committal phenomenology of conscious perceptual experience. The naïve realist holds that it introspectively seems to one as if one's experience itself *suffices* for the actual presence of the mind-independent entities one perceives, and if such apparent objects of experience are not actually present, then one's experience doesn't have the sort of conscious character that it introspectively seems to have.

Martin argues that this naïve realist view best articulates how sensory experience seems to us to be through introspective reflection. As we've seen, the non-relationalist may claim that the relationalist misdescribes, or at least overdescribes, the committal aspect of the phenomenology of perceptual experience. The non-relationalist is liable to claim that we can adequately accommodate the respect in which conscious perceptual experience is committal with respect to the question of whether a mind-independent object of experience is actually present, without having to endorse naïve realism, and indeed, without having to agree that naïve realism best articulates how one's conscious experience introspectively *seems* to be. Against this, Martin argues that reflection on the phenomenology of sensory imagination can help to reveal that the naïve realist hasn't overdescribed the committal aspect of the phenomenology of conscious perceptual experience. Reflection on the phenomenology of sensory imagination can reveal that there are reasons to favour the relationalist characterisation of the committal phenomenology of perceptual experience, over the competing non-relationalist alternative.

Martin's argument for this claim has the following structure:

(i) He starts by comparing and contrasting the different ways in which the naïve realist and the 'intentionalist' attempt to accommodate the fact that the phenomenology of conscious perceptual experience is committal with respect to the actual presence of mind-independent objects in one's environment. As Martin uses the term, the 'intentionalist' is a non-relationalist who claims that our perceptual experiences have representational contents with veridicality conditions. So the contrast he draws between the naïve realist and the 'intentionalist'

corresponds to the contrast I have been drawing between the relationalist, disjunctivist view of the committal phenomenology of conscious perceptual, and the non-relationalist alternative.
(ii) Next, Martin argues for a thesis about visualising – the 'dependency thesis', which states that to visualise an F is to imagine a visual experience of an F.[2]
(iii) He then argues that the truth of the dependency thesis should lead the intentionalist and the naïve realist to make different predictions about the phenomenology of visualising, given their different accounts of the committal phenomenology of conscious perceptual experience. So, he claims, the phenomenology of visualising can be regarded as a test of these competing views.
(iv) Finally, he argues that the phenomenology of our episodes of visualising favours the naïve realist account.

I have already outlined the competing ways in which the naïve realist and the non-relationalist characterise the committal aspect of the phenomenology of conscious perceptual experience, so let's now proceed to the second stage of Martin's argument: his argument for the 'dependency thesis' about visualising.

When one visualises an object or scene, one engages in a conscious activity with a phenomenology that seems to correspond, in certain respects to a visual experience of that object or scene. This sort of episode of sensory imagining doesn't have the committal phenomenology of conscious visual experience. That is to say, when one visualises an object, the phenomenology of that episode isn't committal on the question of whether there is such an object actually present before one. So, for example, if no such object is actually present, then one wouldn't say that the episode of imagining was in any way misleading. Nonetheless, it seems that the phenomenology of the *sensory, imagistic* character of the episode of visualising bears some relation to the conscious character of visual experience. According to those who advocate the dependency thesis, the phenomenological correspondence in question is to be explained, at least in part, in terms of the idea that when one visualises an object, one imagines a visual experience of that object. The episode of visualising doesn't actually have the conscious character of a visual experience of the object, but it nonetheless involves a distinctive way of representing the conscious character of a visual experience of the object.

To get a sense of the respect in which it may be said that we have available to us distinctive way of representing the conscious character of an experience without actually being in a state that has the conscious character of the experience in question, consider the following sort of case, which Martin discusses: a case in which one imagines what it is like to feel a sensation (such as an itch) on some part of one's body (e.g. one's thigh). One can talk about, and think about, feeling an itch on one's thigh without actually feeling one; and this way of representing an itch needn't involve imagining, 'from the inside', what it would be like to feel one. But one can also represent an itch on one's thigh by imagining what it would be like to feel the sensation: one can imaginatively project a sensation of that kind onto one's thigh. And when one does so, there is certain kind of correspondence between the phenomenology of the episode of imagining and the phenomenology of the experience one would have if one actually felt such an itch on one's thigh. Now when one represents the conscious character of the sensation in this distinctive way, one isn't thereby in a state that actually has the conscious character of an itch. As Martin notes, 'it does not seem right to say that in this case one is still feeling an actual itch, albeit one that is less intense in character than itches not brought about through imagining' (2002: 406). So, although there is a certain kind of correspondence between the phenomenology of the episode of imagining and the phenomenology of feeling such a sensation, an explanation of this phenomenological correspondence shouldn't commit to the claim that the episode of imagining actually has the conscious character of the sensation it represents.

Now in the case of imagining, from the inside, what it is like to feel a bodily sensation, it seems relatively uncontroversial to say that one is thereby imagining the conscious character of something experiential, namely the feeling of the sensation. However, those advocating the dependency thesis commit to a more general and controversial claim, the claim that when one sensorily imagines an object or scene one is thereby imagining an experience of that object or scene. So, for example, those advocating the dependency thesis would claim that when you visualise an apple you are thereby imagining a visual experience of an apple. Why think that there is reason to commit to this more general claim?

In arguing for the dependency thesis, Martin appeals to certain perspectival aspects of visualising that appear to correspond with certain perspectival features of visual experience. He notes that one often visualises from a point of view, and gives as an example a case in which one visualises a red light and a green light, with the red light being visualised as to the left of the green light. He claims that if you now visualise the reverse – so you visualise the green light to the left of the red light – then there is a difference in your episode of visualising, and furthermore, what is visualised is different. Now the two situations that are visualised can only count as different if there is a *point of view* relative to which the one light is to the left and the other light is to the right. But is this point of view itself imagined?

If the point of view relative to which the lights are being imagined as being to the left and right is not itself imagined, then one will be imagining the lights to be to one's *actual* left and to one's *actual* right. This is something one could do: one might imaginatively project the imagined lights onto locations to the left and right in one's actual environment. But Martin suggests that this is not necessary and nor is it the simplest case of visualising the lights. In the simplest case (e.g. when one closes one's eyes and visualises the lights), one does not imagine the lights to be to one's *actual* left and to one's *actual* right, occupying positions in one's *actual* environment. Rather, in the simplest case, the point of view relative to which the lights are imagined as being to the left and right is itself imagined. What is represented when one visualises in this way, is not position of the lights relative to one's current, actual location, but rather the position of the lights relative to an *imagined* perspective on them. According to Martin, one visualises the lights as being to the left and right through imagining a point of view relative to which they are to the left and right, and one imagines this point of view through imagining a *visual experience* with the appropriate perspectival feature, i.e. one in which lights are experienced as being to the left and right. So in certain central cases of visualising, one visualises objects through imagining a visual experience of them. He writes,

> [W]hat difference need there be in the imagined scene in order for what has been imagined to be different in the two cases? . . . The two situations count as different only where there is a point of view relative to which the one object is to the left and the other to the right, or *vice versa*. So, if we absent a point of view from the imagined scene, then what appears in visualising to be a difference in the scene imagined, and not just a difference in one's state of mind, cannot be so . . . if one does have to imagine a point of view within the scene, then one thereby must be imagining an experience within that scene.
>
> (2002: 408–409)

One might object to this dependency thesis about visualising on the following grounds. Often when one visualises objects or events, imagining an experience of those objects and events need be no part of one's imaginative project. When I visualise the red and green lights, I need not be supposing that there is in that imagined situation me, or anyone else, having a visual experience of those lights. Indeed, I might be supposing that there is no one there to perceive the lights. Given that I need not be supposing that there is someone having a visual experience of those lights, doesn't an endorsement of the dependency thesis commit one to an implausible view of what is imagined in simple cases of visualising? Doesn't the advocate of the dependency thesis *overpopulate* the imagined situation, with *experiences* of objects, in addition to the objects that are visualised?

In order to see how an advocate of the dependency thesis might respond to this objection, it will be helpful first to address the following question. Is it possible to accept the dependency thesis without committing to the claim that when one visualises an object one thereby *supposes that* there occurs in the imagined scene an experience of that object? Something all parties are likely to agree with is that one can put the sensory imagery that is associated with visualising to a variety of different imaginative and cognitive purposes, and the different uses to which one puts such imagery won't simply be determined by the sensory character of that imagery. For example, one might visualise a scene in which a man is wearing a top hat. Now one might suppose that the man being visualised is a magician and that there is a rabbit concealed under his hat. When one makes the supposition that there is a rabbit present in the visualised scene, this need not make any difference to the sensory imagery one deploys when one imagines in this way. And in general, when one engages in some imaginative project, the suppositions one does and doesn't make aren't fixed by the sensory character of the imagery one deploys.

When you visualise the magician, you could suppose that you are in the imagined scene, looking at the magician, occupying the perspective from which the magician is visualised. Alternatively, you might suppose that someone other than you is occupying that perspective. But equally, you need not be making any suppositions about anyone occupying that perspective. And indeed, you need not be making any suppositions about the presence in that scene of a visual experience. But is that latter claim something that an advocate of the dependency thesis could accept? A point one might press against the advocate of the dependency thesis here is the following. According to the dependency thesis, whenever one visualises an object one thereby imagines an experience of that object. So if, when one visualises the object, one doesn't make any suppositions about the presence of a visual experience in the imagined scene, then in what sense has one imagined a visual experience of the object?

The key to Martin's proposal about visualising, as I understand it, is that when one visualises an object one thereby represents, in a distinctive kind of way, the conscious character of a visual experience of that object, just as when one imagines from the inside feeling an itch on one's thigh, one represents the conscious character of an itch in a distinctive kind of way. Representing a visual experience in this distinctive way, I take it, isn't meant to be equivalent to making a supposition about a visual experience. One can make suppositions about a visual experience without visualising anything, just as one can make suppositions about an itch on one's thigh without actually imagining from the inside what it would be like to feel one. Now the particular claim about visualising that Martin wishes to defend in his argument for the dependency thesis is one that is concerned with the *imagistic* aspects of visualising, rather than any non-imagistic suppositions one might make in deploying such imagery. So someone who accepts the dependency thesis that Martin is concerned to defend may claim that when one visualises an object, one thereby represents, in a distinctive kind of way, the conscious character of a visual experience of that object, and the visual experience one thereby represents is an imagined experience, insofar as it isn't a visual experience one is actually having. But any suppositions one does and doesn't make when one represents a visual experience in this way – any use to which one puts the imagery generated when one represents a visual experience in this way – is a further matter. So while it is true that when one visualises an object one thereby represents the conscious character of a visual experience of that object, in doing so one needn't be making any non-imagistic suppositions about the occurrence of a visual experience in the scene imagined.

On this understanding of what an advocate of the dependency thesis minimally commits, one could accept the thesis without committing to the claim that when one visualises an object one thereby *supposes that* there occurs in the imagined scene an experience of that object. For the question of whether there occurs in the imagined scene a visual experience of the object need be of no concern to one when one visualises the objects and puts the imagery generated to use in the imaginative project one is engaged in. The non-imagistic suppositions one makes when one puts the imagery to use may simply centre on the visualised objects, rather than with the question of whether experiences are occurring in the imagined scene (and, if so, who is having them). So in accepting the dependency thesis, one accepts that when one visualises the green and red lights one thereby represents, in a distinctive way, the conscious character of a visual experience of the lights, but when visualising the lights in this way, one need not be *supposing that* there is anyone in the imagined situation having a visual experience of those lights.

Let's assume that the advocate of the dependency thesis is simply making a proposal about the *imagistic* aspects of visualising, rather than any non-imagistic suppositions one might make in deploying such imagery. So let's grant that someone advocating the thesis can consistently maintain that when one visualises an object one need not be making any non-imagistic suppositions about the occurrence of a visual experience in the scene imagined. Still, it may be said, the thesis commits to an implausible view of the phenomenology of the imagistic aspects of visualising. For it might be said that when one visualises an object, for example an apple, the imagistic, sensory character of one's episode of imagining is not neutral with respect to the question of whether one has thereby imagined that object. That is, the imagery itself is not neutral with respect to the question of whether or not one has thereby imagined a scene containing an apple. However, if the dependency thesis is correct, then the imagery one deploys in visualising an apple is simply a matter of one's representing the conscious character of a visual experience of an apple; and in representing the conscious character of a visual experience of an apple, one won't have done enough to imagine a scene containing an apple. This is because one can have a visual experience of an apple whether or not an apple is present. So if the dependency thesis were correct, in order to imagine a scene containing an apple through visualisation, one would need not just the imagery, but also the further non-imagistic supposition that the visual experience one thereby represents is veridical: a case of *seeing* an apple.

From Martin's point of view, this would be a cogent line of objection to the dependency thesis if the non-relationalist's account of the conscious character of perceptual experience were correct. But this line of objection wouldn't have force if the naïve realist's account of the conscious character of perceptual experience were correct. And this is precisely why he regards reflection on the phenomenology of visualising as a test of competing views of the committal phenomenology of conscious perceptual experience.

Recall that a key point of dispute between the naïve realist disjunctivist and her non-relationalist opponents centres on the appropriate characterisation of the committal phenomenology of conscious perceptual experience. According to the naïve realist, it introspectively seems to one as if the conscious character of a visual experience of a mind-independent object itself *suffices* for the actual presence of that mind-independent object. If that mind-independent object is not present (as in the case of hallucination), then one's experience doesn't have the conscious character that it introspectively seems to have. According to her non-relationalist opponents, the naïve realist overdescribes the committal phenomenology of conscious perceptual experience. According to the non-relationalist, the respect in which conscious perceptual experience is committal over the actual presence of such an object is to be explained in terms of the causal/functional role of the perceptual state one is in when one has a conscious perceptual experience. In virtue of being in a psychological state with that functional role it perceptually seems to one as if the mind-independent object of experience is present. The distinctive causal/functional role of this psychological state isn't altered or neutralised when one introspects one's experience, and so as one introspects it will still seem to one as if the mind-independent object of experience is present. This is a functional role that the state can have whether or not the object of experience is actually present. If the object of experience is not present then one's environment won't be the way it perceptually seems to one to be. But introspection doesn't support the further claim that in such a case one's *experience* isn't the way it introspectively seems to be; it doesn't introspectively seem to one as though one's conscious experience itself *suffices* for the presence of the mind-independent object.

Now if the dependency thesis is correct, and if the non-relationalist is correct in her characterisation of the committal phenomenology of conscious perceptual experience, then we should predict that the imagery one deploys in visualising an apple won't in itself be sufficient for imagining a scene containing an apple. One should rather predict that the imagery deployed in visualising an apple will be neutral on the question of whether one has thereby imagined an apple. For according to the non-relationalist, in merely representing the conscious character of a visual experience of an apple one won't have done enough to imagine an apple, given that the conscious character of a visual experience of an apple doesn't suffice for the actual presence of an apple. In order to imagine a scene containing an apple, one would need the further stipulation of a non-imagistic supposition that the conscious visual experience represented in so imagining is veridical. On the other hand, if the naïve realist's characterisation of the committal phenomenology of conscious visual experience is correct, then no such non-imagistic supposition is needed. In representing the conscious character of a visual experience one will have done enough to imagine an apple. For according to the naïve realist's account of the committal phenomenology of conscious perceptual experience, the conscious character of a visual experience of an apple itself suffices for the actual presence of an apple. That's why if no such apple is present then one's experience doesn't have the conscious character it introspectively seems to have.

Martin suggests that the phenomenology of visualising is in keeping with what the naïve realist would predict. That is to say, the imagery one deploys in visualising an apple is not neutral with respect to the question of whether one has imagined a scene containing an apple. One might deploy the imagery involved in visualising an apple in order to represent a scene that doesn't contain an apple. For example, one might deploy that imagery as a way of representing a hallucination of an apple. But in such a case, a non-imagistic supposition that the experience is a hallucination is required. Without that non-imagistic supposition, one will have imagined a scene containing an apple.

3.3 Objections to Martin's argument

Let us now review some of the key moves in Martin's argument, in order to attain a clearer view of the various points at which opposition to the argument might arise.

(a) Competing accounts of the committal phenomenology of conscious perceptual experience are outlined: the naïve realist account, and the account offered by her non-relationalist opponent. According to the naïve realist, the conscious character of perceptual experience suffices for the actual presence of the mind-independent object of experience, and so if no such object is present, then the experience doesn't have the conscious character it seems to have. According to the non-relationalist, the conscious character of perceptual experience doesn't suffice for the actual presence of the mind-independent object of experience. If the object of experience is not present, then things are misleading, for the environment isn't the way it perceptually seems to be. But this aspect of the phenomenology is accommodated by the causal/functional role of the psychological state one is in whenever one has a perceptual experience (whether that experience is a genuine perception or a complete hallucination), and we don't need to commit to the further claim that in the case of hallucination the experience itself isn't the way it introspectively seems to be.

(b) Martin argues for the dependency thesis, according to which when one visualises an F one represents, in a distinctive way, the conscious character of a visual experience of an F.

(c) Martin argues that the truth of the dependency thesis should lead the naïve realist and her non-relationalist opponent to make different predictions about the phenomenology of the imagery deployed in visualising, given their differing accounts of the committal phenomenology of conscious perceptual experience. The naïve realist should predict that the imagery deployed in visualising an F will be sufficient to imagine a scene containing an F. One may use such imagery to represent a situation that doesn't contain an F, for example when one imagines hallucinating an F, but in such a case a non-imagistic supposition that there isn't an F in the scene imagined is required. On the other hand, the non-relationalist should predict that the imagery deployed in visualising an F won't be sufficient to imagine a scene containing an F. In order to imagine a scene containing an F, one will need the further non-imagistic supposition that the experience represented is veridical.

(d) Martin claims that the imagery deployed in visualising an F is just as the naïve realist would predict. The imagery deployed in such visualising is not neutral with respect to the question of whether one has thereby imagined a scene containing an F.

Given that the dependency thesis is controversial, and given that it is crucial to the success of Martin's argument, Move (b) above is a natural target for an opponent of naïve realism.[3] An opponent of the dependency thesis may concede that there is a certain correspondence between visualising an F and having a visual experience of an F. However, she may argue that this correspondence can be captured without committing to the dependency thesis, and by instead appealing to a correspondence in the *contents* of visual experience and visual imagination. On such a view, aspects of the content of visual experience are replicated in the case of visual imagination, but in the case of visual imagination one takes an 'imagining' attitude to the content in question. And this is why visualisation doesn't have the committal phenomenology of perceptual experience.

Someone taking this line will need a response to the following claim that Martin invokes in his defence of the dependency thesis. When one visualises the red and green lights, one need not be imagining that the lights occupy locations in one's actual environment, to one's actual left and right, where these are positions relative to one's actual location. But if visualising simply involved taking an imagining attitude to a content that a visual experience might have, then the content of the episode of visualising would locate the lights relative to one's actual location.

An opponent of the dependency thesis might at this point just choose to reject what Martin takes to be a datum, i.e. the claim that in so visualising one need not be imagining the lights as occupying locations relative to one's *actual* position. Alternatively, an opponent of the dependency thesis might claim that when one visualises the lights one does imagine a perspective on the lights (a perspective whose centre of origin does not pick out one's actual location), but this can be done without imagining a visual experience of those lights. This line of response seems to be one that Tyler Burge has in mind in the following quote:

> [Martin] begins by rightly noting that visualizing an object involves taking an imagined visual perspective on the object – for example, visualizing it from a perspective according to which the object is to the left. It is quite true that one could have such a perspective on the object only if one were to have an experience of the object. It does not follow that if one imagines something from a perspective one *could have* only if such and such were the case (only if one were experiencing the object from that perspective, or only if there were an experience of the object from that perspective), then in imagining something from that perspective one *must imagine* such and such to be the case.
>
> (2005: 63)

I suggested earlier that in defending the dependency thesis, Martin is concerned to defend a proposal about the *imagistic* aspects of visualising, rather than any non-imagistic suppositions one might make in deploying such imagery. So there's a sense in which an advocate of the dependency thesis can agree with Burge here, insofar as someone advocating the thesis can consistently maintain that when one visualises an object one need not be making any non-imagistic suppositions about the occurrence of a visual experience in the scene imagined. This advocate of the dependency thesis may claim that in visualising an object one represents the conscious character of a visual experience of that object, but one need not be making any suppositions about anyone occupying the perspective of the visual experience one represents, and in that sense one need not be imagining *that* one is occupying the perspective and having the visual experience in the imagined scene. So it's not clear that this line of objection has traction against the sort of dependency thesis that Martin is defending.

An opponent of Martin's argument may instead choose to target Move (c) above. I have in mind here someone who agrees with the dependency thesis, and so agrees that

(i) in visualising an F one represents a visual experience of an F, and who also agrees that
(ii) the phenomenology of one's episode of visualising an F is committal with respect to the question of whether one has imagined a scene containing an F; but someone who nonetheless asserts that
(iii) the non-relationalist has no problem in accommodating this aspect of the phenomenology of visualising.

This opponent of Martin's argument may say that when one visualises an F one imagines a *veridical* perception of an F. In so imagining, one guarantees the presence of an F in the scene one thereby imagines.

Arguably, someone taking this line would have to deny that in visualising an F one is merely representing the conscious character of a visual experience of an F. For on the non-relationalist view of conscious character, that would *not* suffice for imagining a scene containing an F. One option for a proponent of this line of argument would be to claim that we are incapable of merely representing the conscious character of a visual experience of an F. For we can only imagine the conscious character of a visual experience of an F when we also imagine the experience to be veridical. And here one might wonder why there should be this limitation on our powers of imagination.

Alternatively, a proponent of this line of argument might claim that we can represent the conscious character of a visual experience of an F without imagining the experience to be veridical, but when we do so, the imagistic character of the episode of imagining *is* neutral on the question of whether one has thereby imagined a scene containing an F. But it is perhaps better to regard the latter line of argument as targeting Move (d) above.

I think we also find this line of argument against Martin in Burge's discussion. He writes the following when he assumes for the sake of argument that the dependency thesis is correct:

> I hold that the imagery does not by itself guarantee the presence of the imagined scene rather than a mere imagined experience of the scene, possibly an illusory experience . . . [Assuming the dependency thesis] we have to be imagining a *veridical* experience of what is being visualized. The imagined veridicality is not derivative from the imagery itself. *Visualizing something with a given imagery has to do with how the imagery is used.*
> (2005: 66)

In effect, to take this line of response is simply to deny what Martin takes to be a phenomenological datum, i.e. the claim that the *imagery* deployed in visualising an F is not in itself neutral with respect to the question of whether one has thereby imagined an F. Here an opponent of Martin's argument may claim that he has overdescribed the phenomenology of the imagery deployed in visualising, just as the naïve realist has overdescribed the committal aspect of the phenomenology of conscious perceptual experience.

Finally, it should be noted that it is in principle possible for one to accept the key moves of Martin's argument that I outlined above – (a) to (d) – without committing to naïve realism. One could accept the various claims that Martin makes about the phenomenology of visualising, and so agree that conscious perceptual experience introspectively *seems* to have the sort of committal phenomenology that the naïve realist articulates, while nonetheless maintaining that we need to adopt a non-relationalist account of the metaphysics of such experience. That is to say, one could adopt a position according to which introspective reflection turns out to be misleading. Although it introspectively seems to one as if naïve realism is true, it isn't true.

As I mentioned at the start of the chapter, the adoption of this sort of concessive stance would appear to weaken significantly the dialectical position of the non-relationalist. Once it is conceded that it introspectively seems to one as if naïve realism is true, the disjunctivist is in a good position to argue that the fact that a hallucination can be introspectively indiscriminable from a genuine perception should not in itself oblige us to provide the same account of the conscious character of each. We can instead adopt a view according to which the genuine perceptions actually have the conscious character that they introspectively seem to have, while the introspectively indiscriminable hallucinations merely seem to have that conscious character. That is not to say that once one has conceded that it introspectively seems to one as if naïve realism is true, then there can be no considerations that tell against a naïve realist account of the metaphysics of the conscious character of veridical perception. The point is just that some of the standard arguments against naïve realism will lose their force, for example those that simply appeal to the introspective indiscriminability of genuine perception and hallucination, and those that simply rest on puzzlement at the suggestion that a conscious perceptual experience can fail to have the conscious character that it introspectively seems to have.

In Chapter 2 we looked at ways in which a disjunctivist about the conscious character of perceptual experience may attempt to block certain arguments that purport to show that her favoured view of conscious perception is untenable. I noted that the success of that defensive manoeuvre wouldn't in itself show that the disjunctivist's favoured view of conscious perception was sufficiently motivated. In this chapter we've looked at an argument that tries to motivate that positive view of conscious perception. It is an argument that rests on phenomenological considerations, an argument that purports to show that naïve realism best articulates how conscious perceptual experience seems to us to be through introspective reflection. In the next chapter we'll look at further arguments that have been appealed to in support of the naïve realist, relationalist view of the conscious character of conscious perception. These are arguments that purport to show that we need to adopt the relational, naïve realist view if we are to adequately accommodate the way in which conscious perception performs certain key explanatory roles.

3.4 Chapter summary

In this chapter we considered whether introspective reflection supports the naïve realist's account of the phenomenal character of veridical perception, and we critically examined an argument that M. G. F. Martin has presented in support of the claim that it does. With this argument, Martin attempts to show that introspective reflection on the phenomenology of sensory imagination can provide a way of revealing shortcomings in the non-relationalist's attempts to accommodate certain aspects of the phenomenology of conscious perception.

First of all, we outlined some phenomenological claims that might be appealed to in support of a relational account of the phenomenal character of perception, and we considered what a representationalist could say in response to them. We noted that when we consider the resources that are available to the representationalist in accommodating the deliverances of introspective reflection, we need to bear in mind that she may appeal not only to the representational content of the psychological state one is in when one has a conscious perceptual experience, but also to the distinctive causal/functional and rational role of that psychological state.

We compared and contrasted the different ways in which the relational, naïve realist and the representationalist attempt to accommodate the 'committal' phenomenology of conscious perceptual experience, i.e. the respect in which the phenomenology of conscious perceptual experience is committal on the question of whether the object of experience is actually present in the subject's environment. According to the naïve realist's characterisation of this committal aspect of the phenomenology of perceptual experience, it introspectively seems to one as if one's experience itself suffices for the actual presence of the object of experience; and if the apparent object of experience is not present, then one's experience doesn't have the sort of conscious character that it introspectively seems to have. Whereas, according to the representationalist's characterisation of the committal phenomenology of perceptual experience, introspective reflection does not support the claim that one's experience itself suffices for the actual presence of the object of experience. According to the representationalist, if the object of experience is not present, then things will be misleading in so far as one's environment won't be the way that it perceptually seems to one to be. But introspective reflection doesn't support the further claim that in such a case one's *experience* isn't the way it seems to be.

We then introduced an argument by M. G. F. Martin that purports to show that that there is reason to favour the naïve realist's account of the committal phenomenology of conscious perceptual experience. The argument first seeks to establish a thesis about visualising – the 'dependency thesis' – which states that to visualise an F is to imagine a visual experience of an F. The argument then suggests that the truth of the dependency thesis should lead the representationalist and the naïve realist to make different predictions about the phenomenology of visualising, given their different accounts of the committal phenomenology of conscious perceptual experience. So the suggestion is that the phenomenology of visualising can be regarded as a test of these competing views. And Martin's argument then concludes that the phenomenology of our episodes of visualising favours the naïve realist account.

We outlined the various considerations that might be appealed to in support of each of these steps in the argument, and we then considered objections that have been raised against the argument.

Notes

1 For discussion of the claim that our perceptual experiences have non-conceptual content, see Evans 1982, Peacocke 1992, Dretske 1981, Cussins 1990, Tye 1995, Heck 2000, Crowther 2006.
2 For an influential discussion of this idea, see Williams 1973. For endorsement of the view, see Peacocke 1985, and Vendler 1984.
3 Objections to the dependency thesis are raised by Noordhof 2002, Currie and Ravenscroft 2002, and Burge 2005.

Further reading

The argument from Martin that we have been discussing in this chapter is to be found in his 2002. Further discussions of his naïve realism can be found in his 1997, 1998, 2004, and 2006. For an influential discussion of the dependency thesis about sensory imagination, see Williams 1973. For an endorsement of the view, see Peacocke 1985 and Vendler 1984. For objections to the dependency thesis, see Noordhof 2002, Currie and Ravenscroft 2002, and Burge 2005. For further critical discussion of Martin's argument, see Dorsch 2010.

References

Burge, Tyler, 2005, 'Disjunctivism and perceptual psychology', *Philosophical Topics*, 33: 1–78.

Crowther, Thomas, 2006, 'Two conceptions of conceptualism and nonconceptualism', *Erkenntnis*, 65: 245–276.

Cussins, A., 1990, 'The connectionist construction of concepts', in M. Boden (ed.), *The Philosophy of Artificial Intelligence*. Oxford: Oxford University Press.

Currie, G., and Ravenscroft, I., 2002, *Recreative Minds*. Oxford: Oxford University Press.

Dorsch, Fabian, 2010, 'Transparency and imagining seeing', *Philosophical Explorations*, 13 (3): 173–200.

Dretske, Fred, 1981, *Knowledge and the Flow of Information*. Cambridge, MA. MIT Press.

Evans, Gareth, 1982, *The Varieties of Reference*. Oxford: Clarendon Press.

Heck, R. G., 2000, 'Nonconceptual content and the space of reasons', *Philosophical Review*, 109: 483–523.

Martin, M. G. F., 1997, 'The reality of appearances', in M. Sainsbury (ed.), *Thought and Ontology*. Milan: Franco Angeli, pp. 77–96.

——, 1998, 'Setting things before the mind', in A. O'Hear (ed.), *Contemporary Issues in the Philosophy of Mind*. Cambridge: Cambridge University Press, pp. 157–179.

——, 2002, 'The transparency of experience', *Mind and Language*, 17: 376–425.

——, 2004, 'The limits of self-awareness', *Philosophical Studies*, 120: 37–89.

——, 2006, 'On being alienated', in Tamar S. Gendler and John Hawthorne (eds), *Perceptual Experience*. Oxford: Oxford University Press, pp. 354–410.

Noordhof, P., 2002, 'Imagining objects and imagining experiences', *Mind and Language*, 17: 426–455.

Peacocke, Chrisopher, 1985, 'Imagination, experience and possibility', in J. Foster and H. Robinson (eds), *Essays on Berkeley*. Oxford: Clarendon Press, pp. 19–35.

——, 1992, *A Study of Concepts*. Cambridge, MA: MIT Press.

Tye, M., 1995, *Ten Problems of Consciousness*. Cambridge, MA: MIT Press.

Vendler, Zeno, 1984, *The Matter of Minds*. Oxford: Oxford University Press.

Williams, B., 1973, 'Imagination and the self', in *Problems of the Self*. Cambridge: Cambridge University Press, pp. 26–45.

4

NAÏVE REALISM, PERCEPTUAL ACQUAINTANCE, AND PERCEPTUALLY BASED THOUGHT

So far we have been focusing on a form of disjunctivism that is adopted in defence of a particular account of the phenomenal character of conscious perception – namely, a naïve realist account. According to this naïve realist view, the conscious perceptual experience that you have when you genuinely perceive the world is a relational phenomenon. The mind-independent entities in your environment that you perceive are constituents of that relation, and hence constituents of your experience, and when you genuinely perceive your environment, the *phenomenal, conscious character* of your experience is constituted, at least in part, by those mind-independent aspects of the environment that you perceive. Endorsement of this account of genuine perception leads to a disjunctivist view of the conscious character of perceptual experience. Those adopting this disjunctivist stance deny that genuine perceptions and hallucinations have the same conscious character. They hold that genuine perceptions of the environment actually have the conscious character that introspectively indiscriminable hallucinations merely seem to have.

In this chapter we will be looking at ways in which these debates about the conscious character of perception are connected with debates about the role played by conscious perception in enabling us to acquire knowledge of, think about, and refer to, the mind-independent entities in our environment that we perceive. In particular, we will be focusing on a line of argument that is to be found in John Campbell's work for the following claim: only the naïve realist can provide an adequate account of the role that conscious perception plays in enabling one to think about the mind-independent objects and qualities one perceives, precisely because only the naïve realist provides an adequate account of the phenomenal character of conscious perception.[1] Given that one will need to commit to a disjunctivist view if one is to adopt the naïve realist account of phenomenal character, this would amount to an argument for the claim that one will need to endorse disjunctivism if one is to provide an adequate account of the distinctive role that conscious perception plays in enabling us to think about our surroundings.

In order to clarify Campbell's proposal, it will be helpful first to focus on a substantive assumption behind the argument that he presents for it. That is the assumption that the phenomenal character of conscious perceptual experience plays a crucial role in explaining our capacity to think about the mind-independent entities in our surroundings that we perceive.

4.1 The explanatory role of the phenomenal character of perception

In Chapter 2 I outlined some of the reasons that Burge presents for thinking that there are representational perceptual state-kinds, common to genuine perception and causally matching hallucination, which play a crucial explanatory role in the science of perception. According to Burge, these perceptual states play a key role in explaining how a subject's perceptual (e.g. visual) system enables her to acquire information about her immediate environment. As I also mentioned in Chapter 2, a widely contested issue in the philosophy of perception is whether it is possible to account for the phenomenal character of conscious perceptual experience if we simply restrict ourselves to the postulation of psychological states with representational content. Some argue that we won't be able to accommodate aspects of the phenomenology of conscious perceptual experience by simply postulating the right combination of representational states, with the right kinds of representational contents, playing the right kinds of functional roles. Of these some endorse a naïve realist account of phenomenal character, while others claim that we will need to appeal to non-representational phenomenal properties of experience – qualia – if we are to account for the phenomenal character of perceptual experience. But a question to be addressed by any of those who deny that such representational states suffice to fix the phenomenal character of perceptual experience is the following: what role, if any, should one assign to the phenomenal character of perceptual experience in an account of the role that perception plays in enabling one to think about, and acquire knowledge of, the mind-independent environment? For can't an appeal to the representational content of perceptual states bear that explanatory burden?

If one postulates the obtaining of perceptual representational states in one's account of perception, then one would appear to be able to accommodate the notion that when one perceives the world one is thereby in psychological states that are directed to objects, properties and events in one's immediate environment. So in postulating these representational states one would appear to be well placed to accommodate the functional, explanatory role played by successful perception in enabling one to form beliefs about, navigate, and interact with, one's immediate environment.

Moreover, if one postulates the obtaining of perceptual representational states one can accommodate a respect in which successful perception involves the obtaining of a perceptual *relation*, a relation that obtains between the subject of perception and the particular, individual entities in her environment that she perceives. For in the case of successful perception, the individual entities perceived are causally responsible for the obtaining of the perceptual states that veridically represent them, and it may be said that the obtaining of this *causal* relation can serve to determine which particular entities are represented by the content of the subject's perceptual states, and hence serve to determine which particular entities the subject is perceptually related to. So, arguably, in simply postulating such representational states one has the resources to explain how it is that successful perception can put its subject in a position to refer *demonstratively* to the particular objects and events in her environment that she perceives, as 'this F', or 'that F'. In this case, when it comes to explaining our capacity to think demonstratively about the mind-independent entities in our environment that we perceive, it is not clear that any crucial explanatory role need be assigned to the sort of conscious perceptual relation that the naïve realist posits in her account of the phenomenal character of conscious perception. More generally, given the rich explanatory resources that the postulation of such representational states makes available to us, why think that the conscious *phenomenal* character of experience has *any* essential role to play in explaining our ability to refer to, think about, and acquire knowledge of, the mind-independent entities that we consciously perceive?

There is an assumption behind this question that ought not to go unchallenged: the assumption that we would be warranted in postulating such perceptual representational states if we lacked conscious perceptual experiences that had phenomenal character. For one might think that if a subject didn't undergo conscious perceptual experiences with the sorts of phenomenal characters that our perceptual experiences have, then we wouldn't be warranted in attributing to that subject perceptual states that represent the sorts of entities in our environment that we perceive. But a further question to press at this point is to ask why this should be so. Can we not envisage the possibility of a subject who lacks phenomenal consciousness but who is nonetheless able to navigate and interact with her environment just as well as we do, and also talk about and refer to the entities in her environment to which we refer? And wouldn't the sophistication of this subject's behavioural responses to her environment warrant us in attributing to her perceptual states with representational contents that represent the sorts of objects and qualities that we perceive? Moreover, as long as that subject had the capacity to be in perceptual states with representational contents that represent the sorts of objects, properties and events that we perceive, wouldn't she be equally well placed to think about and acquire knowledge of the entities in our environment that we consciously perceive? If not, why not? Is there any reason to think that a subject's capacity to represent the environment would be in any way compromised if she lacked perceptual experiences with the sorts of phenomenal characters that our perceptual experiences possess? Indeed, is there any reason to reject a position that's been labelled 'separatism',[2] which commits to the following: all 'intentional' aspects of mind (i.e. all aspects of mind in virtue of which our mental states/events are about, or directed upon, other things) are independent of, and entirely separable from, phenomenal aspects of mind (i.e. those aspects of mind for which there is something it is like for one to undergo them or be in them)?

It seems relatively uncontroversial to accept that we can use terms to refer successfully to items we have never perceived, and to accept further that we can talk knowledgeably about such items in doing so. However, in the case of at least certain terms it is intuitive to think that it is our *conscious sensory* experience of the referents of those terms that provides us with a distinctive conception of what such terms refer to. For example, consider our conscious visual awareness of the colours of objects. It's intuitive to think that the sighted can have a certain kind of understanding of the colour terms which is lacking in a subject who was born blind and who has never had visual experiences of colours. This is not to say that a blind subject could not successfully refer to, and talk knowledgeably about, colours. The suggestion is rather that having had conscious visual experience of, say, red things, the sighted subject is in a position to have a distinctive conception of what the term 'red' refers to that is lacking in a subject incapable of consciously perceiving that quality.

Note in particular, the suggestion here is that it is *phenomenally conscious* sensory experience of the colour that provides for that distinctive conception of what is being referred to. So, for instance, suppose it were possible for there to be a subject who was perceptually sensitive to the colours of objects, but who didn't have phenomenally conscious experiences when perceiving such objects. This subject, we are supposing, is able to perceptually discriminate the colours of objects (i.e. she is able to respond differentially to the colours possessed by objects in her environment), and she may be able to use colour terms to give accurate reports of the colours of objects in her environment. However, according to the supposition, she does all of this without ever having *phenomenally conscious* experiences of the colours of objects. So, for example, she has never had a phenomenally conscious visual experience of the colour red. The intuition that many share is that this subject would lack the distinctive conception of the colour red that is possessed by those of us who have had phenomenally conscious visual awareness of the colour. Perception of the colour that wasn't phenomenally conscious would not be enough to provide for that distinctive conception. But what might explain this intuition? Should we hold that such a subject would lack the distinctive conception of the colour red possessed by those of us who have had phenomenally conscious visual experiences of the colour because such a subject would lack a certain form of *knowledge* of the colour red, a distinctive variety of knowledge of the colour red that can only come with phenomenally conscious awareness of that quality?

Let's first consider what might be said in response to this question by those who claim that the difference between us and the subject who lacks phenomenally conscious visual experiences of the colour red is to be explained by the fact that our visual experiences of the colour possess distinctive non-representational phenomenal properties, i.e. qualia. Advocates of this position may claim that we can concede that there is a distinctive variety of knowledge that a subject would lack if she didn't have phenomenally conscious visual experiences of the colours, but that is simply knowledge of *what it is like* to have phenomenally conscious visual experiences of colours. The subject who doesn't have phenomenally conscious visual experience of the colour red doesn't know what it is like to see the colour red, because she lacks knowledge of the *qualia* possessed by the experiences that we have when we perceive that colour. So according to this view, the epistemic impoverishment that's involved here is primarily to be thought of as ignorance of qualities of the *experiences* that we happen to have when we perceive colours – i.e. ignorance of the non-representational, phenomenal qualities of the experiences we have – rather than ignorance of the qualities of mind-independent objects in the world that we, as phenomenally conscious subjects, perceive. In lacking knowledge of the qualia possessed by the visual experiences that we have when we consciously perceive the colour red, such a subject will be ignorant of a particular psychological effect that a certain quality of mind-independent objects has on us. But from this it doesn't follow that she would lack the ability to think about, refer to, and acquire knowledge of, the quality of mind-independent objects that has that effect on us.

Those advocating this view might concede that the distinctive phenomenal character of the visual experience that we have when we perceive the colour red can have a role to play in explaining a distinctive way in which we think about that quality, for advocates of this sort of view may grant that there is a *concept* of the colour red that is associated with phenomenally conscious visual experiences of the colour. That is to say, they may hold that:

(a) there is a distinctively visual *phenomenal* concept of the colour red that one can only possess if one knows what it is like to see that colour, and
(b) one can only know what it is like to see the colour if one has had visual experiences with the relevant qualia; but possession of this distinctively visual phenomenal concept of the colour red isn't required for thinking about, and acquiring knowledge of, any of the mind-independent qualities of the mind-independent objects that we perceive when we have phenomenally conscious perceptual experiences.

The ability to think about, and acquire knowledge of, any such mind-independent qualities of objects depends on the capacity to be in mental states that represent them, and such representational mental states need not be phenomenally conscious.

As we'll see, from Campbell's point of view a serious flaw in the above proposal is its failure to assign the appropriate epistemic role to the phenomenal character of conscious perception. According to the above proposal, in having phenomenally conscious visual experiences of colours, what we gain epistemically, and would otherwise lack, is knowledge of certain qualities of our perceptual experiences, whereas, according to Campbell, in having phenomenally conscious visual experiences of colours what we gain epistemically, and would otherwise lack, is knowledge of qualities of mind-independent objects. But before we turn to Campbell's view in any detail, I want to focus on some of the assumptions behind the qualia view that I've just outlined. Doing so will help clarify the dialectic between Campbell and his opponents.

4.2 Qualia and phenomenal concepts

I said that advocates of the sort of qualia view I outlined may hold that:

(a) there is a distinctively visual *phenomenal* concept of the colour red that one can only possess if one knows what it is like to see that colour, and
(b) one can only know what it is like to see the colour if one has had visual experiences with the relevant qualia.

Let's start by focusing on the second of those claims. Why assume that if a subject doesn't undergo phenomenally conscious visual experiences with the relevant qualia, then that subject won't be in a position to know what it is like to have such experiences? According to the view I summarised, the subject who has phenomenally conscious visual experience of the colour red is in a position to acquire knowledge of what it is like to see red, because she is in a position to acquire knowledge of non-representational phenomenal properties of visual experience – i.e. qualia – that determine what it is like for one to perceive the colour. So our question is, why assume that knowledge of the relevant qualia would be inaccessible to a subject who didn't undergo experiences that possess such qualia? Why assume that a subject would have to have visual experiences that actually instantiate such qualities in order to acquire the relevant knowledge of them?

There is a related question we might ask about a familiar thought experiment, Frank Jackson's (1982) thought experiment involving Mary, the brilliant scientist, who has not seen the colour red, but who learns, from the confines of a black and white room, all the physical information there is to obtain about what happens when we see the colour red. Many share the intuition that Mary will learn something new about seeing red when she leaves her black and white room and actually sees the colour for the first time. She will learn *what it is like* for one to see the colour red. This is something she wasn't in a position to know prior to having that visual experience. But why is that?

Some take Jackson's thought experiment to pose a significant problem for physicalism,[3] but let's put aside the question of whether this thought experiment can be used as the basis of a cogent argument against physicalism, and consider instead a variant of the thought experiment. Let us suppose that when Mary learns about the visual perception of colours from the confines of her black and white room, she also acquires a body of theoretical knowledge about the *qualia* possessed by the phenomenally conscious perceptual experiences that subjects have when they see the colours of objects. For example, she learns about the effects that such non-representational phenomenal properties of experience have on subjects when they undergo experiences that possess them. She does this without actually having experiences that instantiate such qualia. She acquires all the relevant information 'in black and white', as it were. Is there a form of knowledge of such qualities that she will lack until she actually has an experience that instantiates those qualities? And would this mean that knowledge of what it is like to have such experiences would be inaccessible to her until she had such experiences herself? If so, why?

According to one line of thought, when Mary is in her black and white room she may be able to learn a theory about the causal/functional roles played by the qualia that are associated with seeing colours. But what she will lack, until she has herself had experiences that instantiate such qualities, is knowledge of the *intrinsic characters* of the qualities that play the relevant theoretical roles. Only when she undergoes an experience that instantiates the relevant qualia will she be acquainted with those qualia themselves. And it is only such acquaintance with the relevant qualia that can provide her with a source of knowledge about their intrinsic characters – what those qualia themselves are like – which in turn can put her in a position to know what it is like for one to have an experience that instantiates them. So someone endorsing this line of thought need not deny that Mary was able to refer to, and think about, the relevant qualia before she left her black and white room. They may maintain that when Mary was in her black and white room her theoretical conceptions of such qualities put her in a position to refer to them and make knowledgeable claims about them when doing so. But they will hold that it is only when she actually encounters such qualities, through having perceptual experiences that instantiate them, that she is in a position to acquire conceptions of such qualities that aren't merely theoretical.

How should we understand the proposal that a subject 'encounters' and is 'acquainted' with qualia when she has a conscious perceptual experience that instantiates them? Does this form of acquaintance with qualia depend on the obtaining of a psychological state that represents them? Some deny that it does. For instance, Burge suggests that 'The conscious phenomenal aspects of a conscious state are present for, presented to, the individual'(Burge 2007: 403), but he suggests that this 'presentational relation' is not representational (405). According to Burge, the phenomenal aspects of conscious states are 'present for the individual whether or not they are attended to or represented.' He writes,

> Phenomenal consciousness is indeed a presentation to the individual that cannot fail. It cannot fail, not because it is an infallible representation, but because it is not a representation with veridicality conditions at all. It can neither fail nor succeed. Either phenomenal aspects of psychological states are present for, presented to, the individual in consciousness, or they are not. There is no question of right or wrong. It is a matter of presence or absence.
> (406–407)

However, someone advocating this view might maintain that although the presentational relation to qualia does not itself consist in a representation of those qualities, the obtaining of that presentational relation does nonetheless put its subject in a position to represent such qualities in a distinctive way. The obtaining of the relevant presentational relation puts its subject in a position to acquire knowledge of the *intrinsic* character of a quality of her conscious perceptual experience, which provides for a distinctive conception of the quality that isn't merely theoretical (i.e. which isn't merely a conception of that quality as playing a certain kind of causal/functional role). This puts the subject in a position to grasp a *concept* of the quality that she wouldn't otherwise be in a position to grasp.

An important point to note about this position is the following. It suggests that there are certain concepts that one cannot possess if one does not undergo conscious perceptual experiences that instantiate qualia. This in turn suggests that there will be representational contents, constituted in part by such concepts, that one should not attribute to a subject if that subject doesn't have phenomenally conscious experiences. I mentioned earlier that those who hold a 'separatist' view claim that all representational and phenomenal aspects of mind are mutually independent and entirely separable. Separatism will be rejected by those who maintain that one can adequately accommodate the conscious phenomenal character of perceptual experience by simply postulating the right combination of representational states, with the right kinds of representational contents, playing the right kinds of functional roles. But the significance of the point I just noted about the qualia view we are considering, is that it suggests that not all of those who reject separatism need be committed to a representationalist account of the phenomenal character of perceptual experience. The qualia theorist can deny that all representational and phenomenal aspects of mind are mutually independent and entirely separable, for she can maintain that:

(i) there are concepts that a subject can only possess if she has perceptual experiences with phenomenal character, and so she can maintain that
(ii) there are representational contents, constituted by such concepts, which can only be attributed to a subject if that subject has perceptual experiences with phenomenal character, while also maintaining that
(iii) we need to invoke the instantiation of *non*-representational phenomenal properties of experience – i.e. qualia – if we are to account for the phenomenal character of conscious perceptual experience.

This is what puts the qualia theorist in a position to claim that the phenomenal character of the perceptual experiences we have when we see the colour red does have a role to play in explaining a distinctive way in which we can think about the colour. It allows them to maintain that there is a distinctively visual *phenomenal* concept of the colour that can only be grasped by those subjects who have had perceptual experiences with the relevant qualia.

In the next section we will examine Campbell's reasons for rejecting this account of the role played by the phenomenal character of perceptual experience in enabling us to think about the mind-independent objects and properties in our surroundings that we consciously perceive.

4.3 Campbell on the explanatory role of conscious perception

Although there are a number of significant disagreements between Campbell and the qualia theorist, there are points at which the assumptions behind Campbell's approach appear to correspond in certain ways to some of the assumptions behind the qualia view that I've just outlined. According to that qualia view, when a subject has a phenomenally conscious perceptual experience, the subject is acquainted with phenomenal qualities of her experience, and the obtaining of that presentational relation of acquaintance puts the subject of experience in a position to acquire knowledge of the *intrinsic character* of qualities of her experience. The subject is thereby in a position to acquire a conception of such qualities that she wouldn't otherwise be in a position to grasp.

Campbell likewise holds that when one consciously perceives the world, one is acquainted with certain qualities, the obtaining of that presentational relation puts one in a position to acquire knowledge of the intrinsic character of qualities, and one is thereby in a position to acquire a conception of such qualities that one wouldn't otherwise be in a position to grasp. The crucial difference between Campbell's view and the qualia view, however, is that on Campbell's view the qualities in question are qualities *of the mind-independent objects that we perceive*, rather than qualia (i.e. non-representational properties of our experience).

According to Campbell the conscious perceptual experience that you have when you perceive the world is a relational phenomenon, and the mind-independent entities in your environment that you perceive are constituents of that relation, and hence constituents of your phenomenally conscious experience. When you consciously perceive your environment a conscious presentational relation of acquaintance obtains between you and qualities of the mind-independent objects in your environment that you perceive, and the phenomenal character of your experience is constitutively determined, at least in part, by those qualities of mind-independent objects with which you are so acquainted. On Campbell's relational view, we are not to think of perceptual consciousness of an object as a two-place relation between a person and an object, but rather as a three-place relation between a person, a *standpoint*, and an object. He suggests that we need to factor in the notion of a 'standpoint' as our experience of objects is always, in some sense, partial. You always experience an object from a standpoint, and you can experience one and the same object from different standpoints. The notion of standpoint encompasses the position of the perceiver, the modality of perception, and in the case of vision such factors as the relative orientations of the perceiver and the entities she perceives, and whether there is anything obstructing the light between them. However, although Campbell's view factors in this notion of a standpoint, Campbell nonetheless maintains that it is the obtaining of a conscious perceptual relation to the items you perceive that puts you in a position to acquire knowledge of the intrinsic characters of qualities of mind-independent objects, qualities that play a constitutive role in determining the phenomenal character of your perceptual experience.

In endorsing this naïve realist account of phenomenal character, Campbell clearly disagrees with the qualia theorist over the account that should be given of the metaphysics of the phenomenal character of conscious perception. But with that disagreement about the metaphysics we find a disagreement about the *epistemic role* that is played by the phenomenal character of conscious perception. According to the qualia theorist, in having phenomenally conscious perceptual experience of the colour red what we gain epistemically and would otherwise lack is a distinctive form of knowledge of a quality of our experiences, a quale, whereas for Campbell, in having phenomenally conscious perceptions of the colour red, what we gain epistemically – and would otherwise lack – is a distinctive form of knowledge of a quality of mind-independent objects in our environment.

So in Campbell's view, what Mary learns once she leaves her black and white room and has a phenomenally conscious visual perception of the colour red for the first time, is what the colour *red* is like, where that quality is thought of as a quality of mind-independent objects. Mary may have been able to refer to that quality of objects prior to leaving her room, and she may have acquired a body of propositional knowledge about that quality of objects prior to leaving her room. But once she consciously perceives the colour, she has a form of acquaintance with the quality that puts her in a position to acquire a distinctive form of knowledge of the quality that she was previously lacking. This puts her in a position to acquire a conception of what the term 'red' refers to that hadn't been available to her prior to her encounter with that quality in conscious perception.

When Mary has a phenomenally conscious visual perception of the colour red she not only learns what the colour red is like, she also learns what it is like to see the colour red. But in Campbell's approach this is *because* she now knows what the colour red is like. There is something it is like for her to see red insofar as there is something it is like for her to be the subject of the conscious perceptual relation that obtains when she sees that colour; and what it is like for her to be the subject of that conscious perceptual relation is determined, at least in part, by what she is thereby perceptually related to. Red is not a quality of her experience, it is a quality of the object she seems to perceive, but what that quality is like – the intrinsic character of that quality – determines, at least in part, what it is like for her to be consciously acquainted with it.[4]

Campbell argues that reflection on the phenomenology of conscious perception supports his view and undermines the account offered by the qualia theorist: when one has a conscious perceptual experience of something red, the quality one seems to be acquainted with is the colour red, and that quality is presented to one as a quality of the mind-independent objects in one's environment that one perceives. It is not presented to one as a quality of one's experience. But is the qualia theorist really committed to the claim that red is, rather, a quality of one's experience? Is she really committed to the claim that when one consciously perceives something red, the experience one has is itself literally red?

Here advocates of the qualia view may say, and often do say, that they are not committed to a view according to which one literally has a red experience when one sees the colour red. They may rather say that when one sees the colour red, there is something it is like for one to have that experience, one's experience possesses a phenomenal quality – a quale – that determines, at least in part, what it is like for one to have the experience, but the quale in question is not itself to be identified with the colour red. The quale in question is a phenomenal property of the experience that is associated with seeing red things, but which is not to be identified with the property of being red.

However, the challenge that Campbell and others press against the qualia theorist at this point is to suggest that when one attempts to attend introspectively to the relevant quale, one appears to fail. The quale that is posited is supposed to be distinct from, not identical with, the quality of being red. But when one tries to discern introspectively the relevant property of one's experience, all one seems to find is the colour red. That is to say, it doesn't seem as though one can shift one's focus of attention from the colour red that one seems to perceive to some other property – some property of one's experience that is associated with seeing that colour, and which determines what it is like for one to see that colour, but which is itself distinct from that colour.

Do such phenomenological reflections succeed in undermining the qualia theory? In defence of the qualia view one might reason as follows. It is introspectively obvious that there is something it is like for one to see the colour red, and one can have an experience with that phenomenal character whether or not one is actually acquainted with something red; it is possible for one to have an experience with that phenomenal character when one is hallucinating, or having an illusion as of something red. So there must be *qualities of one's experience* that determine what it is like for one to see something red. If one isn't persuaded that the phenomenal character of the perceptual experience that one has when one sees something red can be exhaustively accounted for by simply postulating states with representational content, then one should be led to posit *non*-representational properties of experience – qualia – that contribute to determining what it is like for one to have the experience. So there will be reason to posit such qualities even if it seems, from the inside, so to speak, as though one cannot shift the focus of one's introspective attention from the colour red to the quale that determines what it is like for one to see that colour.

The suggestion implicit in the above line of reasoning is that qualia can be introduced as *theoretical* entities that we need to posit in order to account for the phenomenal character of experience; and the fact that it doesn't seem, from the inside, as though we can single out such qualities introspectively, does not undermine our reasons for introducing them. However, a problem with this line of reasoning is that it *does* appear to be in tension with the account of the distinctive *epistemic role* of the phenomenal character of experience that I suggested the qualia theorist may wish to endorse.

Recall that according to that account, in having a phenomenally conscious visual experience of red, what one gains epistemically, and would otherwise lack, is a distinctive form of knowledge of the qualia possessed by such an experience. For when one has a phenomenally conscious visual experience of red one is acquainted with the relevant qualia, and the obtaining of that presentational relation puts one in a position to acquire knowledge of the intrinsic character of those qualities. One is thereby in a position to acquire a conception of such qualities that isn't merely theoretical. This is the conception of such qualities that wasn't available to Mary when she was in her black and white room. However, if this presentational relation of acquaintance really does hold when one has a phenomenally conscious experience of something red, and if this relation is supposed to afford one knowledge of the intrinsic character of the qualia one's experience possesses, then presumably one ought to be able to attend introspectively to those qualities of one's experience, the qualia with which one is so acquainted.

From Campbell's point of view, the intuition that there is a distinctive form of knowledge that is made available to Mary when she leaves her black and white room and consciously perceives the colour red for the first time, is sound. The intuition that the phenomenal character of Mary's experience makes available that distinctive form of knowledge is also sound. But, Campbell argues, reflection on the phenomenology of experience shows that the qualia theorist's attempt to accommodate those intuitions fails. For one finds that one cannot single out introspectively the qualities of experience that one should expect to discover if the qualia theory were correct. Rather, one instead discerns the quality that one would expect to discover if the naïve realist account of phenomenal character were correct, i.e. the colour red. So if we agree that Mary does acquire knowledge of the intrinsic character of a quality when she leaves her black and white room and has a phenomenally conscious visual experience of the colour red for the first time, and if we agree that she acquires that distinctive form of knowledge through being acquainted with that quality, then why not say that the quality in question is the quality that she seems to be acquainted with in having that experience – i.e. the colour red – a quality of the mind-independent objects we perceive? We'll consider the reasons one might have to reject that suggestion in due course. Before we do that, however, I want to fill in some further details of the account that Campbell recommends.

In the previous section I suggested that not all of those who reject the 'separatist' claim that all intentional and phenomenal aspects of mind are mutually independent and entirely separable need be committed to a representationalist account of the phenomenal character of perceptual experience. The qualia theorist can reject separatism by defending the proposal that some of our psychological states have representational contents that are constituted, at least in part, by concepts that can only be grasped by the subject who has perceptual experiences that possess qualia. Campbell rejects representationalist accounts of phenomenal character, and he also rejects qualia accounts of phenomenal character. But he too rejects separatism. For he recommends a form of empiricism about concept possession that is incompatible with the separatist view, an empiricism that assigns a crucial role to *phenomenally conscious* perceptual experience in an account of our possession of certain concepts.[5] His own empiricist account of our possession of such concepts crucially requires a commitment to a naïve realist account of the phenomenal character of conscious perception.[6] So, for Campbell, the naïve realist account of the phenomenal character of conscious perception plays a key role in explaining what is wrong with the separatist claim that all intentional and phenomenal aspects of mind are mutually independent and entirely separable.

Why does Campbell's empiricist account of concept possession require a commitment to naïve realism? This is because that account of concept possession crucially depends on an *epistemic* role that is assigned to the phenomenal character of conscious perception, and Campbell argues that only the naïve realist is in a position to accommodate the relevant epistemic role. So in Campbell's view, the epistemic role that is played by conscious perception isn't simply that of explaining how we can come to know various *truths* about objects and qualities in our environment, but also that of explaining what puts us in a position to possess the distinctive *concepts* of such objects and qualities that we have in the first place.

Sticking for now with the example of our grasp of the concept of the quality of redness, the thought is this. There may be various truths about that quality that one can comprehend without ever having been acquainted with the quality in conscious perception, and one may also be able to acquire knowledge that such propositions are true without ever having been acquainted with the quality in conscious perception. So one may be able to refer to, and come to know various truths about, the quality red without ever having been acquainted with the quality in conscious perception. But what one gains epistemically when one is acquainted with the quality in conscious perception is knowledge of the intrinsic character of the quality one had previously been referring to: what that quality itself is like. This affects one's understanding of the term that one uses to refer to that quality. One now knows what one is referring to in using that term in a way that one didn't before. One thereby possesses a concept of the quality that one didn't previously possess.

Now Campbell extends this proposal to the various objects and qualities we perceive in conscious perception: the objects and qualities that, in his naïve realist account, play a constitutive role in determining the phenomenal character of the perceptual experiences that we have when we consciously perceive them. He suggests that there is a distinction to be marked between:

(a) our conception of the *functional* role of a mind-independent object or quality — that is to say, our conception of the range of effects that can occur when various inputs are given to a situation involving that mind-independent object or quality, and
(b) our conception of the *categorical* object or quality itself — that is to say, our conception of the underlying object or quality which occupies that functional role.

Campbell proposes that we experience objects and properties *as categorical*, rather than merely as 'clouds of dispositions' and 'mere complexes of functional connections',[7] and he contends that only the naïve realist is in a position to accommodate the role played by conscious perception in enabling us to grasp our conceptions of the *categorical* mind-independent objects and qualities we perceive. Moreover, he contends that only the naïve realist can provide an adequate account of the perceptual *demonstrative* concepts that we apply to the mind-independent objects we consciously perceive.

The proposal is this. When you consciously perceive your environment, there obtains a conscious perceptual relation to the mind-independent objects and qualities you perceive, which determines, in part, the phenomenal character of your experience, and which acquaints you with mind-independent categorical objects and qualities in your surroundings. You are thereby in a position to single out through conscious attention a particular object with which you are so acquainted, and apply a demonstrative term – for example 'this' or 'that' – to it.[8] It is the obtaining of that conscious perceptual relation of acquaintance that puts you in a position to acquire a distinctive conception of what you are referring to in your use of that demonstrative term. You know the meaning of the demonstrative term you use (i.e. what the term stands for – its semantic value), because the obtaining of that conscious perceptual relation puts you in a position to acquire knowledge of which entity you are thereby referring to. It puts you in a position to acquire knowledge of the *categorical* mind-independent object that you are thereby referring to.

A further, but connected, proposal that Campbell then argues for is this: only the naïve realist can provide an adequate account of the role that conscious perception plays in enabling us to think about the categorical objects we perceive in our environment *as mind-independent*. The line of thought that Campbell offers in support of this proposal is roughly as follows. When you demonstratively refer to objects that you perceive, you can engage in reasoning about the objects you refer to, and such reasoning can reflect your grasp of the mind-independence of those objects. For example, you can reason about such an object in ways that reflect the fact that you are treating the object as one and the same object that is encountered through different sense-modalities, at different times, and by different people. This in turn reflects your grasp of the idea that the object being referred to has its identity constituted in a way that is independent of its relation to your perception of it. That is, in treating the object referred to as numerically identical to an object encountered by another subject, or as numerically identical to an object that you encountered on a previous occasion, you reflect your grasp of the idea that the object can exist when it isn't perceived by you, or indeed by anyone.

According to Campbell, the pattern of your use of the demonstrative in such reasoning is explained by (and, in particular, is caused and justified by) your knowledge of what the demonstrative refers to. Since it is the obtaining of the conscious perceptual relation of acquaintance that provides you with that source of knowledge, the obtaining of that relation of conscious perceptual acquaintance plays a crucial role in both causing and justifying the pattern of your use of the demonstrative in the reasoning you engage in. That pattern of use reflects your grasp of the criteria of identity of the object referred to, for example it reflects your grasp of the standard for judging whether the object referred to is numerically identical with an object encountered on a previous occasion; and this in turn reflects your grasp of the object as being mind-independent. So, in Campbell's view, the conscious perceptual relation that the naïve realist posits in her account of the phenomenal character of perception turns out to play a crucial role in explaining what provides us with our conception of the objects we perceive as mind-independent. And this leads Campbell to propose that only the naïve realist can provide an adequate account of the role that conscious perception plays in enabling us to think about the objects we perceive in our environment as mind-independent.

In the next section we will consider some of the objections that have raised against Campbell's account.

4.4 Objections to Campbell's proposal

There are various strands to Campbell's account of the role that the phenomenal character of conscious perception plays in enabling us to think about the mind-independent objects and qualities in our environment that we perceive, and in his discussions of this issue one finds arguments for claims which differ in the strengths of their commitments. So it's worth bearing in mind that some of the objections that might be levelled against certain aspects of his account may leave other aspects of his account untouched. Let us first consider what might be said against the proposal I just introduced – the proposal that only the naïve realist can provide an adequate account of the role that conscious perception plays in enabling one to think about the objects we perceive *as mind-independent*.

One response to this proposal is to claim that conscious perception enables us to think about the objects that we perceive as mind-independent because our conscious experiences present those objects as mind-independent, and we can accommodate the idea that conscious experience presents such objects as mind-independent if we grant that our perceptual experiences are psychological states that have *conceptual* contents which *represent* those objects as mind-independent.[9] One doesn't have to be a naïve realist to accommodate the idea that our experiences have such conceptual contents, and so it's not correct to claim that only the naïve realist can provide an adequate account of the role that conscious perception plays in enabling one to think about the objects of perception as mind-independent.

From Campbell's point of view, a problem with this alternative proposal is that it fails to accommodate the way in which our conscious perception of objects *explains* our ability to grasp concepts of those objects. If we claim that our perceptual experiences are psychological states that have conceptual contents, then we presuppose the grasp of concepts that an appeal to conscious perception is supposed to explain. According to Campbell we need to think of conscious perception of an object as more primitive than thought about that object. Only so can we appropriately accommodate the role that conscious perception plays in enabling us to grasp concepts of the objects we perceive. So we need to accommodate the idea that when we consciously perceive an object we stand in a relation to that object that is more primitive than thought about the object, but which nonetheless brings the object into the subjective life of the thinker in a way that makes possible thought about that object.[10] If we hold a view in which our perceptual experiences are psychological states that have conceptual contents, then we fail to accommodate the idea that conscious perception of an object is more primitive than thought about that object. In which case we fail to accommodate an explanatory role that conscious perception plays.

Those who reject the empiricist view of concept possession that Campbell is committed to may be happy to deny that conscious perception plays that explanatory role, in which case they may be happy to deny that when we consciously perceive an object we stand in a relation to that object that is more primitive than thought about that object. However, there will also be some opponents of naïve realism who maintain that they too can accommodate the idea that conscious perception of an object is more primitive than thought about that object. They can do so by invoking the claim that the representational contents of the perceptual states that obtain when we consciously perceive the world are *non*-conceptual. In this view, it may be said that our ability to think about the objects we consciously perceive can be grounded in, and explained by, the non-conceptual representation of those objects in conscious perception.[11]

Campbell rejects this proposal because he suggests that it fails to accommodate the idea that the *phenomenal character* of conscious perception plays a crucial role in enabling us to think of the objects we perceive as mind-independent. Campbell argues that the advocate of this view isn't able to explain why it is only *phenomenally conscious* states that could have such non-conceptual contents. They aren't able to offer any good reason to deny that any kind of non-conceptual content that could be ascribed to phenomenally conscious perceptual experience could also, in principle, be ascribed to perceptual states that aren't phenomenally conscious. So when they appeal to the non-conceptual representational content of experience in explaining how conscious perception enables us to think of the objects we perceive as mind-independent, they neglect to accommodate the crucial role that is played by the *phenomenal character* of conscious perception in enabling us to think of such objects as mind-independent.

One might respond to Campbell's complaint by attempting to meet his challenge; that is, by attempting to articulate and defend a conception of the non-conceptual representational content of perceptual experience that can accommodate the idea that only phenomenally conscious perceptual experiences can have such contents. I'll be saying more about that option shortly. But an alternative response to his complaint is to question whether the phenomenal character of conscious perception really does have an *essential* role to play in explaining our capacity to think of the objects we perceive as mind-independent. While it may be intuitive to think that a subject who lacked phenomenally conscious visual experiences of red things would not be in a position to think of the colour red in the way that we do, is it really so obvious that a subject who lacked phenomenally conscious perceptual experiences would not be in a position to think about the objects she perceives as mind-independent? One might argue that their grasp of the mind-independence of the objects they perceive would be reflected in the patterns of reasoning they engage in, and having phenomenally conscious perceptual experiences isn't an essential requirement for engaging in such reasoning.

At this point, the dispute between Campbell and his opponent may turn on whether the phenomenal character of conscious perception really does play a crucial role in *justifying* (as well as causing) the relevant patterns of reasoning, as Campbell suggests, and whether one can only be said to grasp the mind-independence of the objects one perceives if one is so justified. Among the central questions one would need address in order to make further progress on this debate are the following. Can an appeal to a naïve realist account of the phenomenal character of perception adequately explain how our conscious perception of objects can justify, as well as cause, the patterns of reasoning we engage in when we treat such objects as mind-independent? If so, is the appeal to a naïve realist account of the phenomenal character the *only* way of explaining how perception can justify such patterns of reasoning? And in any case, do we need to assign to perception this sort of *justificatory* role if we are to accommodate our grasp of the mind-independence of the objects we perceive? We shan't be pursuing those difficult issues any further here, for I want now to focus on a more limited proposal that Campbell seems to be committed to.

As I said earlier, there are various strands to Campbell's account of the role that the phenomenal character of conscious perception plays in enabling us to think about the mind-independent objects and qualities in our environment that we perceive, and some of the objections that might be levelled against certain aspects of his account may leave other aspects of his account untouched. For example, even if one maintains, contra Campbell, that the phenomenal character of conscious perception does not play an essential role in enabling us to think of the objects we perceive *as mind-independent*, one might still, nonetheless, find plausible the suggestion that the phenomenal character of conscious perception does have an essential role to play in explaining our capacity to grasp at least *some* of the concepts we possess, for example our concepts of the *categorical* mind-independent objects we perceive, or perhaps more minimally our concepts of certain observable qualities, such as the colours of objects. So even if one isn't persuaded by the case Campbell presents for the claim that only the naïve realist can provide an adequate account of the role that conscious perception plays in enabling one to think demonstratively about the objects of perception *as mind-independent*, there remains the question of whether his arguments show that only the naïve realist can provide an adequate account of the role that conscious perception plays in enabling us to acquire (*at least some of*) the conceptions that we have of the objects and qualities in our environment that we perceive.

Let us now consider what might be said against Campbell by someone willing to concede that it is appropriate to endorse an empiricist account of at least some of our concepts – for example our concept of the colour red – in particular, someone who accepts that we possess a concept of the colour red which can only be possessed by the subject who has *phenomenally conscious* experiences of the colour that are like ours. Those who accept this claim would be rejecting separatism. They would be granting that we have a way of thinking about the colour red that is only available to subjects who have phenomenally conscious experiences that are like ours. So they would be denying that all phenomenal and intentional aspects of mind are mutually independent and entirely separable.

I suggested that those who invoke qualia in their accounts of the phenomenal character of experience may be able to reject separatism. However, it is worth noting that simply invoking qualia in one's account of the phenomenal character of perceptual experience won't *in itself* be enough to establish that separatism is false. For example, consider a view which holds that the qualia that are possessed by our conscious perceptual experiences serve as *vehicles* of representation. Such a view is consistent with the claim that the representational contents that our phenomenally conscious perceptual experiences possess could also, in principle, be attributed to perceptual states that have very different qualia to ours, or indeed to perceptual states that lack qualia entirely. In general, vehicles of representation can have very different non-representational properties and yet represent exactly the same states of affairs, for example spoken and written words can serve as vehicles of representation that have exactly the same propositional contents even though sounds and written words have very different non-representational properties. So if a qualia theorist wants to reject separatism, they will need to explain why it is that *only* perceptual states with the qualia that our conscious perceptual experiences possess can serve as vehicles of the representational contents that our conscious perceptual experiences possess. Alternatively they will need to explain why a difference in the vehicle of representation should result in a difference in the conception one has of the item represented by that vehicle.

I have already suggested what a qualia theorist might say in response to that challenge. That response invoked the idea that when one has a phenomenally conscious experience one is *acquainted* with the qualia possessed by that experience. That presentational relation of acquaintance puts one in a position to acquire knowledge of the intrinsic character of the relevant qualia, which in turn puts one in a position to acquire a conception of those qualia that one wouldn't otherwise be in a position to grasp. With this claim established, the qualia theorist can then say that we possess conceptions of qualities we perceive – for example of the colours of objects – that are associated with this distinctive form of knowledge that we have of the qualia that our perceptual experiences possess. They can then maintain that we possess *phenomenal* concepts of qualities we perceive which can only be possessed by subjects who have experiences with the sorts of phenomenal characters that our experiences have. This suggests that one doesn't have to endorse a naïve realist account of the phenomenal character of perception in order to accommodate the idea that we possess a concept of the colour red which can only be possessed by the subject who has *phenomenally conscious* experiences of the colour.

However, as we've seen, a challenge faced by this particular proposal is to respond to the phenomenological objection to the view that Campbell and others have pressed. This is the objection that when one has a perceptual experience of something red, it doesn't seem as though one can shift one's focus of attention from the colour red that one seems to perceive to some other property, some property of one's experience that is associated with seeing that colour, and which determines what it is like for one to see that colour, but which is itself distinct from that colour. If a presentational relation of acquaintance really does hold when one has a phenomenally conscious experience of something red, and if this relation is supposed to afford one knowledge of the intrinsic character of the quale one's experience possesses, then one would have expected that one would be able to attend introspectively to that quality of one's experience – the quale – with which one is so acquainted.

Is there an alternative way of accommodating the idea that we possess a concept of the colour red that can be possessed only by subjects who have phenomenally conscious perceptual experiences that are like ours, a way of accommodating the idea which doesn't commit to qualia and which doesn't commit to a naïve realist account of the phenomenal character of conscious perception? Why not say rather that we can accommodate the idea simply by appealing to the representational contents of the perceptual states that obtain when we consciously perceive the colour red?

Implicit in such a proposal is the assumption that we would not be warranted in attributing to a subject perceptual states with the representational contents that our conscious perceptual experiences possess unless that subject underwent perceptual experiences with the phenomenal characters that our conscious perceptual experiences have. So a challenge faced by this kind of proposal is that of explaining why the attribution of perceptual states with representational contents should be constrained in this way. They need to articulate a conception of representational content that would have that constraint as a consequence. And articulating and defending such a conception of representational content is not a straightforward matter.

The advocate of this proposal cannot appeal to the obtaining of a relation of conscious perceptual acquaintance with a quality in their account of what is required for a subject to perceptually represent the qualities that we perceive in the way that we do. The advocate of this proposal, we are assuming, is someone who rejects naïve realism, and so someone who denies that the obtaining a conscious perceptual relation of acquaintance plays a role in determining the phenomenal character of our perceptual experiences. They can instead appeal to causal relations that obtain between the qualities we perceive and our perceptual states, and they can appeal to the functional roles that such perceptual states play in our cognitive economy. But then the challenge they face is to explain why a subject would have to have phenomenally conscious perceptual experiences like ours in order to be in perceptual states that stand in the relevant causal relations and play the relevant functional roles.

Given the difficulties associated with meeting this challenge, should we conclude that Campbell's naïve realist proposal is, after all, best placed to accommodate the idea that we possess concepts of qualities we perceive (e.g. concepts of colours of objects) that can only be possessed by subjects who have phenomenally conscious perceptual experiences that are like ours? Some will reject Campbell's proposal, because they reject the account of the metaphysics of colour that it assumes. Some will maintain that it is a mistake to think that the sort of sensory quality that appears to be revealed to us in our conscious perceptual experience of the colour red is a *mind-independent*, *categorical* quality of mind-independent objects that we perceive. Some argue that this 'naïve' view of colour is undermined by what we have learnt from physics about physical bodies and their qualities. They suggest that physics teaches us that such categorical sensory qualities are not instantiated by mind-independent reality, so it cannot be correct to hold that the phenomenal character of the perceptual experience that you have when you consciously perceive the colour red is to be explained by the obtaining of a relation of conscious perceptual acquaintance with a mind-independent categorical quality of physical objects.

Campbell's response to this line of objection is to suggest that we can acknowledge that there is something fundamental to the description of our surroundings that the physicist provides us with, while insisting, nonetheless, that physical reality can be described 'at many levels', and the physical is only one level of description, even if it is a particularly fundamental level of description. He argues that in characterising the qualitative world we encounter in experience we are describing how things are at a level that is different to the level of description used by the physicist. But this doesn't mean the qualities we thereby characterise are not mind-independent categorical qualities of mind-independent objects. On Campbell's view of colour, redness is not simply a disposition to produce certain conscious experiences in us. Redness is the categorical ground of that disposition. And although colours may be supervenient on the physical, the categorical quality of redness is not to be identified with some micro-physical property of objects.[12]

Adam Pautz has raised the objection against naïve realist accounts of colour perception that empirical research in the science of colour vision suggests that postreceptoral neural processing can make a contribution to the phenomenal character of our perception of colours that goes beyond any objective property or state of the world that the visual system detects. He argues that there is empirical evidence that should lead us to accept that even under ideal viewing conditions, the phenomenal character of our perception of colours is much better correlated with neural patterns in the brain, rather than anything in external physical world.[13]

Campbell's account of the metaphysics of colour is certainly controversial, but even if one is happy to accept Campbell's account of the metaphysics of colours, a further worry one might have with his proposal is the following. It's plausible to think that the concept of the colour red that we possess could also be possessed by the subject who suffers illusions and hallucinations of the colour. Indeed, there's plausibility to the claim that our concept of the colour could be grasped by a subject who was able to perceptually imagine the colour red. So if we are not willing to reject such plausible claims, we'll either have to say that one is acquainted with the colour red in each of those circumstances, or we'll have to say that conscious perceptual acquaintance with the colour red is not, after all, required for grasping the concept of the colour red that we possess.

If one insists that one is acquainted with the colour red whenever one suffers an illusion or hallucination of the colour, and whenever one perceptually imagines the colour, then arguably one will either have to adopt a view on which the experiences that one has in those circumstances are themselves red, or one will to accept a view on which one is acquainted with red sense-data whenever one has such experiences. For many the preferred option will be to deny that we really are consciously acquainted with the colour red when we have such experiences. So for many of those who want to preserve the intuition that the concept of the colour red that we possess could also be possessed by the subject who only suffers illusions and hallucinations of the colour, or who can perceptually imagine the colour, the preferred option will be that of denying that conscious perceptual acquaintance with the colour red is required for grasping the concept of the colour red that we possess. And if we concede that conscious perceptual acquaintance with the colour red is not, after all, required for grasping the concept of red that we possess, then it seems we have reason to reject Campbell's proposal that only the naïve realist can provide an adequate account of the role played by the phenomenal character of conscious perceptual experience in enabling us to grasp concepts of the qualities we perceive (e.g. concepts of the colours of objects).

What can the naïve realist say in response to this line of objection? One possible line of response is to maintain that if a subject is in a position to acquire the concept of red that we possess, then this can only be because that subject is in a position to know what it is, or would be, like to have conscious perceptual acquaintance with the colour red. According to this line of response, we need to make *essential reference* to the relation of *conscious perceptual acquaintance* with the colour red in our explanation of what puts such a subject in a position to acquire our conception of the colour red. That is, we need to make essential reference to the kind of phenomenal character that the naïve realist claims our perceptual experiences have when we succeed in consciously perceiving the world. Those responding in this way will insist that a subject can only acquire the conception of red that we possess if she is in a position to know what it is, or would be like, to have an experience with that naïve realist phenomenal character. So if illusions/hallucinations of the colour red can put a subject in a position to acquire the concept of red that we possess, and if episodes of perceptual imagination can put a subject in a position to acquire the concept of red that we possess, then this would only be because such experiences put their subject in a position to know (or in the case of perceptual imagination, constitute knowledge of) what it is like to have an experience with that naïve realist phenomenal character.

In her explanation of how perceptual imagination of the colour red can put one in a position to know (or amount to a form of knowledge of) what it is, or would be, like to have an experience that has a naïve realist phenomenal character, the naïve realist might invoke the dependency thesis that I discussed in the previous chapter. Recall that those who endorse the dependency thesis claim that when one perceptually imagines an object, quality or scene, one thereby represents, in a distinctive way, the phenomenal character of the perceptual experience one would have if one were to consciously perceive that object, quality or scene. In advocating the dependency thesis, the naïve realist may then say that although the conscious episodes that occur when one perceptually imagines the colour red do not actually have the phenomenal character of the experience that one has when one consciously perceives the colour red (and so although one is not actually consciously acquainted with the colour red when one perceptually imagines the colour), such episodes of imagining nonetheless *represent*, in a distinctive way, the phenomenal character of conscious perceptions of the colour red, and this form of representation can put one in a position to know (or amount to a form of knowledge of) what it is, or would be, like to consciously perceive the colour.

As for cases of perceptual illusion/hallucination of the colour red, the naïve realist may say that the subject who undergoes such experiences may be in a position to know what it is, or would be, like to have an experience that has a naïve realist phenomenal character, because although such experiences don't actually instantiate a naïve realist phenomenal character, they nonetheless introspectively seem to have that phenomenal character. So, while the illusory/hallucinatory experience doesn't actually have the naïve realist phenomenal character that it introspectively seems to have, the fact that it introspectively seems to have that phenomenal character can, nonetheless, put one in a position to know what it would be like to have an experience with naïve realist phenomenal character.

Note that the naïve realist who responds in this way will be granting the following claim: experiences that don't actually have the naïve realist phenomenal character can put a subject in a position to know what it is, or would be like, to have an experience with a naïve realist phenomenal character. And once that claim is conceded, it might be argued that we are not obliged to accept that our veridical perceptions have a naïve realist phenomenal character. Perhaps veridical perceptions, like hallucinations, put one in a position to know what it would be like to have an experience with a naïve realist phenomenal character, but without actually instantiating that naïve realist phenomenal character. However, note that to take this line is to grant a concession of sorts to the naïve realist. In taking this line one would be conceding that if our veridical perceptions don't have a naïve realist phenomenal character, then such experiences don't have the sort of phenomenal character that they introspectively seem to have. And as we've seen, once this concession is made, the dialectical position of those opposing naïve realism is significantly weakened.[14]

Now if the naïve realist responds in this way, and grants that actual conscious perceptual acquaintance with the colour red isn't required for knowing what it would be like to be consciously acquainted with that colour, does that after all mean that she thereby allows that a subject who wasn't phenomenally conscious could in principle know what it would be like to consciously perceive the colour red, and so acquire the conception of the colour red that we possess? Not if she maintains that only a *phenomenally conscious* condition of a subject can put that subject in a position to acquire the relevant knowledge, i.e. not if she maintains that it is only a *phenomenally conscious* hallucination/illusion, or episode of perceptual imagination, that can put a subject in a position to know what it is, or would be like, to consciously perceive the colour red. But note, then, that the tenability of this naïve realist response depends on the tenability of a naïve realist view that can accommodate the idea that a hallucination is a phenomenally conscious experience that doesn't have the phenomenal character of a veridical perception, but which nonetheless puts its subject in a position to know what it is, or would be like, to have an experience with the phenomenal character of a genuine perception. In Chapter 6 we'll be considering whether the naïve realist has a problem in accommodating a conception of hallucination that fits that description.

4.5 Chapter summary

In this chapter we considered ways in which debates about the conscious character of perception are connected with debates about the role played by conscious perception in enabling us to acquire knowledge of, think about, and refer to, the mind-independent entities in our environment that we perceive. In particular, we focused on a line of argument in John

Campbell's work for the following claim: only the naïve realist can provide an adequate account of the role that conscious perception plays in enabling one to think about the mind-independent objects and qualities one perceives, precisely because only the naïve realist provides an adequate account of the phenomenal character of conscious perception

First of all we discussed whether there is any reason to think that the *phenomenal character* of conscious perception plays a crucial role in explaining our capacity to think about the mind-independent objects and features in our environment that we perceive. Here we considered the suggestion that it is *phenomenally conscious* sensory experience of colours that provides for our distinctive conceptions of what our colour terms refer to, and we considered what could be said to accommodate this suggestion by those who hold that the phenomenal character of conscious perceptual experiences is to be explained by appeal to the instantiation of qualia. In particular, we discussed a view in which

(a) there is a distinctively visual *phenomenal* concept of the colour red that one can only possess if one knows what it is like to see that colour, and
(b) one can only know what it is like to see the colour if one has had visual experiences with the relevant qualia.

We then considered Campbell's reasons for rejecting such accounts, and we discussed the arguments he presents for holding that only a naïve realist account of phenomenal character can accommodate an epistemic role that conscious perception plays in grounding the concepts we possess of the mind-independent objects and qualities we perceive. We saw that Campbell recommends a form of empiricism about concept possession that is incompatible with a 'separatist' view – i.e. a view that holds that all intentional and phenomenal aspects of mind are mutually independent and entirely separable – and we saw that for Campbell, the naïve realist account of the phenomenal character of conscious perception plays a key role in explaining what is wrong with the separatist view. We also saw how Campbell argues for the further claim that only the naïve realist can provide an adequate account of the role that conscious perception plays in enabling us to think about the objects we perceive in our environment *as mind-independent*.

We considered various objections to Campbell's proposal – including objections raised by those who hold that our perceptual experiences have representational contents – and we discussed some of Campbell's responses to them. We also discussed how some will reject Campbell's proposal because they reject the account of the metaphysics of colour that it assumes.

Notes

1 Campbell 2002a, 2002b, 2005, 2011, and 2014.
2 For discussion of, and opposition to, 'separatism', see Horgan and Tienson 2002. For a collection of papers relevant to what has become known as the 'phenomenal intentionality' research programme, see also Kriegel 2013.
3 The thought here is the following: Mary knows all the physical facts concerning human colour vision before she leaves her black and white room. There is a fact about human colour vision that she doesn't know until she leaves the room and actually has a visual experience of something red. Therefore, there are non-physical facts concerning human colour vision. Jackson's argument has generated a great deal of discussion. For a survey of the literature, see Nida-Rümelin 2009.
4 For similar endorsement of this claim see Langsam 2011. Langsam argues that 'our observation of the world . . . does not merely inform us that certain objects have certain properties; it tells us something about those properties' (37). He also holds a relational view of experience on which 'the object one experiences is literally part of one's experience' (42), and according to which observable properties determine the phenomenal character of experience. And in his view, 'the nature of red partly explains what it is like to experience red' (39).
5 See Campbell 2002a: 139.
6 The same is true of Bill Brewer. Brewer (2011) argues that it is through explaining our grasp of concepts of the objects we perceive that conscious perceptual experience makes possible thought about such objects, and he argues that only a naïve realist relational view of the phenomenal character of conscious perception can accommodate that explanatory role.
7 Campbell 2002a: 134–135.
8 For Campbell's discussion of the role that perceptual attention plays in enabling us to demonstratively refer to entities that we perceive, see his 2002a. For further discussion, and a distinctive development of, the proposal that perceptual attention plays an epistemic role in fixing demonstrative reference to perceived objects, see Dickie 2011.
9 For arguments for the claim that our perceptual experiences have conceptual contents, see McDowell 1994, Sedivy 1996, and Brewer 1999.

10 Campbell 2002a: 6.
11 For this sort of criticism of Campbell's argument, see Cassam 2011 and Cassam's contribution to Campbell and Cassam 2014.
12 For Campbell's account of colour, see Campbell 1994 and 2005a. A number of different accounts of colour have been advanced. For some important proposals and discussions of this topic, see Hardin 1993, Johnston 1992, Jackson 1996, Tye 2000, Cohen 2004, Kalderon 2007, and Byrne and Hilbert 2007.
13 See Pautz 2006, 2011, 2013.
14 The earlier discussions of this point can be found in 2.2 and 3.3.

Further reading

Campbell's arguments for holding a naïve realist account of the phenomenal character of perception can be found in Campbell and Cassam 2014 and Campbell 2002a, 2002b, 2005b, and 2011. For objections to Campbell's arguments, see Cassam's contribution to Campbell and Cassam 2014. See also Cassam 2011. Further objections are raised against Campbell's arguments in Burge 2005. For a response to Burge, see Campbell 2010.

For Brewer's argument that only a naïve realist relational view of the phenomenal character of conscious perception can accommodate the role that conscious perception plays in explaining our grasp of concepts of the objects we perceive, see his 2011. (See also his 2004 and 2006.) For Langsam's appeal to perceptual acquaintance, see his 1997 and 2011.

For discussion of, and opposition to, 'separatism', see Horgan and Tienson 2002. For a collection of papers relevant to what has become known as the 'phenomenal intentionality' research programme, see also Kriegel 2013. For Burge's reflections on phenomenal consciousness, see his 2007.

For Campbell's account of colour, see Campbell 1994 and 2005a. For some important proposals and discussions of colour, see Hardin 1993, Johnston 1992, Jackson 1996, Tye 2000, Cohen 2004, Kalderon 2007, and Byrne and Hilbert 2007. For Pautz's objections to naïve realism based in the science of colour perception, see his 2006, 2011, and 2013.

References

Brewer, Bill, 1999, *Perception and Reason*. Oxford: Oxford University Press.
———, 2004, 'Realism and the nature of perceptual experience', *Philosophical Issues*, 14 (1): 61–77.

——, 2006, 'Perception and content', *European Journal of Philosophy*, 14 (2): 165–181.
——, 2011, *Perception and Its Objects*. Oxford: Oxford University Press.
Burge, Tyler, 2005, 'Disjunctivism and perceptual psychology', *Philosophical Topics*, 33: 1–78.
——, 'Reflections of two kinds of consciousness', in *Foundations of Mind*. Oxford: Oxford University Press.
Byrne, A. and Hilbert, D. R., 2007, 'Color primitivism', *Erkenntnis*, 26: 3–21.
Campbell, J., 1994, 'A simple view of color', in J. Haldane and C. Wright (eds), *Reality, Representation and Projection*. Oxford: Clarendon Press, pp. 257–269.
——, 2002a, *Reference and Consciousness*. Oxford: Oxford University Press.
——, 2002b, 'Berkeley's puzzle', in Tamar Szabo Gendler and John O'Leary Hawthorne (eds), *Conceivability and Possibility*. Oxford: Oxford University Press, pp. 127–144.
——, 2005a, 'Transparency vs revelation in color perception', *Philosophical Topics*, 33: 105–115.
——, 2005b, 'Précis of *Reference and Consciousness*, and replies to Neil Manson and Georges Rey', *Philosophical Studies*, 126: 103–114, 145–153, 155–162.
——, 2011, 'Relational vs. Kantian responses to Berkeley's puzzle', in J. Roessler, H. Lerman, and N. Eilan, (eds), *Understanding Perception, Causation and Objectivity*. Oxford: Oxford University Press.
Campbell, John and Cassam, Quassim, 2014, *Berkeley's Puzzle: what does experience teach us?* Oxford: Oxford University Press.
Cassam, Q., 2011, 'Tackling Berkeley's puzzle', in N. Eilan, H. Lerman, and J. Roessler (eds), *Understanding Perception, Causation and Objectivity*. Oxford: Oxford University Press.
Cohen, J., 2004, 'Color properties and color ascription: a rationalist manifesto', *The Philosophical Review*, 101: 451–488.
Imogen Dickie, 2011, 'Visual attention fixes demonstrative reference by eliminating referential luck', in Christopher Mole, Declan Smithies, and Wayne Wu (eds), *Attention: philosophical and psychological essays*. Oxford: Oxford University Press, pp. 292–321.
Hardin, C. L., 1993, *Color for Philosophers*. Indianapolis: Hackett.
Horgan, Terence and Tienson, John, 2002, 'The intentionality of phenomenology and the phenomenology of intentionality', in D. Chalmers (ed.), *Philosophy of Mind: classical and contemporary readings*. Oxford: Oxford University Press.

Jackson, F., 1982, 'Epiphenomenal qualia', *Philosophical Quarterly*, 32: 127–136
——,1996, 'The primary quality view of color', *Philosophical Perspectives*, 10: 199–219.
Johnston, M., 1992, 'How to speak of the colors', *Philosophical Studies*, 68 (3): 221–263.
Kalderon, M., 2007, 'Color pluralism', *The Philosophical Review*, 116: 563–601.
Kriegel, Uriah, 2013, *Phenomenal Intentionality*. Oxford: Oxford University Press.
Langsam, Harold, 1997, 'The theory of appearing defended', *Philosophical Studies*, 120: 33–59.
——, 2011, *The Wonder of Consciousness: understanding the mind through philosophical reflection*. Cambridge, MA: MIT Press.
McDowell, John, 1994, *Mind and World*. Cambridge, MA: Harvard University Press.
Nida-Rümelin, Martine, 2009, 'Qualia: the knowledge argument', Edward N. Zalta (ed.), *The Stanford Encyclopedia of Philosophy* (forthcoming) <http://plato.stanford.edu/archives/sum2015/entries/qualia-knowledge/>.
Pautz, Adam, 2006, 'Sensory awareness is not a wide physical relation: an empirical argument against externalist intentionalism', *Nous*, 40 (2): 205–240.
——, 2011, 'Can disjunctivists explain our access to the sensible world?', *Philosophical Issues*, 21: 384–433.
——, 2013, 'The real trouble for phenomenal externalists: new empirical evidence for a brain-based theory of consciousness', in Richard Brown (ed.), *Consciousness Inside and Out: phenomenology, neuroscience, and the nature of experience*. The Netherlands: Springer, pp. 237–298.
Sedivy, Sonia, 1996, 'Must conceptually informed perceptual experience involve nonconceptual content?', *Canadian Journal of Philosophy*, 26 (3): 413–431.
Tye, M., 2000, *Consciousness, Color and Content*. Cambridge, MA: MIT Press.

5

EPISTEMOLOGICAL DISJUNCTIVISM

Thus far we have primarily been concerned with forms of disjunctivism that are adopted in defence of an account of the phenomenal character of conscious perception, and in particular, forms of disjunctivism that are adopted in defence of naïve realist accounts of the phenomenal character of conscious perception. In the previous chapter, epistemic concerns also came into play, as we discussed Campbell's contention that only a naïve realist account of phenomenal character can accommodate an epistemic role that conscious perception plays in grounding the concepts we possess of the mind-independent objects and qualities we perceive. In this chapter we will continue to examine epistemological motivations for disjunctivism, but we will leave to one side debates about the putative role played by the phenomenal character of perception in grounding our possession of *concepts* of the items we perceive. We will instead focus on forms of disjunctivism that are adopted in defence of the role played by perception in providing us with *propositional* knowledge about our surroundings, knowledge *that* things are thus and so in our environment.

The philosopher most associated with this sort of epistemological motivation for disjunctivism is John McDowell, and this chapter will largely be devoted to outlining and assessing McDowell's view.[1] There are a number of different elements to McDowell's positive account of perceptual knowledge, and I shan't be discussing all of them. In particular, I shan't be discussing McDowell's epistemological arguments for the claim that conscious perceptual awareness, in self-conscious subjects, involves the actualisation of subject's conceptual capacities. I shall be limiting the focus of the discussion to those aspects of McDowell's approach that I take to be most pertinent to the disjunctivism in his view.

McDowell has argued that we need to adopt disjunctivism in order to secure the right account of the role that successful perception plays in providing us with propositional knowledge about our surroundings. According to McDowell, this is because the right account of perceptual knowledge depends upon the rejection of a common kind claim – a claim about what is common to cases of successful perception and subjectively indistinguishable hallucination. In particular, McDowell argues that we need to reject the following 'highest common factor' assumption:

> When you successfully perceive your environment, the warrant that you have for making judgements about your environment is no better than, no stronger than, the warrant that you would have for making such judgements if you were having a subjectively indistinguishable hallucination.

In this chapter we'll be considering the significance of this highest common factor (HCF) claim, what arguments can be given in support of the claim, how one might try to resist them, and why one might want to resist them. Before we embark on that discussion there are a couple of points to note about the claim.

The first is this. Those who accept the sort of highest common factor claim that McDowell targets need not deny that there is a significant epistemological difference between the situation you are in when you successfully perceive your environment, and the situation you are in when you are having a subjectively indistinguishable hallucination. For those who accept the claim might maintain that when you successfully perceive your environment you are (normally) in a position to acquire propositional knowledge about your environment, whereas when you hallucinate you are not. What those who accept the HCF claim will deny, however, is that this epistemological difference is to be explained in terms of a difference in the sort of epistemic grounds for judgement *that you have access to* in each case. They insist that the epistemic grounds for world-directed judgement that you have access to in the case of successful perception are *no better than* the epistemic grounds for judgement that you have access to in the case of a subjectively indistinguishable hallucination. In consequence they hold that when you successfully perceive your environment, the epistemic grounds that you have access to for making judgements about your environment, are compatible with the falsity of those judgements. When you perceive your environment, the warrant that you have access to for making world-directed judgements leaves open the possibility that those judgements are false.

By contrast, those who, like McDowell, reject the HCF claim maintain the following:

(a) there is a significant epistemic asymmetry between the case in which you successfully perceive your environment and the case in which you have a subjectively indistinguishable hallucination;
(b) this epistemic asymmetry is to be explained, at least in part, by appeal to an asymmetry in the epistemic grounds for judgement that you have access to in each case; and
(c) when all goes well and you successfully perceive your environment, you have access to *conclusive* grounds for judgements about your environment, i.e. epistemic grounds for judgement that don't leave open the possibility that those judgements are false.

The second point to note is that the 'highest common factor' claim that McDowell is concerned to resist is one that is expressed in epistemic terms. The common factor claim that McDowell targets doesn't explicitly commit to any particular proposal about the phenomenal character of conscious perception. So one might question whether one would need to accept a disjunctivist account of the phenomenal character of perception in order to resist this highest common factor claim. The question of whether one can consistently reject this HCF claim by granting that there are significant epistemic differences between the experiences involved in cases of genuine perception and subjectively indistinguishable hallucination, while maintaining that there are *no* significant *psychological* differences between such experiences is one we shall be considering in due course. This issue will be relevant to an assessment of the question of whether an advocate of McDowell's epistemological disjunctivism needs to commit to any form of 'metaphysical' disjunctivism.

First, though, we will need to clarify further the sort of epistemological proposal that McDowell is concerned to defend, and to that end it will be helpful to discuss in more detail the general idea that there can be an epistemic asymmetry between certain 'good' situations, in which things are as they appear to be, and certain 'bad' situations, which aren't good, and yet which are indistinguishable for their subjects from those good situations.

5.1 Epistemic asymmetries between 'good' and 'bad' cases

At this stage I'd like to introduce a rather rough and abstract characterisation of so-called 'good' and 'bad' situations, so we can consider good and bad situations that aren't restricted to – or specific to – cases of perceptual judgement. Let us say that a 'good' situation is one in which things really are as they seem, or appear, to the subject to be, and let us say that a 'bad' situation is a situation that is indistinguishable from the good situation, and in which things aren't as they seem – or appear – to be in the good situation. Moreover, let us say that a 'bad' situation is indistinguishable from a good one just in case when one is in the bad situation one is not in a position to activate knowledge that one is not in the good situation.

Now consider the following sceptical line of thought. If there is a bad situation that is indistinguishable from the good one, then even when you are in the good situation you won't be able to tell that your situation is good, in which case, you won't be able to know that things really are as they appear to be: in order to know that your situation is a good one, you must be able to rule out the hypothesis that your situation is a bad one. And if the bad situation is indistinguishable from the good one, then even if your situation is in fact good, you won't be able to rule out the hypothesis that your situation is bad.

The particular characterisation I gave of what makes a bad situation indistinguishable from a good one leaves open the following line of response to this argument. Indistinguishability, so characterised, does not imply a match in epistemic significance. And we can see why by considering points that Bernard Williams once noted. According to Williams,

> The idea of one's being able to tell *whether* S seems to entail the conjunction of two things:
>
> (a)   One can tell that S when S;
> (b)   One can tell that not-S when not-S.
>
> We may be tempted to think that (a) and (b) must go together. The vital point . . . is that they do not necessarily go together.
>
> (1978: 310)

Williams notes that for certain values of 'S', one of these conjuncts can obtain without the other. For example, suppose that 'S' is 'one is dead', or 'one is in dreamless sleep', or 'one is severely drunk'. You cannot tell that you are dead when you are dead, but from this it doesn't follow that you cannot tell that you are not dead when you are not dead. You cannot tell that you are in dreamless sleep when you are in dreamless sleep, but from this it doesn't follow that you cannot tell that you are not in dreamless sleep when you are not in dreamless sleep. You may be unable to tell that you are severely drunk when you are severely drunk, but from this it doesn't follow that you are unable to tell that you are sober when you are sober.

Consider the latter case. Let's call the 'good' situation one in which it seems to you as though you are sober, and things really are as they seem to be: you are sober. Let's say that severe drunkenness is the 'bad' situation. It could be held that severe drunkenness is a situation that is indistinguishable from the 'good' one in the following respect: when you are severely drunk your condition is such that you are not in a position to activate knowledge that you are not sober. According to this characterisation of indistinguishability, severe drunkenness is a 'bad' situation that is indistinguishable from the 'good' one. Suppose we were to apply the sceptical line of thought that I outlined above. In this case, it seems we have reason to reject the following step in that argument: if the bad situation is indistinguishable from the good one, then even if your situation is in fact good, you won't be able to rule out the hypothesis that your situation is bad. So here we appear to have a counterexample to the general claim that there must be a match in epistemic significance — there must be an epistemic symmetry — between good situations and bad situations that are indistinguishable from good ones.

The indistinguishability of a bad situation, as I characterised that notion, does not in itself imply any such match in epistemic significance.

Accepting this much, one might nonetheless maintain that matters are very different when it comes to assessing the question of whether there is an epistemic symmetry between a good case in which one successfully perceives one's environment, and a bad case in which one is having a subjectively indistinguishable hallucination. In cases like 'being dead', 'being in dreamless sleep', and 'being severely drunk', there are rather obvious explanations to be given of why, in such 'bad' situations, one is not in position to activate knowledge that one is not in the good situation, and such explanations are consistent with the proposal that in the good situations one's epistemic position is rather different. If you are dead, you do not exist to activate any knowledge. If you are in dreamless sleep, although you are alive, you are not in a position to make any judgements. If you are severely drunk, although you may be in a position to make judgements, your drunken condition impacts your ability to make *rational* judgements. None of these explanations apply in the case of a subject who is awake, sober, and having a hallucination that is subjectively indistinguishable from a successful perception. So in the latter case we lack such grounds for denying that there is an epistemic symmetry between the good and bad situations.

Before we return to the case of perceptual knowledge, and McDowell's stance on perceptual knowledge, I want to consider a further example of a good and bad situation, one which it may be more intuitive to regard as involving an epistemic asymmetry. Consideration of this example may help to clarify certain aspects of McDowell's proposal about perceptual knowledge.

Let us consider a form of scepticism that targets your claim to know that you have *phenomenally conscious* perceptual experience. In this case the bad situation is as follows. Although you may think that you have phenomenally conscious perceptual experience, you do not. You are a phenomenal zombie. Although you lack phenomenally conscious experience, you are functionally very similar to a subject who has phenomenally conscious perceptual experience. You are disposed to believe that you have phenomenally conscious experience, you think that you have good reason to believe that you have phenomenally conscious perceptual experience, for you think that introspection reveals to you that you have phenomenally conscious perceptual experience, and you are disposed to give rich descriptions of the phenomenal character of your experience when asked to do so. However, although you are so disposed, and although you interact with your environment successfully, and communicate with others effectively, you do not in fact enjoy phenomenally conscious experiences. And in this bad situation, given the functional roles played by the mental states you are in, you are not in a position to activate knowledge that you are not phenomenally conscious.

Now consider the following sceptical line of argument:

(a) The bad situation (i.e. being a phenomenal zombie) is indistinguishable from the good situation (i.e. having phenomenally conscious experience) in the following respect: when one is in the bad situation, one cannot tell that one is not in the good situation, for one cannot activate knowledge that one is not in the good situation. Moreover, in the bad situation, one would believe that one was in the good situation.
(b) Given (a), if one were in the bad situation one would not notice that one was not in the good situation, and one would believe that one was in the good situation.
(c) Given (b), you cannot now rule out that you are not in the bad situation.

Before we consider how one might respond to this line of argument, let us consider a related argument, an argument that doesn't target your claim to *know* that you have phenomenally conscious experience, but which is rather concerned to establish a claim about the epistemic grounds you have access to for judging whether or not you have phenomenally conscious experience. The argument proceeds as follows:

(i) Suppose for *reductio* that the following is true: when you are in the good situation you have access to epistemic grounds for judging whether or not you have phenomenally conscious experience that are absent in the bad situation.
(ii) If the above supposition were true, then if you were in the bad situation you would be in a position to notice that you lacked access to such epistemic grounds for judgement; in which case you would be in a position to tell that you were not in the good situation.
(iii) However, it follows from our characterisation of the bad situation that if you were in the bad situation you would not notice that you were not in the good situation, and you would believe that you were in the good situation.

(iv) So in order to avoid contradiction we should reject our starting supposition: the supposition that when you are in the good situation you have access to epistemic grounds for judging whether or not you have phenomenally conscious experience that are absent in the bad situation.
(v) So we should accept that the epistemic grounds that you have access to for making judgements about whether or not you have phenomenally conscious experience are no better than, no stronger than, the epistemic grounds that you would have access to if you were a phenomenal zombie.
(vi) In which case we should accept that in the case of your judgement that you are having a phenomenally conscious experience, the epistemic grounds that you have access to for making that judgement leave open the possibility that your judgement is false.
(vii) This need not imply that you do not know that you are having a phenomenally conscious experience. Your judgement that you are having a phenomenally conscious experience may be warranted, and if you are in the good situation the belief you so acquire might amount to knowledge. However, the epistemic grounds for judgement that you have access to in the good and bad situations are the same; and so we should accept that even if you are in the good situation, you only have access to *non-conclusive*, grounds for judging that you are having phenomenally conscious experience.

In the case of this particular example of good and bad situations, I suspect that many will want to maintain that the right response to the initial sceptical argument (which targets your claims to *know* that you are having phenomenally conscious experience) is to explain why we should not be persuaded by the second argument (which purports to establish that the epistemic grounds that you have access to for making judgements about whether or not you have phenomenally conscious experience are no better than, no stronger than, the epistemic grounds that you would have access to if you were a phenomenal zombie).[2]

I suspect that many will be unpersuaded by the second argument, because it is intuitive to think that the epistemic grounds that you now have access to for judging whether you are having a phenomenally conscious experience would be absent if you were in the bad situation. If you are having a phenomenally conscious experience, then that fact is made manifest to you through introspection. Your introspective intake doesn't fall short of the fact that you are having a phenomenally conscious experience, in the following respect: your introspective intake is incompatible with the absence of phenomenally conscious experience. So your introspective intake provides you with *conclusive* grounds for judging that you are having a phenomenally conscious experience. The epistemic grounds that you have access to for so judging don't leave open the possibility that your judgement is false. A phenomenal zombie wouldn't have access to such epistemic grounds for judgement. In lacking phenomenally conscious experience, the phenomenal zombie would lack the epistemic grounds for judgement that you have access to.

Those who find this sort of characterisation of the good situation compelling will have cause to question the move from premise (i) to premise (ii) in the argument I outlined: they will want to maintain that in the good situation you have access to epistemic grounds for judgement that would *not* be available to a subject in the bad situation, and they will want to maintain that this is consistent with the claim that the subject in the bad situation would fail to notice that she lacked such epistemic grounds for judgement.

Why does the subject in the bad situation fail to notice that she lacks the relevant epistemic grounds for judging that she is phenomenally conscious? One answer we can give to this question is that the subject in the bad situation has something in common with the subject in the good situation. Given her functional similarity to the subject in the good situation, she is disposed to believe that she has access to epistemic grounds for judging that she is having a phenomenally conscious experience. Indeed, in being so disposed she may be disposed to believe that she has access to *conclusive* grounds for judging that she is having a phenomenally conscious experience. She shares that disposition with the subject in the good situation. There is a sense, then, in which we may say that for each subject it seems to her as though she is having a phenomenally conscious experience.

However, those who find compelling the characterisation of the good situation that I outlined will want to say the following: although there may be a sense in which it seems to each subject as though she is having a phenomenally conscious experience, there are rather different explanations to be given of why this is so in each case. In the case of the subject in the good situation, it seems to her as though she is having a phenomenally conscious experience, and she is disposed to judge that she is having a phenomenally conscious experience, because she is *introspectively aware of* her phenomenally conscious experience. The fact that she is having a phenomenally conscious experience is made manifest to her through introspection. Whereas, in the case of the subject in the bad situation, it seems to her as though she is having a phenomenally conscious experience, because she is merely disposed to believe that her situation is good. The fact that we can give these very different explanations of the dispositions of the subjects who are in such good and bad situations offers us a way of making consistent the following two claims:

(a) in the good situation you have access to epistemic grounds for judgement that would not be available to you in the bad situation, and
(b) the subject in the bad situation would be ignorant of the fact that she lacked such epistemic grounds for judgement.

This in turn offers us a way of blocking the move from premise (i) to premise (ii) in the argument I outlined.

Here is another way of framing the stance of those inclined to respond in this way. There is an epistemically distinguished class of cases – the good cases – in which one has access to *conclusive* grounds for judging that one is having a phenomenally conscious experience. If your situation belongs to that epistemically distinguished class, then you have access to conclusive grounds for judging that you are having a phenomenally conscious experience, because the fact that you are having a phenomenally conscious experience is made manifest to you through introspection. This is consistent with the idea that there can be cases in which a subject is deceived into thinking that her situation belongs to that epistemically distinguished class. That is to say, the fact that it is possible, in principle, for a subject to be deceived into thinking that her situation belongs to the epistemically distinguished class, doesn't entail that there can be no such epistemically distinguished class of cases at all. Once we realise this, we can see that the move from premise (i) to premise (ii) in the argument I outlined is illegitimate.

As we shall see, McDowell appears to want to make a similar defensive move when responding to some of the objections that have been raised against his favoured account of the role that perception plays in providing us with propositional knowledge of our surroundings. It is to that account that we now turn.

5.2 McDowell's epistemological disjunctivism

McDowell gives the following characterisation of the basic shape of his epistemological disjunctivism:

> In perceptual experience a subject has it appear to her that things are a certain way in her environment. In some cases ('good' cases), the experience makes it manifest to the subject that things are that way; in others ('bad' cases), the appearance that things are that way is a *mere* appearance. An experience in which the appearance that things are a certain way is a mere appearance can be such that the subject cannot tell that it is not an experience of the first kind. The point of my epistemological disjunctivism is that this indiscriminability does not imply a match in epistemic significance.
>
> (2013: 259–260)

As I noted earlier, a number of those who are opposed to McDowell's epistemological disjunctivism may be happy to agree that there is a significant epistemological difference between a 'good' case in which one successfully perceives one's environment, and an indiscriminable 'bad' case in which one hallucinates. For they might maintain, contrary to the sceptic, that one is in a position to acquire perceptual knowledge of one's environment in the good case, and that this is a privilege one isn't afforded in the indiscriminable bad case. In that respect, they may agree with McDowell that such 'indiscriminability does not imply a match in epistemic significance'. In order to see where the real disagreement between McDowell and his opponents lies, we need to turn to McDowell's account of the warranting, justificatory role played by perceptual experience in the acquisition of such perceptual knowledge.

According to McDowell, when one visually perceives one's environment, aspects of objective reality are perceptually 'present to one', 'visibly *there* for one' (2010: 245), and one's perceptual experience in the 'good' case thereby 'makes manifest' to one that things are a certain way in one's environment. One can imagine critics of McDowell insisting that they are also able to accommodate the idea that in the good situation aspects of the environment are perceptually 'present to one', 'visibly *there* for one', without having to commit to any form of disjunctivism. However, one will miss what is distinctive of McDowell's position if one doesn't discern the particular epistemic gloss that he gives to his use of such phrases. When aspects of the environment are said to be 'perceptually present' to you, and your perceptual experience thereby 'makes manifest' to you that things are a certain way in your environment, then, according to McDowell, you have *conclusive* warrant for believing things to be that way. That is to say, the warrant that is provided by your perceptual experience is incompatible with the belief's falsity. As McDowell puts it, 'If an aspect of objective reality is perceptually present to someone, there is no possibility, compatibly with her experience's being as it is, that she might be wrong in believing that things are as her experience is revealing them to be' (2010: 245).

One might think of the suggestion here as somewhat akin to the respect in which introspection might be said to 'make manifest' to you that you are having a phenomenally conscious perceptual experience. As discussed in the previous section, I think many are likely to find intuitive the suggestion that the introspective warrant you have for believing that you are undergoing a phenomenally conscious experience is conclusive. Your introspective warrant doesn't leave open the possibility that you are in the position of the phenomenal zombie. Such warrant is incompatible with the falsity of your belief. There is an epistemic asymmetry between your situation, and the situation of the phenomenal zombie. You are in a position to know that you have phenomenally conscious experience, and the zombie is not; but moreover, and crucially, this fact is to be explained by appeal to a further fact about the asymmetry of your situations. You have access to conclusive epistemic grounds for believing that you are having a phenomenally conscious experience, and the phenomenal zombie doesn't. So it would be a mistake to maintain the following: the epistemic grounds that you have access to for making judgements about whether or not you have phenomenally conscious experience are no better than, no stronger than, the epistemic grounds that you would have access to if you were a phenomenal zombie.

McDowell appears to want to make analogous claims about the perceptual warrant that we have in the so-called 'good' cases of perception. He claims that there is an epistemic asymmetry between the situation you are in when you successfully perceive your environment, and the situation you are in when you have a subjectively indistinguishable hallucination. In the former situation you are in a position to acquire knowledge of your environment, and in the latter situation you are not; but moreover, and crucially, this fact is to be explained by appeal to a further fact about the asymmetry of the two situations. In the good situation you have access to *conclusive* perceptual warrant for believing things about your environment.

In the bad situation, you don't. So McDowell proposes that it would be a mistake to maintain that in the good situation the warrant that you have access to for making judgements about your environment is no better than, no stronger than, the warrant that you would have access to if you were having a subjectively indistinguishable hallucination. To quote McDowell, it would be a mistake to hold the following:

> if someone knows something about her environment through an experience, it must be partly by virtue of something additional to the experience itself; the warranting power of the experience is no better than the warranting power of an experience that would be indiscriminable from it but would not make the corresponding knowledge available, so the experience leaves open the possibility that a belief grounded on it is not a case of knowledge.
> (2013: 260)

According to McDowell, one would only embrace the latter option if there didn't seem to be any alternative (2010: 251). And he argues that his disjunctivism 'shows how, in spite of temptations to believe the contrary, perceptual warrants can be conclusive' (2013: 271).

In order to defend this position McDowell needs to show that we can consistently maintain the following two claims:

(i) in the good situation (successful perception) you have access to conclusive epistemic grounds for perceptual judgement that would not be available to you in the bad situation (subjectively indistinguishable hallucination), and
(ii) if you were in the bad situation you would fail to notice you lacked such epistemic grounds for judgement.

In the previous section I suggested that if we are to be persuaded of the tenability of this kind of epistemic asymmetry between good and bad situations (i.e. an asymmetry that is due to a difference in the warrant one has access to in each case), we might expect some explanation of the purported fact that the subject in the bad situation fails to notice that she lacks access to the sort of conclusive warrant that she would have access to in good situation. So what can McDowell say about this?

McDowell can say that the subject in the bad situation fails to notice that she lacks the relevant conclusive epistemic grounds for judgement, because she has something in common with the subject in the good situation. In the bad situation it perceptually appears to the subject as if things are thus and so in her environment, and this is equally true of the subject in the good situation. That is why the subject in the bad situation cannot discriminate her situation from the good one. The point of McDowell's disjunctive conception of perceptual experience is to insist that there are, nonetheless, rather different accounts to be given of the perceptual appearances that are involved in each case. In the good situation it perceptually appears to the subject that things are thus and so in her environment because aspects of the environment are perceptually present to her, and in a way that makes manifest to her that things are that way. In the bad situation, meanwhile, it appears, but merely appears, to the subject as if her situation is the good one.

Here McDowell deploys the kind of defensive move that I outlined at the end of the previous section. The strategy is to insist that there is an epistemically distinguished class of cases – the good cases – in which one has access to *conclusive* grounds for judging that things are thus and so in one's environment. If your situation belongs to that epistemically distinguished class, then you have access to conclusive grounds for making judgements about your environment because facts about the layout of your environment are made manifest to you through perception. This is consistent with the idea that there can be cases in which a subject is deceived, by misleading appearances, into thinking that her situation belongs to that epistemically distinguished class. That is to say, the fact that it is possible, in principle, for a subject to be deceived into thinking that her situation belongs to the epistemically distinguished class, doesn't entail that there can be no such epistemically distinguished class of cases at all.

Is there any reason to think that this sort of defensive manoeuvre cannot be plausibly applied in the case of the perceptual warrant one has for making judgements about one's environment? Compare the proposal that you have access to conclusive epistemic grounds for judging that you are having a phenomenally conscious experience, epistemic grounds that would not be available to the phenomenal zombie. One might think that what makes this suggestion plausible is the following: built into the descriptions of these 'good' and 'bad' situations is the fact that there is a significant *psychological* difference between the subjects occupying each situation. The subject in the good situation undergoes perceptual experience that has phenomenal properties, and the subject in the bad situation doesn't. Moreover, it is plausible to think that the psychological features (phenomenal properties) which are present in the case of the subject in the good situation, and absent in the case of the subject in the bad situation, are psychological features to which the subject in the good situation has introspective access. This enables the subject in the good situation to introspectively discriminate her situation from the bad one. It could be said, then, that there is a certain respect in which the two situations (good and bad) are not, after all, genuinely introspectively indiscriminable: although the subject in the bad situation is unable to introspectively discriminate her situation from the good one, the subject in the good situation is able to introspectively discriminate her situation from the bad one; and she is in a position to do so, because there is an introspectively discernible feature that her experience possesses, which would be lacking if she were in the bad situation.

Many will maintain that things are rather different in the case of the good and bad situations that involve successful perception and subjectively indistinguishable hallucination. It is not built into the description of these good and bad situations that there is a significant psychological difference between the subjects occupying each: while it might be said that there is a psychological *description* of the subject in the good situation ('she *sees* aspects of her environment') which isn't true of the subject in the bad situation, it is by no means obvious that there are psychological features that are present in the case of the subject in the good situation, and absent in the case of the subject in the bad situation, to which the subject in the good situation has *introspective* access. So it is by no means obvious that the perceptual experience of the subject in the good situation possesses an introspectively discernible feature that would be absent if she were in the bad situation. In this case, then, it might be said that it is far less plausible to maintain that the subject in the good situation is able to *introspectively* discriminate her situation from the bad one. The situations are genuinely, and *symmetrically*, introspectively indiscriminable. Just as the subject in the bad situation is unable to introspectively discriminate her situation from the good one, the subject in the good situation is unable to introspectively discriminate her situation from the bad one. And so it might be said that since there is no obvious 'internal', introspectively accessible, psychological difference between the subjects in each situation, it is, in this case, far less plausible to hold that the subject in the good situation has access to epistemic grounds for judgement that are not accessible to the subject in the bad situation.

One assumption behind the above line of argument is that the subject who successfully perceives her environment and the subject who has a subjectively indistinguishable hallucination are psychologically the same. A second assumption is that if two subjects are psychologically the same then the epistemic grounds for judgement that each has access to are the same. One response to that line of argument is to reject the first assumption, by allying epistemological disjunctivism with a form of metaphysical disjunctivism. To adopt this stance would be to deny that the subjects in good and bad cases are psychologically identical, by denying that they have perceptual experiences of the same kind. Indeed at points McDowell does appear to be asserting that the sort of perceptual experience that the subject has in the good situation isn't one she would be having if she were in the bad situation. For example, he writes, 'If an aspect of objective reality is perceptually present to someone, there is no possibility, *compatibly with her experience's being as it is*, that she might be wrong in believing that things are as her experience is revealing them to be' (2010: 245; my emphasis).

Critics of this defensive move may complain that even if the subjects in good and bad situations are not psychologically identical, it's not plausible to maintain that the perceptual experience of the subject in the good situation possesses an *introspectively accessible* feature that would be absent if she were in the bad situation. They may object that even if the disjunctivist insists that there is *some* psychological difference between the subjects in good and bad situations, we should be reluctant to accept that there is an *introspectively accessible*, psychological difference between the subjects in each situation. For if the perceptual experience of the subject in the good situation possesses an introspectively accessible feature that would be absent if she were in the bad situation, then the subject in the good situation should be able to introspectively discriminate her situation from the bad one. But the subject in the good situation is *not* able to *introspectively* discriminate her situation from the bad one. The perceptual experience one has when one successfully perceives one's environment is introspectively indiscriminable from some possible hallucination.

From the point of view of those who accept a disjunctivist view of the phenomenal character of perception (e.g. those who accept a naïve realist account of the phenomenal character of perception), the above line of reasoning is question-begging. Such disjunctivists will maintain that the experiences involved in the good and bad situations do not have the same phenomenal character. In the bad situation the subject's experience introspectively seems to her to have the (naïve realist) phenomenal character that her experience would have if she were in the good situation; but it lacks that phenomenal character. Although the experience involved in the bad situation doesn't have the sort of phenomenal character that it seems to have, it doesn't follow from this that the experience in the good situation lacks the (naïve realist) phenomenal character that it seems to have. So there is no reason to deny that in the good situation one has introspective access to a feature of one's experience that hallucination lacks and merely seems to possess.

Although it is not clear that McDowell is committed to a naïve realist account of the phenomenal character of conscious perception, he does adopt a stance that is similar to the naïve realist defence that I just outlined. In defending his disjunctive conception of perceptual experience he opposes the idea of 'a self-contained subjective realm, in which things are as they are independently of external reality' (1986: 151). It is a mistake, he thinks, to regard subjectivity as 'confined to a tract of reality whose layout would be exactly as it is however things stood outside it' (1986: 151). He recommends an alternative view on which how things are with you subjectively in the good situation is not independent of the fact that an aspect of the environment is made manifest to you, and revealed to you, by your experience. According to that conception 'a subject's inner world does not have the characteristic Cartesian independence from the outer world' (2010: 245). In the good case, 'how things are in that world [i.e. the subject's inner world] cannot be fully specified without a commitment as to how things are in the subject's environment' (2010: 245). So in the good case, we are to 'picture the inner and outer realms as interpenetrating, not separated from one another by the characteristically Cartesian divide' (1986: 150).

On the assumption that one has direct reflective access to how things are with one subjectively, this suggests a picture according to which, in the good situation one *does* have direct reflective access to a feature of one's experience that is lacking when one hallucinates. In the bad situation – i.e. in the case of hallucination – one is not only misled about the layout of one's environment, one is also misled about the kind of experience one is having; for one seems, but merely seems, to be having an experience that cannot be fully specified without a commitment to how things actually are in one's environment. The hallucinatory experience merely seems to have, yet lacks, the 'interpenetration' of the 'inner and outer realms' that is characteristic of the experience one has in the good situation. The experience thereby misleadingly presents itself as belonging to the epistemically distinguished class of experiences that one undergoes in the good situation.

Note that to adopt this view is to accept that one can be misled as to how things are in the subjective realm. Just as one is fallible in one's capacity to tell, via perception, how things are in one's environment, one is fallible in one's capacity to tell how things are with one subjectively. When one is uncertain as to whether or not one is successfully perceiving one's environment, one may still be able to tell how things appear to one to be – one may be in a position to judge knowledgably that it perceptually appears to one that such and such is the case. But on the disjunctivist view, what one can know of such a perceptual appearance, *specified in that neutral way*, is equivalent to a disjunctive fact: such perceptual appearances are 'either objective states of affairs making themselves manifest to subjects, or situations in which it is as if an objective state of affairs is making itself manifest to a subject, although that is not how things are' (McDowell 2008: 381). If one isn't in a position to know whether one is successfully perceiving one's environment, one isn't in a position to know which particular disjunct obtains. So on this disjunctivist view, one denies that what one can know when one has knowledge of a *neutral* specification of one's experience is all there is to know about how things are with one subjectively. For on this disjunctivist view, it is a mistake to assume that how things are with one subjectively is 'a self-standing configuration in the inner realm, whose intrinsic nature should be knowable through and through without adverting to what is registered ... by the difference between the disjuncts' (McDowell 1986: 151).

Here one might object on the grounds that it is unclear how the adoption of what appears to be a metaphysical disjunctivist stance is supposed to bring with it any significant epistemic gains. Suppose we grant that in the good situation one cannot fully specify how things are with one subjectively without committing to how things actually are in one's environment; and so suppose we thereby grant that there is a difference in how things are with one subjectively in good and bad situations. The cost is to concede that one has a merely fallible capacity to know how things are with one subjectively: according to that disjunctivist supposition, given that one is fallible in one's capacity to tell via perception how things actually are in one's environment, it follows that one is fallible in one's capacity to tell how things are with one subjectively. In consequence, it might be argued, whether one is in the good situation or the bad situation, the most one can be sure of is the obtaining of a disjunctive fact: either one is having an experience in which an aspect of one's environment is made manifest to one, or one is having an experience that merely seems to be of that kind. One cannot be sure which of the disjuncts obtains. And if one can only be sure of the disjunctive fact, then one doesn't, after all, have access to conclusive epistemic grounds for making judgements about one's environment.

McDowell's response to this line of objection is to acknowledge that perception is a fallible capacity, but to insist, nonetheless, that this is consistent with maintaining that it is a fallible capacity to get into positions in which one has access to *conclusive* grounds for beliefs about one's environment: 'That is what the capacity is a capacity to do, and that is what one does in non-defective exercises of it, exercises in which its acknowledged fallibility does not kick in' (2010: 245). The idea here, I take it, is that once we acknowledge that it is appropriate to give an *epistemic* specification of what a given fallible capacity is a capacity to do, we can see that it is a mistake to assume that defective and non-defective exercises of that capacity must be epistemically symmetrical.[3] Non-defective exercises of that epistemically specified capacity belong to an epistemically distinguished class of cases that the defective cases fail to yield (and only seem to yield). Once we realise that the fallibility of such a capacity does not entail that defective and non-defective exercises must be epistemically symmetrical, we are in a position to accommodate the idea that non-defective exercises of the capacity yield *conclusive* warrants. So this opens up the following line of response to the objection raised in the previous paragraph. One's capacity to tell, via perception, how things are in one's environment is fallible. So too is one's capacity for self-knowledge, i.e. one's capacity to tell whether one is having the kind of experience that yields conclusive warrant for making judgements about one's environment. But it is a mistake to assume that the fallibility of one's perceptual capacity entails that defective and non-defective exercises are epistemically symmetrical; and the same is true of one's fallible capacity for self-knowledge. According to McDowell, we need to avoid the 'faulty inference' from the acknowledged fact that one's perceptual capacity is fallible to the conclusion that defective and non-defective exercises of that capacity are epistemically symmetrical, 'not only in connection with its guise as a capacity for knowledge about one's environment, but also in connection with its guise as a capacity for self-knowledge – knowledge that one's experience is revealing an aspect of objective reality to one' (2010: 246).

He writes,

> Granted, one cannot discriminate cases in which one is being fooled from cases in which one is not being fooled, at least at the time; if one could one would not be fooled. But it is a form of that same mistake about fallibility to infer that when one is not being fooled, one's experience does not put one in a position to know that one is not being fooled. One's experience *does* put one in a position to know that, in an exercise of one's admittedly fallible capacity. When the capacity stumbles, as – being fallible – it can, one is being fooled, of course without knowing it. But when the capacity does not stumble and one is not being fooled, one is in a position to know, in an exercise of one's fallible capacity, that one is not being fooled – to know that one's experience is revealing things to be a certain way, thereby providing one with an indefeasible [i.e. conclusive] warrant to believe things are that way.
>
> (2010: 246)

When it comes to an assessment of McDowell's epistemological disjunctivist view, a great deal will hinge on the question of whether we should agree that he has correctly identified what our perceptual capacity is a capacity to do.[4] Should it be given the epistemic characterisation he proposes, a capacity to get into positions in which one has access to *conclusive* grounds for beliefs about one's environment? Part of McDowell's defensive strategy, I take it, is to argue that merely pointing to the fallibility of our perceptual capacity cannot in itself be enough to establish that the epistemic characterisation of the capacity that he proposes is false. However, of course that doesn't mean that the epistemological disjunctivist stance is not subject to further difficulties and problems. In the next section we will consider some further objections that have been raised against the view.

5.3 Objections to McDowell's epistemological disjunctivism

One line of objection to McDowell's epistemological disjunctivism is that by rejecting the highest common factor claim he appears to commit to what many would regard as a counterintuitive position on the question of the justificatory status of the world-directed perceptual beliefs of a subject in the bad situation. To reject the highest common factor claim is to reject the following thesis: when you successfully perceive your environment, the warrant that you have for making judgements about your environment is no better than – no stronger than – the warrant that you would have for making such judgements if you were having a subjectively indistinguishable hallucination. One line of thought in support of this highest common factor claim rests on the suggestion that the world-directed perceptual beliefs that a subject acquires in the bad situation are no less justified than the corresponding perceptual beliefs that a subject acquires in the good situation. And, so the objection goes, if the subject's perceptual beliefs in the bad situation are no less justified than the subject's perceptual beliefs in the good situation, then it can't be correct to claim that the warrant that the subject has for her perceptual beliefs in the good situation is better than – stronger than – the warrant that the subject has for her perceptual beliefs in the bad situation.

Let us first consider why one might find intuitive the suggestion that the perceptual beliefs that a subject acquires in the bad situation are no less justified than the corresponding perceptual beliefs that the subject acquires in the good situation. Consider the perspective of a subject in the bad situation, who is awake, rational, and to whom it perceptually appears that p. For such a subject, what is the epistemically appropriate response to the question of whether p? Suppose someone were to suggest that it is epistemically appropriate for her to suspend judgement over p. Here we might ask: what grounds does she have for doubting that things are as they perceptually appear to her to be? And in particular, does she have any grounds for doubt that are *absent* in the case of the subject in the good situation? On the assumption that the subjects share the same background beliefs, many will find it implausible to insist that the subject in the bad situation has grounds for doubt that are not present in the case of the subject in the good situation. Either both subjects have grounds for doubt (e.g. perhaps grounds for doubt that a sceptic could persuade one of), in which case the suspension of judgement may be an epistemically permissible response for both subjects, or neither has the kind of grounds for doubt that makes suspension of judgement an epistemically appropriate response.

Suppose we now assume that in the case of the subject in the bad situation, suspending judgement over the question of whether p is not an epistemically appropriate response. What then is the epistemically appropriate response? Believing that not-p is clearly not an epistemically appropriate option, as the subject in the bad situation lacks any grounds to believe that not-p. On the assumption that there is an epistemically appropriate response available to the subject in the bad situation, believing that p appears to be the only epistemically appropriate response. So, the only epistemically permissible option available to the subject in the bad situation is to believe that p.

Is the subject in the bad situation warranted in giving less credence to the proposition that p than the subject in the good situation? Here it might be argued that if the subject in the bad situation were warranted in giving less credence to the proposition that p, this would suggest that she is in a position to notice that her epistemic position isn't what it would be if she were in the good situation. However, if her situation is genuinely indiscriminable from the good situation, she is not in a position to notice that her epistemic position isn't what it would be if she were in the good situation, in which case she isn't warranted in giving less credence to the proposition that p.

The conclusion of this line of reasoning is that the only epistemically permissible option open to the subject in the bad situation is to believe that p and give whatever credence she would give to that proposition if she were in the good situation. If indeed that is the only epistemically permissible option open to her, then it seems counterintuitive to maintain that her belief is unjustified, and, moreover, it seems counterintuitive to maintain that her belief is any less justified than the belief of the subject in the good situation. This suggests that there is, after all, an epistemic match, of sorts, between the subjects in the good and bad situations. Both are epistemically entitled to the belief that p, and both are *epistemically entitled* to give the same degree of credence to the proposition that p.[5] This in turn, it might be argued, should lead us to accept that an account of what makes a subject's perceptual belief one to which the subject is epistemically entitled (and hence justified), should appeal to what is common to the subjects in the good and bad situations, and not to anything that is distinctive of the experience of the subject in the good situation. If we further assume that we should simply be appealing to this notion of epistemic entitlement in an account of what warrants the subject's perceptual belief in the good situation, we appear to arrive at the sort of view to which McDowell's epistemological disjunctivism is directly opposed:

> if someone knows something about her environment through an experience, it must be partly by virtue of something additional to the experience itself; the warranting power of the experience is no better than the

warranting power of an experience that would be indiscriminable from it but would not make the corresponding knowledge available.

(2013: 260)

One response to this line of objection is to argue that while there is an epistemic match, of sorts, between subjects in the good and bad situations, this is, nonetheless, consistent with the kind of epistemic asymmetry that the epistemological disjunctivist seeks to defend. The concession is to grant that there is a match in the epistemically permissible options available to each subject. What is resisted, however, is the following claim: when it comes to an account of what the subjects have, epistemically, in common, we shouldn't be appealing to anything that is distinctive of the epistemic position of the subject in the good situation; and in particular, we shouldn't be appealing to the claim that the subject in the good situation has access to *conclusive* epistemic grounds for her belief.

The thought behind this line of response is the following. While it may be true that the only epistemically permissible option available to the subject in the bad situation is to believe that p and give whatever credence she would give to that proposition if she were in the good situation, this fact is to be explained *derivatively* in terms of the epistemically distinctive and privileged position a subject is in when she is in the good situation. In particular, it is to be explained in the following terms: when a subject is in the good situation she has access to conclusive grounds for making judgements about her environment; and when a subject is in the bad situation, although she doesn't have access to conclusive grounds for judgement, it seems to her as though she does, and she isn't in a position to activate knowledge that she doesn't. That is why the only epistemically permissible option available to the subject in the bad situation is to believe that p and give whatever credence she would give to that proposition if she were in the good situation.

According to this response, while there is a match in the epistemically permissible options available to the subjects in the good and bad situations, this is consistent with maintaining that rather different accounts are to be given of what warrants the perceptual beliefs of each subject. Only the subject in the good situation has access to conclusive epistemic grounds for her perceptual belief. Such warrant isn't available to the subject in the bad situation. It merely seems to be available. Given that the subject in the bad situation isn't in a position to tell that such warrant isn't available, the only epistemically permissible option available to her is to treat the situation as if it were the good one. So conceding that there is a match in the epistemically permissible options available to each subject is consistent with saying that the following asymmetry obtains: in the good situation the subject's experience provides her with conclusive grounds for judgement, and in the bad situation the subject's experience doesn't provide her with conclusive grounds for judgement. It merely seems to do so.

A further challenge to this disjunctivist stance proceeds as follows. Suppose, for the sake of argument, that when you successfully perceive your environment you do have access to conclusive epistemic grounds for making judgements about your environment. If the epistemic grounds for judgement that you have access to are indeed conclusive, then presumably that should mean that when you successfully perceive your environment the warrant that you have for your perceptual judgements is not open to possible defeat; and so when you successfully perceive your environment you can have no legitimate grounds for doubting that you are perceiving. However, one *can* have legitimate grounds for doubting that one is successfully perceiving one's environment even when one is successfully perceiving one's environment.[6] For example, the testimony of others could, in principle, provide you with overwhelming reason to believe (mistakenly) that you are not perceiving; or at least provide you with reason to suspend judgement over the question. So even when you do in fact succeed in perceiving your environment, the warrant that your experience provides you with *is* open to possible defeat, and so that warrant is not conclusive. And once we concede that the warrant that your experience provides you with when you successfully perceive your environment is less than conclusive, then we have no clear reason to reject the highest common factor claim.

Does McDowell's epistemological disjunctivism imply that whenever one succeeds in perceiving one's environment, one has conclusive warrant for one's world-directed perceptual belief that is *not subject to possible defeat*? And does this in turn imply that whenever one succeeds in perceiving one's environment, one can have no legitimate grounds for doubting that one is perceiving? McDowell holds that warrant for belief is 'conclusive', in the relevant sense, 'if and only if the believer's having that warrant is incompatible with the belief's not being true' (2013: 267). But he does not think that having such warrant 'licenses one in refusing to consider apparent grounds for supposing that one's experience is not one of perceiving' (2013: 270).

In McDowell's view, a self-conscious subject won't be in a position to acquire knowledge that things are thus and so via perception if she is not 'sensitive to the requirements of doxastic responsibility' (1994: 429). And a subject who is sensitive to the requirements of doxastic responsibility must be 'responsive to the rational force of independently available considerations' (1994: 429). So she must be suitably sensitive to counterevidence when it is presented to her. Given this requirement, she must be suitably sensitive to apparent grounds for thinking that her experience is not one of perceiving, even when she is in fact perceiving. This means that a doxastically responsible subject who is in fact perceiving, could be persuaded (e.g. by the misleading testimony of another subject) into thinking that she is hallucinating, or into thinking that it is likely that she is hallucinating. In such a case, on McDowell's view, the subject is persuaded (by misleading apparent counterevidence) into thinking that she is not having (or may not be having) the kind of experience she seems to be having. She is persuaded into thinking (mistakenly) that she does not (or may not) have access to conclusive epistemic grounds for making judgements about her environment, even though it seems to her as though she does. The experience she is having is, in fact, the experience it seems to be. This is why it is appropriate to call the presented counterevidence misleading. So the experience she is having does in fact provide her with conclusive grounds for making judgements about her environment, and so it does put her in a position to know things about her environment. However, because of the misleading apparent counterevidence that has been presented to her, 'She has been deprived of awareness that she is in such a position' (2013: 269).

According to this defence of the disjunctivist position, there can be cases in which the experience you have when you successfully perceive your environment provides you with access to conclusive warrant for perceptual beliefs about your environment (warrant that is incompatible with the falsity of those beliefs), but in which you have also been presented with misleading apparent counterevidence that deprives you of awareness that you have access to such conclusive warrant. In such circumstances you are deprived of awareness that your experience puts you in a position to know things about your environment. Although you do not actually acquire knowledge about your environment via perception, you are still, nonetheless, having an experience that puts you *in a position to know* things about your environment. At one point, McDowell comments that 'for some purposes the notion of being in a position to know something is more interesting than the notion of actually knowing it' (1982: 390, fn. 37).

However, it can be argued that there can also be cases of the following kind: one is successfully perceiving one's environment, one is presented with counterevidence that undermines any world-directed perceptual beliefs one might potentially form on the basis of one's experience, but where the counterevidence in question is accurate, and *not* misleading. For example, consider a case in which one is participating in a psychological experiment and one is reliably informed by the experimenter of the fact that during the experiment only 50 per cent of one's perceptual experiences will be veridical. It's plausible to hold that in such circumstances, even on those occasions when one's perceptual experiences are veridical, one is not justified in forming world-directed perceptual beliefs on their basis: given the circumstances, the epistemically appropriate thing to do is suspend judgement over whether one is veridically perceiving. Suppose the disjunctivist grants that in such circumstances the subject does not acquire knowledge of her environment via perception. Can she nonetheless plausibly maintain that the subject's veridical perceptions, when they occur, still put her in a position to know things about her environment? Isn't it a stretch to maintain that in such circumstances one's veridical perceptions would provide one with *conclusive* warrant for making judgements about one's environment? In which case, shouldn't the disjunctivist concede that the experience one has when one successfully perceives one's environment is not in itself sufficient to provide one with conclusive grounds for making judgements about one's environment?

McDowell's response to this sort of case is to concede that in the circumstances described the experience the subject has when she veridically perceives her environment does not put her in a position to know things about her environment. Such experiences do not provide their subject with conclusive warrant for making judgements about her environment. But the conclusion McDowell draws from this is that such experiences, although veridical, do not count as cases of 'perceiving'.[7] He draws this conclusion on the basis of the particular epistemic characterisation he gives of what our perceptual capacity is a capacity to do. It is a (fallible) capacity to get into positions in which one has access to *conclusive* grounds for beliefs about one's environment. If, in the circumstances described, the subject's veridical perceptual experiences do not put her in a position to acquire knowledge of her environment by providing her with conclusive warrant for making world-directed perceptual judgements, then they do not count as non-defective exercises of that capacity. In which case they do not count as cases of successful perceiving. McDowell writes,

> For an experience to be one of perceiving, in the sense that is relevant to my disjunctivism, it must be an act of a capacity to have environmental realities present to the subject in such a way as to provide the subject with conclusive warrant for an associated belief. An experience had in circumstances in which there is good reason to believe apparent perceptions are not trustworthy is not an experience of perceiving, even if it happens to be veridical. So if our subject had been in such a situation, her experience would not have been an experience of perceiving, and it would not have provided her with conclusive warrant for the belief.
>
> (2013: 269)

A further point to note about the kind of case we are considering is this. In the kind of experimental conditions I described, the subject's perceptual experiences are untrustworthy, and the fact that they are untrustworthy is independent of the subject's being apprised of that fact. Arguably, if the subject was unaware that she was participating in such an experiment, any world-directed perceptual beliefs she acquired would not count as cases of knowledge, even if they were true; for any true beliefs she formed would have been luckily true, where the luck that would have been involved is of a kind incompatible with knowledge.[8] Suppose, then, that the disjunctivist says that a subject counts as 'perceiving' her environment only if her experience provides her with conclusive warrant for world-directed perceptual beliefs, and that an experience provides its subject with conclusive warrant for world-directed perceptual beliefs only if it puts her in a position to acquire knowledge about her environment on that basis (whether or not the subject actually does form the relevant beliefs and acquire the relevant knowledge). What should such a disjunctivist say about other well-known cases in which unusual environmental conditions result in the subject's not being in a position to form true beliefs about her environment in a way that satisfies the relevant 'no luck' requirement for knowledge, for example a case in which one sees a barn, believes on that basis that there is a barn before one, but is unaware that there happen to be lots of barn façades in the area?[9]

At points McDowell appears to suggest that such cases are not to be counted as instances of successful 'perceiving', in his sense. (E.g. see McDowell 1982: 390, fn 37.) Many are likely to find counterintuitive the suggestion that in the circumstances described the subject does not perceive the barn before her. There is a use of 'S sees that p' that only applies when S knows that p. According to that use of the phrase, seeing that p is a way of knowing that p. Given that use of the phrase, it may be appropriate to say that the subject, in the circumstances just described, does not *see that* there is a barn before her. However, McDowell does not want to equate 'perceiving' in his sense, with actually knowing things about one's environment. For according to McDowell, perceiving, in his sense, puts one in a position to know things about one's environment, even if one doesn't actually acquire the relevant item of perceptual knowledge. So is the only option here for McDowell to insist that the subject does not perceive the barn, despite the counterintuitive ring to that claim?

There may be alternatives open to the disjunctivist. She can claim that the subject does perceive the barn, because her experience does put her in a position to acquire a great deal of knowledge about the barn's visible properties, even if the environmental conditions prevent her from being able to tell that it genuinely is a barn. A disjunctivist might hold that in the circumstances, the subject is, after all, able to exercise successfully her capacity for perception, even if we give an epistemic characterisation of what our perceptual capacity is a capacity to do. What the subject is unable to exercise successfully (given the unusual environmental conditions) is a particular *perceptual-recognitional ability* that she would otherwise normally be able to deploy, i.e. an ability to tell by sight whether an entity she sees is a barn.

Whatever particular proposal the disjunctivist may care to give of such cases, there is a more general, and significant, point to note about the disjunctivist's response to the line of objection we have been considering. Although a disjunctivist of McDowell's ilk may insist that successful perception provides one with conclusive warrant for world-directed perceptual beliefs about one's environment, this does not commit that disjunctivist to holding that if one is veridically perceiving one's environment, one can have no legitimate grounds for doubting that one is perceiving. And that point is relevant to an assessment of whether an adoption of epistemological disjunctivism brings with it any distinctive advantages when it comes to responding to external world scepticism.

5.4 Epistemological disjunctivism and scepticism

Crispin Wright (2002, 2008) has argued that McDowell's epistemological disjunctivism provides us with nothing to address mainstream Cartesian perceptual scepticism.[10] Wright notes that the traditional Cartesian sceptical argument does not rely on the impossibility of direct perceptual acquaintance with the world. And given that it does not rely on the impossibility of direct perceptual acquaintance with the world, it allows that right now you may be having a perceptual experience that involves a fact in the world making itself 'perceptually manifest to you'. What it attempts to undermine is the idea that anything other than agnosticism as to whether or not you are perceiving is warranted, even in this situation. Suppose the disjunctivist is right to maintain that a perceptual appearance that such and such is the case is *either* an experience in which an aspect of one's environment is made manifest to one, *or* an experience that merely seems to be of that kind. And suppose now that it perceptually appears to you that p, and you insist that the experience you are having is an instance of the first disjunct, and hence you know that p. The worry here is as follows: how can that be anything other than begging the question against the sceptic? And in particular, given the disjunctivist's concession that one can (in principle) have legitimate grounds for doubting that one is perceiving even when one is having a veridical perception of one's environment, with what entitlement does the disjunctivist insist that the grounds for doubt raised by the sceptic are not legitimate?

From the disjunctivist's point of view, what the adoption of epistemic disjunctivism enables one to do is block an argument that the sceptic may present for the legitimacy of the sceptical doubt. It enables one to resist sceptical arguments that appeal to the 'highest common factor' conception of experience, a conception of experience according to which successful perceptions and subjectively indistinguishable hallucinations do not differ in their epistemological significance. And in particular, it enables one to resist such arguments without needing to resort to an epistemologically externalist position that holds that the epistemic difference between the good situation and the bad situation is something that may not be reflectively accessible to the subject in the good situation.[11]

Those adopting McDowell's epistemological disjunctivism argue that the sceptic has done nothing to establish that the highest common factor claim is true.[12] The sceptic has done nothing to establish that when you successfully perceive your environment, the warrant that you have for making judgements about your environment is no better than, no stronger than, the warrant that you would have for making such judgements if you were having a subjectively indistinguishable hallucination. So the sceptic has done nothing to establish that one does not have access to conclusive epistemic grounds for world-directed judgement in the good situation. Hence, if an argument for the legitimacy of the sceptical doubt assumes the highest common factor claim, adoption of epistemological disjunctivism blocks that argument.

McDowell notes that in accepting his disjunctive account of experience we need not pretend to have an argument that can prove that we are not being deceived, on any given occasion, using premises we can affirm without begging the question against the sceptic. That is to say, the disjunctive conception does not put one in a position to provide a non-question-begging demonstration that one is perceiving from the *neutral* vantage point of merely affirming the disjunction: either I am having an experience in which an aspect of my environment is made manifest to me, or I am having an experience that merely seems to be of that kind. What the disjunctive account does achieve, though, is to enable us to 'remove a prop' upon which a certain line of sceptical argument depends, and hence block an argument for the legitimacy of the doubt raised by the sceptic. The relevant prop is the assumption that the highest common factor claim is correct.

In order to further clarify and assess what kind of response to the sceptic epistemological disjunctivism offers, it will be helpful to return to the question of whether the epistemological disjunctivist needs to commit to a form of metaphysical disjunctivism, and, if so, what kind. A key element in McDowell's defence of his rejection of the highest common factor claim is his suggestion that it is a mistake to assume that it follows from the fallibility of our perceptual capacity that non-defective exercises of that capacity cannot yield conclusive warrants. If we give an epistemic characterisation of our fallible perceptual capacity in terms of the notions of conclusive warrant and knowledge of our environment, then we make room for the idea that a successful, non-defective exercise of that capacity does not yield anything less than conclusive warrant. Does this sort of defensive manoeuvre involve a commitment to metaphysical disjunctivism?

Some might argue that it doesn't. For it is not clear why we should assume that defective and non-defective exercises of an epistemically characterised capacity cannot involve psychological states of the same metaphysical kind. Consider, for example, the suggestion that it is appropriate to give an epistemic characterisation of one's perceptual-recognitional ability to recognise barns by sight, where that epistemic characterisation is expressed in terms of a capacity to know, by sight, whether something is a barn. One can envisage someone arguing as follows. The fact that the capacity is fallible doesn't imply that successful exercises of the capacity yield anything less than knowledge. In a region in which there are a lot of barn façades around one may not be able to exercise successfully that perceptual-recognitional capacity: in that environment one cannot know by sight whether something is a barn, as opposed to a mere barn façade. But from this it doesn't follow that one cannot successfully exercise the perceptual-recognitional capacity in other, more suitable, environmental conditions; and when one does successfully exercise that capacity one acquires knowledge, for what the capacity is a capacity to do is specified in terms of knowledge, and nothing less than knowledge.[13]

Suppose one were to endorse this general proposal. Should that commit one to holding that the psychological states that one is in when one is in barn façade county are not of the same metaphysical kind as those psychological states one is in when one is in an environment that enables one to exercise successfully that perceptual-recognitional capacity? It is not at all obvious that it should. So if defence of the epistemological disjunctivist position, and rejection of the highest common factor claim, simply rests on the idea that we should give an epistemic characterisation of our (fallible) perceptual capacity, then one might likewise question whether this epistemological disjunctivism requires any commitment to metaphysical disjunctivism.

However, if an epistemological disjunctivist doesn't commit to any form of metaphysical disjunctivism, one might question whether her response to scepticism succeeds in accommodating any pertinent aspects of an internalist approach to epistemology. That may not in itself be an objection to her view, but it might lead one to question whether her disjunctivist response to scepticism has anything distinctive to recommend it that isn't captured by alternative externalist responses to scepticism; and, arguably, McDowell does at points appear to be attempting to be offering a response to scepticism that *can* accommodate certain intuitions that are associated with internalist approaches to epistemology.

Consider again the suggestion that you have access to conclusive epistemic grounds for judging that you are having a phenomenally conscious experience, epistemic grounds that would not be available to the phenomenal zombie. As I noted earlier, part of what makes that suggestion intuitive is the idea that

(a) there is a *psychological* difference between you and the phenomenal zombie, and the idea that
(b) the psychological features that your experience has, and which the zombie's lacks, are features to which you have *introspective* access.

So an account of the epistemic asymmetry between your situation and the situation of the phenomenal zombie is something that is amenable to an internalist approach to epistemology.

One might likewise think that if the disjunctivist's response to perceptual scepticism is to be amenable to an internalist approach to epistemology it too should endorse both the idea that:

(a) * there is a psychological difference between the subject who successfully perceives her environment and the subject who is having a subjectively indistinguishable hallucination, and the idea that
(b) * the psychological features that are present in the case of successful perception, and absent in the case of hallucination, are features to which the subject in the good situation has reflective access.

And to endorse such a proposal would amount to an endorsement of a form of metaphysical disjunctivism.

As I noted earlier, there is a strand to McDowell's epistemological disjunctivist position that appears to commit him to a metaphysical disjunctivist view; and this would suggest that his response to scepticism is, in part, an attempt to accommodate aspects of an internalist approach to epistemology. Indeed, McDowell suggests that his disjunctive conception of perceptual appearances shows a way to detach an internalist intuition (an intuition that 'one's epistemic standing on some question cannot be intelligibly constituted, even in part, by matters blankly external to how it is with one subjectively') from the requirement of providing, in response to scepticism, a non-question-begging demonstration that we do have perceptual knowledge from a *neutral* vantage point that the sceptic will be willing to affirm. But if McDowell is committed to a form of metaphysical disjunctivism, what sort of metaphysical disjunctivist view is this? Is he, for example, committed to a naïve realist account of the phenomenal character of perception?

Consider again the case in which one is participating in a psychological experiment and one is reliably informed by the experimenter of the fact that during the experiment only 50 per cent of one's perceptual experiences will be veridical. It is not clear that a naïve realist has any reason to deny that in such circumstances one's veridical perceptions actually have the naïve realist phenomenal character that they seem to have. So it is not clear that the naïve realist has any reason to deny that the veridical perceptions one has in such circumstances are metaphysically different, in kind, from the perceptual experiences one has when one's experiences put one in a position to acquire world-directed knowledge of one's environment. However, according to McDowell, if one is in the situation of the subject participating in the psychological experiment, one's veridical perceptions do not count as instances of 'perceiving', in his sense. So, if he were to commit to the claim that 'perceivings', in his sense, are different in metaphysical kind from experiences that are not 'perceivings', then that would appear to commit him to a form of metaphysical disjunctivism that isn't straightforwardly equivalent to a naïve realist view.

Suppose that McDowell were to commit to the claim that 'perceivings', in his sense, are different in metaphysical kind from experiences that are not 'perceivings'. A concern that some might have with that position is the following. It is not clear that such a metaphysical difference can be appealed to in order to *explain*, and *account for*, an epistemological difference between those perceptual experiences that are perceivings and those perceptual experiences that are not perceivings. For arguably, any metaphysical difference between the relevant experiences must itself be accounted for and explained in epistemic terms. What makes them metaphysically different just resides in the fact that the one kind of experience puts one in a position to acquire perceptual knowledge of one's environment, and the other kind of experience doesn't.

One further point to note is this. If a commitment to a form of metaphysical disjunctivism really is a key element in the epistemological disjunctivist view, then clearly the fortunes of that view, and its response to scepticism, are tied to the fortunes of the metaphysical disjunctivist stance. And here some may argue that while it is plausible to hold that that there is a psychological difference between you and a phenomenal zombie, and while it is plausible to hold that the psychological features that your experience has, and which the zombie's lacks, are features to which you have introspective access, analogous claims are wildly implausible in the case of successful perception and subjectively indistinguishable hallucination. For it might be maintained that a crucial difference between the cases is this. Although the phenomenal zombie may judge that she is in the good situation of having phenomenally conscious experiences, she doesn't know what it would be like to be in that good situation. And the fact that the phenomenal zombie doesn't have access to the epistemic grounds for judgement that you have access to, is connected with the fact that she doesn't know what it would be like to be in your good situation. It is *because* she does not have access to how things are with you subjectively that she is not in a position to know what it would be like to be in your good situation. However, when a subject has a hallucination that is subjectively indistinguishable from a successful perception, matters are rather different. For that sort of bad situation does not prevent its subject from acquiring knowledge of what it would be like to be in the good situation of successfully perceiving her environment.

If that latter claim is correct then a worry that might be pressed is this. If hallucination puts one in a position to know what it would be like to be in the good situation of successfully perceiving one's environment, this is because when one hallucinates one has introspective access to what it is like to be in the good situation. And if, in the bad situation, one has introspective access to what it would be like to be in the good situation, this can only be because there is no difference in what it is like for one to be in the good situation and what it is like to be in the bad. If there is no difference in what it is like for one to be in the good situation and the bad, then this means there is no difference in how things are with you subjectively in each situation. And if there is no difference in how things are with you subjectively in each situation, then when you are in the good situation, you don't, after all, have reflective access to some feature of your experience that would be lacking if you were in the bad situation. In which case, in the good situation, you don't, after all, have access to epistemic grounds for judgement that would be lacking if you were in the bad situation.

There may yet be various ways of responding to this line of objection. But assessment of the possible responses open to the disjunctivist will depend, in part, on whether one can consistently maintain the following two claims:

(a) there is a difference in what it is like for one when one hallucinates and what it is like for one when one successfully perceives one's environment, and
(b) when one hallucinates one is in a position to know what it is like to successfully perceive one's environment.

Does the disjunctivist have to deny at least one of those claims? That is a question we shall be considering in the next chapter, when we examine what accounts the disjunctivist can and should give of illusion and hallucination.

5.5 Chapter summary

In this chapter we considered forms of disjunctivism that are adopted in defence of the role played by perception in providing us with *propositional* knowledge about our surroundings, knowledge *that* things are thus and so in our environment, and in particular we focused on the form of epistemological disjunctivism that has been advocated by John McDowell.

We saw that McDowell's disjunctivism is motivated by a concern to show that we can and should reject the following epistemically expressed 'highest common factor claim': when you successfully perceive your environment, the warrant that you have for making judgements about your environment is no better than, no stronger than, the warrant that you would have for making such judgements if you were having a subjectively indistinguishable hallucination. According to the view that McDowell recommends

(a) there is a significant epistemic asymmetry between the case in which you successfully perceive your environment and the case in which you have a subjectively indistinguishable hallucination;
(b) this epistemic asymmetry is to be explained, at least in part, by appeal to an asymmetry in the epistemic grounds for judgement that you have access to in each case; and
(c) when all goes well and you successfully perceive your environment, you have access to *conclusive* grounds for judgements about your environment, i.e. epistemic grounds for judgement that don't leave open the possibility that those judgements are false.

We first examined ways in which one might defend the claim that there can be epistemic asymmetries between certain 'good' situations, in which things are as they appear to be, and certain 'bad' situations that are indistinguishable from those good situations. We then considered how McDowell applies such ideas in defence of his claim that successful perception provides its subject with *conclusive* grounds for making judgements about her environment. We saw that a key element of McDowell's proposal is the suggestion that once we acknowledge it is appropriate to give an *epistemic* specification of what our fallible perceptual capacity is a capacity to do, we can see that it is a mistake to assume that defective and non-defective exercises of that capacity must be epistemically symmetrical. And in particular, once we realise that the fallibility of such a capacity does not entail that defective and non-defective exercises must be epistemically symmetrical, we are in a position to accommodate the idea that non-defective exercises of the capacity yield *conclusive* warrants. We also saw that McDowell recommends a view on which how things are with you subjectively in the good situation is not independent of the fact that an aspect of the environment is made manifest to you, and revealed to you, by your experience. We noted that a consequence of adopting this view is to accept that just as one is fallible in one's capacity to tell, via perception, how things are in one's environment, one is fallible in one's capacity to tell, via introspection, how things are with one subjectively.

We discussed various objections to McDowell's proposal. According to one line of objection, by rejecting the highest common factor claim McDowell commits to a counterintuitive position on the question of the justificatory status of the world-directed perceptual beliefs of a subject in the bad situation. According to another line of objection, by committing to the claim that we have access to *conclusive* grounds for judgement in the case of veridical perception, McDowell commits to the implausible view that in cases of veridical perception the warrant that you have for your perceptual judgements is not open to possible defeat. We discussed responses to these objections, and in our discussion of the latter objection we noted that for McDowell, some veridical experiences do not count as cases of 'perceiving'. We noted how this appears to commit him to a view of perception that is not equivalent to the account of perception endorsed by the naïve realist.

We then considered whether McDowell's epistemological disjunctivism provides us with anything novel to address mainstream Cartesian perceptual scepticism. Here we discussed whether McDowell's disjunctivist response to perceptual scepticism is amenable to an internalist approach to epistemology, and we connected this issue with the question of whether those espousing McDowell's epistemological disjunctivism need commit themselves to a form of metaphysical disjunctivism.

Notes

1. McDowell 1982, 1987, 2008, 2010, 2013.
2. This, I think, is connected to Timothy Williamson's remark that 'Scepticism about the external world has more intuitive force than scepticism about one's own sensations because we do not usually envisage beliefs about one's own sensations as based on evidence insufficient for their truth' (2000: 169).
3. For a discussion of the significance to the disjunctivist position of the relations between, and dependencies between, perceptual *capacities* and their exercises, see Kalderon 2012. For Kalderon's own disjunctivist account of the epistemic role of veridical perception, which differs in some significant respects from McDowell's, see Kalderon 2011.
4. For discussion of matters relevant to this issue, see Kalderon 2012.
5. For 'entitlement' approaches to an account of perceptual justification, see Dretske 2000, Burge 2003, Wright 2004, Peacocke 2004.
6. For objections to McDowell along these lines, see Burge 2011.
7. For discussion of this issue, see Brogaard 2011.
8. For further and detailed discussion of forms of luck incompatible with knowledge, see Pritchard 2005.
9. This sort of example became widely discussed after Goldman's use of it in his 1976.
10. See also Conee 2007.
11. For discussion of this point, see Pritchard 2012, Part One, Sec. 6.
12. For a related argument for the claim that the sceptic fails to provide a non-question-begging argument for an epistemic symmetry between 'good' and 'bad' cases, see Williamson 2000, Ch. 8.
13. For a similar proposal, see Millar 2007 and 2008.

Further reading

For McDowell's defence of his epistemological disjunctivism, see his 1982, 1987, 2008, 2010, and 2013. For discussion and defence of McDowell's epistemological disjunctivism, see Neta 2008, Pritchard 2008, Sedivy 2008, and Haddock 2011. For a defence of epistemological disjunctivism in general see Pritchard 2012. For further discussion of McDowell's disjunctivism and comparison with Austin 1962, see Thau 2004.

Bernard Williams's discussion of epistemic asymmetries between 'good' and 'bad' cases can be found in Appendix 3 of his 1978. An extremely influential defence of the claim that there are epistemic asymmetries between good cases and bad cases is the 'knowledge first' position that has been articulated and defended by Williamson (see in particular Williamson 2000).

For Burge's criticisms of McDowell's disjunctivism, see Burge 2005 and 2011. For 'entitlement' approaches to an account of perceptual justification, see Dretske 2000, Burge 2003, Wright 2004, Peacocke 2004.

For criticism of the proposal that disjunctivism has anything novel to offer in response to sceptical arguments, see Wright 2002 and 2008, and Conee 2007. For further discussion of this issue see the essays in Part III of Dodd and Zardini 2014.

For a discussion of the significance to the disjunctivist position of the relations between, and dependencies between, perceptual *capacities* and their exercises, see Kalderon 2012. For Kalderon's own disjunctivist account of the epistemic role of veridical perception, which differs in some significant respects from McDowell's, see Kalderon 2011.

For discussion of whether one can endorse epistemological disjunctivism without being committed to metaphysical disjunctivism, see Byrne and Logue 2008, Snowdon 2005, Haddock and MacPherson 2008, Brogaard 2011, and Pritchard 2012. For an explicit endorsement of the proposal that we should accept a form of epistemological disjunctivism about perceptual knowledge without being committed to metaphysical disjunctivism, see Millar 2007 and 2008.

References

Austin, J. L., 1962, *Sense and Sensibilia*. Oxford: Oxford University Press.
Brogaard, Berit, 2011, 'Primitive knowledge disjunctivism', *Philosophical Issues*, 21 (1): 45–73.
Burge, Tyler, 2003, 'Perceptual entitlement', *Philosophy and Phenomenological Research*, 67 (3): 503–548.
——, 2005, 'Disjunctivism and perceptual psychology', *Philosophical Topics*, 33: 1–78.

——, 2011, 'Disjunctivism again', *Philosophical Explorations*, 14 (1): 43–80.
Byrne, Alex and Logue, Heather, 2008, 'Either/or', in Adrian Haddock and Fiona Macpherson (eds), *Disjunctivism: perception, action, knowledge*. Oxford: Oxford University Press, pp. 57–94.
Conee, Earl, 2007, 'Disjunctivism and anti-skepticism', *Philosophical Issues*, 17 (1): 16–36.
Dodd, D. and Zardini, E., 2014, *Scepticism and Perceptual Justification*. Oxford: Oxford University Press.
Dretske, Fred, 2000, 'Entitlement: epistemic rights without epistemic duties?', *Philosophy and Phenomenological Research*, 60 (3): 591–606.
Goldman, A., 1976, 'Discrimination and perceptual knowledge', *Journal of Philosophy*, 72: 771–791
Haddock, Adrian, 2011, 'The disjunctive conception of perceiving', *Philosophical Explorations*, 14 (1): 23–42.
Haddock, Adrian and Macpherson, Fiona, 2008, 'Introduction: varieties of disjunctivism', in Adrian Haddock and Fiona Macpherson (eds), *Disjunctivism: perception, action, knowledge*. Oxford: Oxford University Press, pp. 1–24.
Kalderon, M., 2011, 'Before the law', *Philosophical Issues*, 21 (1): 219–244.
——, 2012, 'Experiential pluralism and the power of perception'. http://www.academia.edu/1495929/Experiential_Pluralism_and_the_Power_of_Perception.
McDowell, John, 1982, 'Criteria, defeasibility and knowledge', *Proceedings of the British Academy*, 68: 455–479.
——, 1986, 'Singular thought and the extent of inner space', in Pettit and McDowell (eds), *Subject, Thought and Context*. Oxford: Clarendon Press, pp. 137–168.
——, 1994, 'Knowledge by hearsay', in Bimal Krishna Matilal and Arindam Chakrabarti, eds, *Knowing from Words: Western and Indian philosophical analysis of understanding and testimony*, pp. 195–224. Synthese Library, 230. Dordrecht, Holland and Boston, MA: Kluwer Academic; reprinted in McDowell (2001), *Meaning, Knowledge and Reality*, Cambridge, MA: Harvard University Press, pp. 414–444.
——, 2008, 'The disjunctive conception of experience as material for a transcendental argument', in Fiona Macpherson and Adrian Haddock (eds), *Disjunctivism: perception, action, knowledge*. Oxford: Oxford University Press, pp. 376–389.

———, 2010, 'Tyler Burge on disjunctivism', *Philosophical Explorations*, 13 (3): 243–255.
———, 2013, 'Tyler Burge on disjunctivism (II)', *Philosophical Explorations*, 16 (3): 259–279.
Millar, Alan, 2007, 'What the disjunctivist is right about', *Philosophy and Phenomenological Research*, 74 (1): 176–198.
———, 2008, 'Perceptual-recognitional abilities and perceptual knowledge', in Adrian Haddock and Fiona Macpherson (eds), *Disjunctivism: perception, action, knowledge*. Oxford: Oxford University Press, pp. 330–347.
Neta, Ram, 2008, 'In defence of disjunctivism', in Fiona Macpherson and Adrian Haddock (eds), *Disjunctivism: perception, action, knowledge*. Oxford: Oxford University Press, pp. 311–329.
Peacocke, Christopher, 2004, *The Realm of Reason*. Oxford: Oxford University Press.
Pritchard, Duncan, 2005, *Epistemic Luck*. Oxford: Oxford University Press.
———, 2008, 'McDowellian neo-Mooreanism', in Fiona Macpherson and Adrian Haddock (eds), *Disjunctivism: perception, action, knowledge*. Oxford: Oxford University Press, pp. 283–310.
———, 2012, *Epistemological Disjunctivism*. Oxford: Oxford University Press.
Sedivy, Sonia, 2008, 'Starting afresh disjunctively: perceptual engagement with the world', in Fiona Macpherson and Adrian Haddock (eds), *Disjunctivism: perception, action, knowledge*. Oxford: Oxford University Press, pp. 348–375.
Snowdon, P. F., 2005, 'The formulation of disjunctivism: a response to Fish', *Proceedings of the Aristotelian Society*, New Series, 105: 129–141.
Thau, Michael, 2004, 'What is disjunctivism?', *Philosophical Studies*, 120 (1–3): 193–253.
Williams, B., 1978, *Descartes: the project of pure enquiry*. London: Penguin.
Williamson, Timothy, 2000, *Knowledge and its Limits*. Oxford: Oxford University Press.
Wright, Crispin, 2002, 'Anti-sceptics simple and subtle: G. E. Moore and John McDowell', *Philosophy and Phenomenological Research*, 65: 330–348.
———, 2004, 'Warrant for nothing (and foundations for free)?', *Aristotelian Society Supplementary Volume*, 78 (1): 167–212.
———, 2008, 'Comment on John McDowell's "The Disjunctive Conception of Experience as Material for a Transcendental Argument"', in A. Haddock and F. Macpherson (eds), *Disjunctivism: perception, action and knowledge*. Oxford: Oxford University Press, pp. 390–404.

6

DISJUNCTIVIST ACCOUNTS OF HALLUCINATION AND ILLUSION

The disjunctivist holds a view of conscious perception that commits her to the following claim: the sort of conscious perceptual experience that you have when you successfully perceive your environment isn't one you could be having if you were hallucinating. To say so much is to commit to an entirely negative claim about hallucination, a claim about what hallucination isn't. A challenge faced by the disjunctivist is to say something more positive about the kind of experience that's involved when you hallucinate; and, for that matter, the kind of experience involved in cases of perceptual illusion. Can the disjunctivist provide satisfactory, *positive* accounts of illusion and hallucination that are consistent with her favoured view of perception? If she can't, then her opponents may argue that she is failing to acknowledge at least some of the constraints that the existence of illusion and hallucination impose on the account we can give of conscious perception; in which case, her favoured view of conscious perception should be rejected. This chapter will be concerned with what disjunctivists say in response to that challenge.

As we shall see, it is by no means obvious that there is a uniform account to be given of the experiences that are involved in all cases of illusion and hallucination; and part of what is at issue is disagreement over which experiences it is appropriate to count as an 'illusion', and what it is that makes such experiences illusory, if they are. One of our tasks in this chapter will be to consider how such debates impact on the options that are open to disjunctivists when it comes to providing accounts of the kinds of experiences that are involved in these different cases of illusion and hallucination.

First though, we will be focusing on a particular variety of hallucination, 'causally matching' hallucination. A causally matching hallucination is one that involves the same kind of proximate cause and brain state as a veridical perception. Certain arguments that relate to this particular class of hallucinations are thought to pose a special problem for those disjunctivists seeking to defend a naïve realist account of the phenomenal character of perception. These arguments put the disjunctivist under pressure to accept both that

(a) there can be a psychological effect that is common to cases of veridical perception and hallucination, and
(b) the occurrence of this common psychological effect is sufficient to account for the kind of experience involved in cases of causally matching hallucination. These arguments then purport to give grounds for thinking that if a disjunctivist accepts both (a) and (b), she also has reason to accept that
(c) the occurrence of this common psychological effect is sufficient to account for the phenomenal character of veridical perception.

And once (c) has been conceded, so the argument goes, any reason for advocating a naïve realist account of the phenomenal character of conscious perception is thereby undermined. Our first task is to consider how this line of objection to naïve realism can be developed. We'll then consider what the naïve realist can say in response.

6.1 A causal argument against naïve realism

In Chapter 1 I outlined two causal arguments for a sense-datum theory of perception. From the second of those arguments we can reconstruct a modified causal argument, which doesn't involve any endorsement of a sense-datum theory, but which rather gives grounds for holding the following more general claim: the sort of psychological effect that is produced in the case of a 'causally matching' hallucination is also produced in the case of genuine perception. Here is how such an argument might proceed.[1]

Consider a case in which a subject, S, visually perceives in her environment a mind-independent material object, O. The obtaining of that state of affairs depends on the occurrence of some psychological effect, E, that O has on S. In particular, S doesn't begin to perceive O until O has produced in S some appropriate psychological effect, E. In the causal chain of events leading to E we can mark distinctions between the more proximate causes of E, and the more distal causes of E. Let 'D' denote a distal cause that involves light being reflected by O, and let 'P' denote the more proximate cause of S's optic nerves being suitably stimulated. Let 'T' denote S's total physical and psychological condition immediately prior to her perception of O.

1 When S perceives O, the proximate cause P of psychological effect E on S is preceded by, and caused by, the distal cause D. But that is not the only way in which an event of kind P can occur. An event of kind P can in principle occur in the absence of O, and in the absence of any mind-independent material objects that are qualitatively similar to O (i.e. in the absence of objects that could be candidate objects of perception for S when she is having an experience subjectively indistinguishable from a genuine perception of O).

2 Condition T can also, in principle, obtain in the absence of O and in the absence of mind-independent material objects that are qualitatively similar to O. Indeed, we can envisage a situation in which T obtains *and* P occurs even though no suitable mind-independent O-like material object is present. In any such situation, the occurrence of P won't be causally sufficient for S to be perceptually aware of a mind-independent material object in her environment.

3 If T obtains and O is absent (and there are no other suitable O-like mind-independent material objects in S's environment to serve as candidate objects of perceptual awareness), then proximate cause P is sufficient to produce in S a perceptual event/state of the kind that occurs when one has a hallucination that is subjectively indistinguishable from a genuine perception of an O.

4   The presence of O (and the fact that O is involved in an event D that is a distal cause of P) does not prevent the proximate cause P from producing the same kind of effect – i.e. the effect of producing in S a perceptual event/state of the kind that occurs when one has a hallucination that is subjectively indistinguishable from a genuine perception of an O.

5   Therefore, when S has a genuine perception of an O, this involves the occurrence/obtaining of a perceptual event/state of the kind that occurs when one has a hallucination that is subjectively indistinguishable from a genuine perception of an O.

This argument gives grounds for thinking that whatever kind of perceptual state/event that occurs/obtains when you have a causally matching hallucination of an F will also be produced when you have a veridical perception of an F, thereby giving us reason to accept that there is a psychological element that is common to veridical perception and causally matching hallucination. The argument makes a number of empirical assumptions. For example, premise (3) makes an empirical assumption about the effect that will be produced on S when P occurs and T obtains and there are no suitable O-like mind-independent material objects in S's environment to serve as candidate objects of perceptual awareness. The assumption is that S will have a hallucination subjectively indistinguishable from a genuine perception of O. And premise (4) assumes that the absence of a distal cause involving O isn't a background causal condition that's required for P to have the effect of producing in S a perceptual event/state of the same kind. While such assumptions are not incontestable, many find them plausible. So does the disjunctivist have to deny what many take to be plausible empirical assumptions in order to defend her favoured view of conscious perception?

Well it's not obvious that the disjunctivist needs to deny the conclusion of this argument. The disjunctivist endorses a view of conscious perception that commits her to the claim that the sort of conscious perceptual experience that you have when you successfully perceive your environment isn't one you could be having if you were hallucinating. She is therefore committed to holding that there are significant psychological differences between the sort of perceptual experience that's involved when you successfully perceive the world, and the sort of perceptual experience that's involved when you have a subjectively indistinguishable hallucination. But it's not obvious that the conclusion of the causal argument outlined above is inconsistent with that thesis. The argument doesn't establish that in the case of veridical perception the occurrence of P produces in S *only* those psychological effects that P would produce in S if O were absent and S were having a causally matching hallucination. The conclusion of the argument appears to commit to a weaker claim: the claim that in the case of veridical perception there is *a* psychological effect produced in S by P which is the kind of effect that P would produce in S if O were absent and S were having a causally matching hallucination. And to establish that there is *a* common psychological effect in cases of veridical perception and causally matching hallucination isn't yet to establish that there are no psychological differences between the cases. In Chapter 2 I outlined some reasons for thinking that a disjunctivist view may be compatible with the proposal that there can be perceptual states/events that are common to cases of successful perception, illusion, and hallucination. Let's review those considerations and assess their bearing on the above argument.

Consider, for example, the commitments of those who advocate a relationalist, naïve realist account of conscious perception. Their proposal is that the conscious perceptual experience that you have when you consciously perceive the world is in itself sufficient to put you in perceptual contact with aspects of your mind-independent environment. For they hold that the conscious perceptual experience that's involved in such cases is sufficient for the obtaining of a *relation* of conscious perceptual awareness – a relation that obtains between you, as subject of experience, and aspects of your mind-independent environment. Moreover, advocates of this naïve realist view assert that the phenomenal character of the experience that you have when you consciously perceive the world is to be accounted for, at least in part, by the obtaining of this relation. They hold that there is something it is like for you to be the subject of the conscious perceptual experience that you have when you consciously perceive your environment insofar as there is something it is like for you to be the subject of the conscious perceptual relation that obtains when you have that experience; and that this is determined, at least in part, by what you are perceptually related to, i.e. by the worldly constituents of the conscious perceptual relation that obtains. So the qualities of the mind-independent entities in your environment that you perceive – what those qualities are like – constitutively determine, at least in part, what it is like for you to be consciously, perceptually aware of them.

Those who endorse this naïve realist view clearly need to accept that an experience of this kind isn't involved when you hallucinate; for the experience you have when you hallucinate is not sufficient to put you in perceptual contact with aspects of your mind-independent environment. The experience you have when you hallucinate isn't sufficient for the obtaining a relation of conscious perceptual awareness, understood as a relation that obtains between you, as subject of experience, and aspects of your mind-independent environment. Does this mean that the naïve realist has to rule out the proposal that there can be perceptual states/events common to cases of successful perception and hallucination?

In Chapter 2 I suggested that a naïve realist could allow that when you succeed in perceiving your environment there obtain perceptual states that are insufficient for the obtaining of a conscious perceptual relation between you, as subject of experience, and aspects of your mind-independent environment. So she can therefore allow that these perceptual states also obtain when you hallucinate. What the naïve realist will need to deny is that the conscious perceptual experience that you have when you perceive your environment is to be *identified* with the perceptual states that can be common to cases of perception and hallucination. She will need to deny that the phenomenally conscious perceptual experience you have when you perceive your environment *just is* some psychological state that can obtain whether or not that relation of conscious perceptual awareness obtains. Moreover, she will have to deny that the phenomenal character of the experience you have when you consciously perceive your environment is to be exhaustively accounted for by the obtaining of any perceptual state that can be common to cases of veridical perception and hallucination.

For instance, suppose it is proposed that when a subject consciously perceives her environment there obtain perceptual states that can be characterised in terms of their functional roles, where the functional role of any such perceptual state is specified in terms of the state's causal relations to other mental states and behaviour. Suppose too it is proposed that a perceptual state of that functionally specified kind can obtain when the subject isn't perceptually aware of anything, i.e. if the subject is hallucinating. It is not clear that such a proposal is inconsistent with a naïve realist view. But what the naïve realist will have to deny is that the conscious perceptual experience one has when one consciously perceives the world *just is* this functionally specified perceptual state. That is, she may grant that a perceptual state of that functionally specified kind *obtains when* one consciously perceives the world, but she will have to maintain that the conscious perceptual experience that one has when one consciously perceives the world is not to be *identified* with this functionally specified perceptual state. Moreover, she will have to insist that the obtaining of this functionally specified psychological state does not suffice to account for the phenomenal character of the perceptual experience that one has when one perceives ones environment. For if she doesn't deny that claim, then she can no longer insist that it is the obtaining of the subject's conscious perceptual relation to the mind-independent environment that accounts (at least in part) for the phenomenal character of the experience she has when she perceives her environment.

As I noted in Chapter 2, if a naïve realist need not deny that perceptual states/events that are insufficient for the obtaining of a conscious relation of perceptual awareness do obtain/occur whenever a subject consciously perceives the world, she might also allow that perceptual states/events with representational content are among them. But given the minimal commitments of the naïve realist view of the phenomenal character of successful perception, what she will have to deny is this: the postulation of such representational states/events can exhaustively account for the phenomenal character of the experience that a subject has when she consciously perceives her environment.

If this assessment of the situation is correct, and so if it is open for the naïve realist to accept that there can be a psychological effect that is common to cases of veridical perception, illusion, and hallucination, why should the above causal argument be thought to make problems for the view? Well, the causal argument not only suggests that there is a psychological effect that is common to cases of veridical perception and causally matching hallucination, it also suggests that we won't need to appeal to anything more than this common psychological effect when it comes to providing an account of causally matching hallucination. This leaves the naïve realist open to the following line of objection. If we don't need to appeal to anything more than this common psychological effect when it comes to providing an account of causally matching hallucination, this must mean that this common psychological effect suffices to account for the *phenomenal character* of causally matching hallucination. But if the psychological effect that is common to veridical perception and causally matching hallucination suffices to account for the phenomenal character of causally matching hallucination, then that common psychological effect will also suffice to account for the phenomenal character of veridical perception. And if the psychological effect that is common to veridical perception and causally matching hallucination suffices to account for the phenomenal character of veridical perception, then we have no reason to accept the naïve realist account of the phenomenal character of veridical perception.

First let us consider how this line of objection might be applied against a naïve realist who accepts that the psychological effect that is common to veridical perception and causally matching hallucination is to be identified with some functionally specified perceptual state of the subject. If the causal argument is correct, then such a naïve realist, we have said, will need to hold that the obtaining of this functionally specified perceptual state is sufficient to account for causally matching hallucination, and that it isn't sufficient to account for the phenomenal character of veridical perception. In defence of that proposal, such a naïve realist may say that she is well positioned to explain various features of causally matching hallucination that we would expect an adequate account of hallucination to accommodate. Here are three such features:[2]

(i) Veridical perceptions and hallucinations can produce similar behavioural effects. For example, in general, if it sensibly appears to you as though a rock is flying towards you, you will duck, irrespective of whether the experience you are having is a veridical perception or a hallucination.
(ii) Veridical perceptions and hallucinations can be introspectively indistinguishable.
(iii) If you have an experience as of a rock flying towards you, and on the basis of that experience you believe that a rock is flying towards you, and you act on that belief and duck, then there is a sense in which your belief and action are rational, irrespective of whether that experience is a veridical perception or a hallucination.

If a naïve realist allows that there can be functionally specified perceptual state kinds that are common to cases of veridical perception and causally matching hallucination, she can accommodate (i) by appealing to the obtaining of such states. Given that the relevant functionally specified perceptual state obtains when a subject has a causally matching hallucination, the behavioural effects of a causally matching hallucination will be similar to the behavioural effects induced by veridical perception. What about claim (ii)? If we understand (ii) as the claim that a subject suffering a hallucination may be unable to tell, via introspection, that she is not genuinely perceiving her environment, such a naïve realist may say the following: if a subject *was* able to tell via introspection that her experience wasn't a veridical perception, then it is unlikely that her experience would have the sort of behavioural and cognitive effects that occur in the case of veridical perception. In which case, when a subject underwent such a hallucination there wouldn't obtain the sort of functionally specified perceptual state kinds that can be common to cases of veridical perception and hallucination. So by granting that there can be functionally specified perceptual state kinds common to both cases, one accommodates the idea that hallucination can be introspectively indistinguishable from veridical perception. And if claim (ii) can be accommodated, the naïve realist may say that this puts her in a position to accommodate claim (iii). If the difference between a hallucination and a veridical perception is something that a subject isn't in a position to detect through introspection, then if a subject were to experience such a hallucination, there is a sense in which it would be rational for her to respond to her situation as though she were perceiving.

However, an objector to this line of defence is likely to press the following question. Is the obtaining of the relevant functionally specified perceptual state kind sufficient to account for the idea that causally matching hallucination involves the occurrence of a *phenomenally conscious* perceptual experience that puts its subject in a position to know *what it is like* to have the veridical perception? For if it isn't, then the naïve realist hasn't yet provided an adequate account of the experience that is involved in the case of causally matching hallucination. And if it is, then why can't we simply appeal to the obtaining of a perceptual state of this kind when it comes to providing an account of the phenomenal character of veridical perception, which would make an appeal to the naïve realist account of the phenomenal character of veridical perception explanatorily redundant?

By analogy consider the position of someone who holds that we can't account for the phenomenal character of conscious perceptual experience without appealing to the instantiation of qualia. Suppose that the proponent of this view grants that when we have a phenomenally conscious perceptual experience there obtain functionally specified perceptual state kinds that can in principle obtain without the instantiation of qualia. Presumably those endorsing such a view should hold that were such a state to obtain without the instantiation of qualia, their subject would *not* be in a phenomenally conscious mental state that put her in a position to know what it is like to have a phenomenally conscious perceptual experience; otherwise, their appeal to the actual instantiation of qualia would appear to be explanatorily redundant.

One possible response to this line of objection against naïve realism is to deny that the proximate cause involved in causally matching hallucination is sufficient to produce a *phenomenally conscious* perceptual experience that is introspectively indiscriminable from a veridical perception. Someone adopting this stance may concede that in the case of causally matching hallucination the proximate cause is sufficient to produce a psychological effect that is common to cases of causally matching hallucination and veridical perception – for example the obtaining of some functionally specified, representational perceptual state – and they may claim that the occurrence of that common psychological effect is sufficient to ensure that its subject isn't in a position to activate knowledge, through introspection, that she is not having a veridical perception; but they will deny that the occurrence of that effect is sufficient to produce a *phenomenally conscious* perceptual experience, and so assert that no such phenomenally conscious perceptual experience is involved in the case of causally matching hallucination.

The tenability of this sort of response obviously rests on the tenability of an empirical assumption about the effect that would be produced in the circumstances outlined in the causal argument. As I presented the causal argument, premise (3) asserts the following: 'If T obtains and O is absent (and there are no other suitable O-like mind-independent material objects in S's environment to serve as candidate objects of perceptual awareness), then proximate cause P is sufficient to produce in S a perceptual event/state of the kind that occurs when one has a hallucination that is subjectively indistinguishable from a genuine perception of an O.' Are we justified in further assuming that in these circumstances P would produce a *phenomenally conscious* perceptual event/state that is subjectively indistinguishable from a genuine perception of an O? William Fish (2009) has argued that the empirical evidence that we have so far gathered does not assure us of that conclusion; so it is open to the naïve realist to simply deny that the psychological effect that is common to cases of hallucination and veridical perception is sufficient to produce a phenomenally conscious perceptual experience.[3] The naïve realist can thereby protect her claim that the phenomenal character of veridical perception cannot be adequately accounted for by appeal to some psychological effect that is common to cases of veridical perception and causally matching hallucination.

It would beg the question against the naïve realist if one simply assumed from the outset that a causally matching hallucination must have the *same* phenomenal character as a veridical perception. But many find it entirely reasonable at least to assume the following: hallucination (including causally matching hallucination) involves the occurrence of a phenomenally conscious event, and moreover a phenomenally conscious event that puts its subject in a position to know what it is like to have a veridical perception. The naïve realist would be in a dialectically stronger position if defence of her account of veridical perception did not depend on rejecting that assumption. So is there any way for the naïve realist to defend her position without committing herself to rejecting that assumption?

Well, suppose that the naïve realist grants that an adequate account of causally matching hallucination should be able to accommodate the proposal that the proximate cause involved in causally matching hallucination is sufficient to produce a phenomenally conscious perceptual experience that is introspectively indiscriminable from a veridical perception, and which puts its subject in a position to know what it is like to have a veridical perception. What positive account of the phenomenal character of the perceptual experience involved could the naïve realist offer? Could she, for instance, say that the phenomenal character of the perceptual experience involved in causally matching hallucination is to be accounted for by appeal to its possession of a certain kind of representational content? Could she appeal to the instantiation of qualia? Could she hold that causally matching hallucination involves an awareness of sense-data? As Martin (2004 and 2006) notes, if the naïve realist does offer *any* such *positive* account of the kind of phenomenal event that occurs when one hallucinates, and if she also accepts, as the causal argument suggests, that this kind of event also occurs in the case of veridical perception, then she will be under pressure to explain why the occurrence of this kind of event doesn't screen off the explanatory role that she assigns to her naïve realist account of the phenomenal character of veridical perception.

One thing to note here is that this line of objection raises a specific difficulty for those disjunctivists who endorse a naïve realist account of the phenomenal character of veridical perception. It's not clear that this line of argument poses problems for those who endorse the following set of claims:

(a) the sort of conscious perceptual experience that you have when you successfully perceive your environment isn't one you could be having if you were hallucinating;
(b) there are significant psychological differences between the sort of perceptual experience that's involved when you successfully perceive your environment, and the sort of perceptual experience that's involved when you have a subjectively indistinguishable hallucination;
(c) there occurs a common psychological effect in cases of veridical perception and causally matching hallucination;
(d) both veridical perception and causally matching hallucination involve experiences that have the same phenomenal character.[4]

Those endorsing the above set of claims might adopt a defence of their position that is Austinian in spirit. They could hold that causally matching hallucination and veridical perception are introspectively indistinguishable because they are qualitatively alike (i.e. they share the same introspectible phenomenal properties), while also maintaining that veridical perception and causally matching hallucination have different natures: they involve experiences of different metaphysical kinds that differ in significant psychological respects. And in defence of the conjunction of those claims they might invoke the following Austinian defensive manoeuvre: from the mere fact that two things are qualitatively alike, it doesn't follow that they are 'generically' alike, for example it doesn't follow that they have the same metaphysical nature.

So, for instance, it may be open to those adopting this Austinian defensive strategy to endorse the account of hallucination that has been proposed by Mark Johnston. Johnston (2004) has proposed that there is a respect in which the objects of hallucination and the objects of seeing are akin. According to Johnston, the objects of a subject's hallucination are complexes of sensible qualities and relations that are not instantiated in the scene before her; whereas the objects of veridical perception are spatiotemporal particulars *instantiating* such complexes. On this view, there is, then, a phenomenal core that is common to veridical perception and hallucination, in both cases the subject of experience is aware of a 'sensible profile', a complex of qualities and relations. Endorsement of that claim, however, may be consistent with maintaining that veridical perception and causally matching hallucination differ in some significant mental respect; for from the fact that two experiences are qualitatively alike (in sharing some common phenomenal core), it doesn't follow that they are generically the same, in which case it may not follow that they are experiences of the same psychological kind.

Arguably, this sort of defensive move doesn't help those disjunctivists who are concerned to defend a naïve realist account of the phenomenal character of veridical perception; the naïve realist insists that veridical perception has a phenomenal character that can't be possessed by a causally matching hallucination. And if the naïve realist allows that it is possible to give some positive account of a phenomenal core that is common to veridical perception and hallucination, she will thereby leave herself open to the objection that this common phenomenal core screens off, and makes explanatorily redundant, the sort of phenomenal character she takes to be distinctive of veridical perception. That is why the causal argument is thought to present a specific difficulty for those disjunctivists who endorse a naïve realist account of the phenomenal character of veridical perception.[5]

6.2 Martin's negative epistemic account of causally matching hallucination

Martin's response to the causal argument is to argue that the naïve realist should deny that it is possible to give a *positive, non-derivative* account of the kind of phenomenal event that occurs when one hallucinates; for it is precisely that concession that leaves the naïve realist susceptible to the screening-off worry.[6] Martin suggests that the naïve realist should, rather, characterise the phenomenal character of causally matching hallucination *derivatively* – in terms of the phenomenal character that is distinctive of veridical perception – a phenomenal character that the hallucination seems to have, but lacks. In particular he suggests that the naïve realist should affirm that in the case of a causally matching hallucination, the phenomenal character of the experience one has is exhausted by its possession of the following negative epistemic property – that of being introspectively indiscriminable from a veridical perception. This counts as an *epistemic* characterisation of the phenomenal character of causally matching hallucination in so far as it appeals to what is *knowable* about the phenomenal character of the hallucination by introspection. It offers a *negative* epistemic characterisation of the phenomenal character of the experience involved, for it appeals to a claim about what *cannot* be known about the phenomenal character of the experience via introspection. The proposal is that a causally matching hallucination has a phenomenal character such that it is *not* possible to *know* via introspection that is not a certain kind of veridical perception. In the case of the causally matching hallucination there is no more to the phenomenal character of such an experience than that.

How does this response help avoid the screening off worry? Surely *both* a veridical perception of an F *and* a causally matching hallucination possess the negative epistemic property of being introspectively indiscriminable from a veridical perception of an F. So why doesn't this common element screen off any explanatory role that the naïve realist might assign to the phenomenal character that she claims only a veridical perception can possess? Martin's response is to suggest that the property of being indiscriminable from an F has an explanatory potential which is *dependent* on the explanatory potential of *being an* F. So the property of actually being a veridical perception, and having the phenomenal character that only a veridical perception can possess, can still be regarded as having a crucial explanatory role to play. According to this naïve realist response, the phenomenal character of causally matching hallucination has its effects in virtue of possessing the negative epistemic property of being introspectively indiscriminable from a veridical perception of an F, and this negative epistemic property is not grounded in some further, positive phenomenal features of the hallucinatory experience. So, any explanatory role assigned to the phenomenal character of causally matching hallucination is *parasitic on* the *distinctive* explanatory role assigned to the naïve realist phenomenal character that only the veridical perception can possess. That is to say, one explains the effects of the hallucination *in terms of* the naïve realist phenomenal character of the veridical perception from which the hallucination is introspectively indiscriminable. In this case, the explanatory role assigned to the naïve realist account of the phenomenal character of veridical perception has not, after all, been screened off.

Martin's negative epistemic proposal about the phenomenal character of causally matching hallucination has been much debated, and a number of objections to his account have been raised.[7] As we shall see, assessment of such objections to Martin's account, and his responses to them, will turn, in large part, on the question of how we should interpret the negative epistemic condition that Martin proposes.

According to one line of objection, Martin's account fails to capture the idea that causally matching hallucinations are phenomenally conscious; for a state that is not phenomenally conscious can satisfy the description of being introspectively indiscriminable from a veridical perception.[8] For example, some suggest that it is conceivable that there could be a phenomenal zombie who lacks phenomenally conscious experience but who is functionally very similar to a subject who has phenomenally conscious perceptual experience. Given the functional roles played by the mental states that the phenomenal zombie is in, the phenomenal zombie may not be in a position to activate knowledge that she is not having a phenomenally conscious perceptual experience. But ex hypothesi, that subject isn't having a phenomenally conscious perceptual experience. And this shows, so the argument goes, that the fact that a perceptual state satisfies the condition of being introspectively indiscriminable from a veridical perception doesn't ensure that such a perceptual state is phenomenally conscious.

The naïve realist might insist that this objection rests on a misunderstanding of her proposal. She might claim that her negative epistemic proposal about causally matching hallucination, when correctly interpreted, does ensure the presence of a phenomenally conscious condition of the subject. But if she is to defend this stance, the naïve realist may need to take steps to distance herself from an assumption that is implicit in the above line of argument, an assumption about what it would take for a subject to have a perceptual state that satisfies her proposed negative epistemic condition.

The objection to Martin's view that I outlined is one that proposes that a subject can satisfy the negative epistemic condition in virtue of being in a psychological state that plays a certain kind of functional role, where the functional role of the state is specified in terms of its typical causes and effects. If the cognitive and behavioural effects of a perceptual state that plays that functional role are inconsistent with the subject's having activated knowledge that she is not having a certain kind of veridical perception, then, the argument assumes, that subject's perceptual state thereby satisfies the negative epistemic condition of being introspectively indiscriminable from a veridical perception. Implicit in the argument is the assumption that the question of whether a perceptual state satisfies the negative epistemic condition can be determined by the cognitive and behavioural *effects* of that perceptual state. The problem that this poses for the naïve realist is that this understanding of what it takes to be in a perceptual state that satisfies the negative epistemic condition does nothing to ensure that the perceptual state that gives rise to the relevant cognitive and behavioural effects, and so which occupies the relevant functional role, is a phenomenally conscious one.

This suggests that if the naïve realist is to insist that her negative epistemic proposal about causally matching hallucination is to be interpreted in a way that ensures the presence of a phenomenally conscious experience, then she should aim to defend an interpretation of that proposal that is subject to the following constraint.

Constraint 1: The question of whether a perceptual state satisfies the relevant negative epistemic condition is not simply fixed by the cognitive and behavioural effects of that perceptual state.

In this case, the naïve realist should dissociate her proposal from an understanding of the negative epistemic condition that would permit the following order of explanation: in the case of causally matching hallucination, the subject satisfies the negative epistemic condition *because* she is in a perceptual state that has certain cognitive and behavioural effects. She should instead seek to defend an interpretation of the negative epistemic condition that commits to the following order of explanation: in the case of causally matching hallucination, certain cognitive and behavioural effects occur because the subject is undergoing an experience that satisfies the negative epistemic condition, that of being introspectively indiscriminable from a certain veridical perception.[9]

Arguably, the naïve realist needs to hold a view that commits to the latter order of explanation if she is to defend her claim that the explanation of the effects to which the causally matching hallucination gives rise is parasitic on the distinctive explanatory role that is assigned to the naïve realist phenomenal character of veridical perception. By maintaining that the causally matching hallucination has its effects *because* it is introspectively indiscriminable from a certain veridical perception, the naïve realist can then say that we are to explain the cognitive effects of a causally matching hallucination by reference to the distinctive explanatory role assigned to the phenomenal character of veridical perception, from which the causally matching hallucination is introspectively indiscriminable. So, for example, consider the proposal that a causally matching hallucination of an F can put its subject in a position to know what it is like to have a veridical perception of an F. Here the naïve realist may say that the explanation of this effect of the hallucination is parasitic on the distinctive explanatory role assigned to the phenomenal character of the veridical perception. That is, the hallucination does not put its subject in a position to know what it's like to have a veridical perception of an F in virtue of having the same phenomenal character as a veridical perception of an F. Rather, it puts its subject in a position to know what it's like to have a veridical perception of an F in virtue of being introspectively indiscriminable from such a perception.

In summary, a conclusion we can draw from this line of objection to Martin's negative epistemic proposal about the phenomenal character of causally matching hallucination is the following. If the naïve realist's intention is that her negative epistemic proposal is to be interpreted in a way that ensures the presence of a phenomenally conscious experience, then she should insist that the claim that a perceptual experience satisfies the negative epistemic condition is not to be understood as equivalent to a claim about the cognitive and behavioural effects to which such an experience gives rise. Her aim should be to defend an interpretation of the negative epistemic condition that satisfies Constraint 1.

So how should we interpret the naïve realist's negative epistemic proposal about causally matching hallucination if it is to be subject to that constraint? What alternative interpretations of the naïve realist's negative epistemic proposal are available? Before we address that question, it will be helpful to consider a further objection that has been raised against Martin's account of causally matching hallucination. Doing so will help to uncover further constraints that an appropriate interpretation of Martin's negative epistemic proposal may be subject to if it is to offer the naïve realist a defensible option.

Siegel (2004) argues that Martin's account fails to accommodate the different kinds of hallucinations that can be experienced by a creature who lacks the conceptual capacities to make introspective judgements about her experience. For example, suppose a dog is having a hallucination. Because the dog lacks the conceptual capacities to make judgements about her experiences, she is not in a position to know that she is not perceiving a tomato. So for the dog this experience is introspectively indiscriminable from a veridical perception of a tomato. However, from this fact alone it does not follow that the dog is having a hallucination as of a tomato. For all that has been said, the dog's hallucinatory experience could be of anything. Each kind of hallucination that the dog can experience will be introspectibly indistinguishable, for the dog, from every kind of veridical perception. But surely we want to avoid the absurd conclusion that all such experiences have the same phenomenal character.

Martin's (2006) response to this form of objection depends, in part, on the claim that a naïve realist can, and should, invoke an *impersonal* notion of introspective indiscriminability in her account of causally matching hallucination. When we say of some individual that she is having an experience that is introspectively indiscriminable from a veridical perception of an F, one way of understanding that claim is as a comment on *that particular* subject's incapacity to tell, via introspection whether her experience is a veridical perception of an F. If we interpret the naïve realist's negative epistemic proposal about causally matching hallucination in this way, then the case of the dog clearly presents a problem; the dog lacks the relevant capacities to tell whether she is having a veridical perception of an F, no matter what kind of experience she is having. However, as Martin notes, this is not the only way of understanding an indiscriminability claim. He compares the way in which we can talk of objects being invisible. He suggests that in certain contexts, when we say that something is invisible, we may not be talking about the way a given individual, or group of individuals, is such that they cannot succeed in seeing the object. We may rather be talking about what *vision* can and cannot discern. Furthermore, in asking what vision can reveal to us, we can ask in terms of how vision actually is, or ways in which vision *could* be. The most extreme claim of invisibility would be concerned with the latter notion. The suggestion is that we should not think that such 'impersonal', 'objective' talk of invisibility need be reducible to claims about what a given subject would or would not see. And, moreover, neither should we assume that such impersonal talk of invisibility need be reducible to claims about what a group of subjects, or even an ideal subject, would or would not see. So similarly, we should not take talk of impersonal introspective indiscriminability as reducible to claims about what a given subject, group of subjects, or ideal subject would or would not come to know through introspection.

How does this help with the case of the dog? One might think that by invoking this sort of impersonal notion of introspective indiscriminability, one thereby articulates a claim about the kind of experience that the dog is having that is not reducible to a claim about the dog's capacity to tell what kind of experience she is having. And this is just what is needed. By analogy, suppose, for example, we say that a subject possesses an object that is visually indiscriminable from a lemon. If this claim is true, then that subject won't be able to tell by sight that the object is not a lemon. But if we are invoking an impersonal notion of visual indiscriminability in making that claim, we are not simply making a claim about *that* subject's inability to tell by sight whether the object is a lemon. We may rather be making a claim about the object that is to be understood in terms of what is discernible about the object *by sight*. And on that understanding, the claim rules out the possibility that the object is a red tomato, even if the subject in question is blind, and so even if the subject in question lacks the capacity to visually discriminate the object from *any* other objects. Moreover, the fact that the object is impersonally visually indiscriminable from a lemon doesn't entail that the object is a lemon. For instance, the object could be a cleverly crafted piece of soap that is made to look exactly like a lemon.

On the face of it, this all seems to fit with what the naïve realist should want to say about causally matching hallucination when she invokes her negative epistemic proposal. So in light of the dog objection, we can perhaps identify a further constraint on the interpretation of the negative epistemic proposal the naïve realist should aim to defend.

Constraint 2: (a) The notion of introspective indiscriminability invoked in the negative epistemic condition is an impersonal one, and (b) we should not take this impersonal notion to be reducible to claims about what a given subject, group of subjects, or ideal subject would or would not come to know through introspection.

However, further comparison with sight – i.e. with an impersonal notion of visual indiscriminability – may lead to a further problem for the naïve realist. When we are told that a subject has an object that is *impersonally* visually indiscriminable from a lemon, it is natural to interpret this claim as one that commits to there being *positive*, visible properties of the object that explains this fact, and in particular, some positive visible features that are shared by that object and a lemon (e.g. its shape, colour, visible texture, and so on). If we now apply the same idea when we invoke the impersonal notion of *introspective* indiscriminability, we will be led to a view on which the causally matching hallucination is introspectively indiscriminable from a veridical perception of an F in virtue of its possessing some positive, introspectible, phenomenal properties that it shares with a veridical perception of an F. And while this accommodates the case of the dog, it does so at the cost of committing the naïve realist to a view of causally matching hallucination that she set out to avoid in that it commits her to a view on which it is possible to provide a positive account of the phenomenal character of causally matching hallucination, where this phenomenal character is also present in the case of veridical perception. And it is this commitment that generates the screening-off worry.

So now it seems we need to stipulate a further constraint that a defensible version of the naïve realist's negative epistemic proposal should be subject to. This is, in effect, a constraint on the way in which Constraint 2 is to be applied.

Constraint 3: The naïve realist needs to invoke a notion of impersonal introspective indiscriminability that doesn't have as a consequence the following: an experience is impersonally introspectively indiscriminable from a veridical perception of an F just in case that experience possesses introspectible phenomenal qualities that it shares with a veridical perception of an F, and which accounts for the introspective indiscriminability of that experience from the veridical perception.

Is there a coherent interpretation of the negative epistemic proposal that satisfies these various constraints? In order to assess that question it will be helpful to consider again the sort of defensive disjunctive strategy that is adopted by Hinton.

Let's start by comparing Hinton's defensive strategy with what I earlier called the Austinian defensive strategy. This is something I commented on in Chapter 2. According to what I called the Austinian defensive strategy, one can maintain that veridical perception and hallucination are introspectively indistinguishable and yet generically (and so psychologically) different, because from the mere fact that two things are qualitatively alike, it doesn't follow that they are 'generically' alike. As I noted, to adopt this strategy is to leave open the proposal that veridical perception and hallucination are introspectively indistinguishable because they are qualitatively alike, for example because they share the same introspectible phenomenal properties. By contrast, Hinton's defensive strategy is to question an assumption that goes unchallenged in the Austinian move. That is the assumption that veridical perception and introspectively indistinguishable hallucination are qualitatively alike. Hinton suggests that from the fact that two experiences are introspectively indiscriminable, it doesn't follow that they must share the same introspectible, phenomenal, 'worn-on-the-sleeve' qualities. In the case of perceptible objects, we don't assume that two objects have to have some perceptible property in common in order for the one to be mistaken for the other. So why, Hinton asks, should we assume that our experiences have to have introspectible phenomenal properties in common in order for them to be mistaken for one another? Why should it not *just seem* as if they had such properties in common (1967: 225)?

The sort of claim about hallucination that Hinton gestures towards here seems to be the one the naïve realist needs in order to avoid the screening off worry in the case of causally matching hallucination. The naïve realist needs to deny that a causally matching hallucination is introspectively indiscriminable from a veridical perception of an F in virtue of possessing the same introspectible phenomenal properties as a veridical perception of an F. In adopting the Hintonesque disjunctive strategy she can say the following. When a subject has a causally matching hallucination that has a phenomenal character introspectively indiscriminable from a veridical perception of an F, it may seem to her as if her experience has the phenomenal character of a veridical perception of an F. But this is not because she is introspectively aware of phenomenal properties that the experience shares with the veridical perception; it *merely seems* to the subject as though that is the case.

Let us consider again an analogous claim that can be made about the objects of sight. When a subject has an illusory experience and misperceives a white object as red, that object may be visually indiscriminable for that subject from a red object. But it doesn't follow from this that the subject is perceiving some colour property of the object that it shares with a red object, and which explains the fact that it is visually indiscriminable from a red object. The object merely seems to have a property in common with a red object. Many would think that this is a perfectly coherent claim to make with respect to the objects of sight; it is possible for objects to be visually indiscriminable from one another because they seem, but *merely seem*, to have properties in common.

However, an aspect of this analogy with the objects of sight looks to be unhelpful for the naïve realist. In the case of the misperceived object it seems we should say the following:

(a) The object actually has some colour property (its whiteness) that is distinct from the colour it seems to have (redness), and the colour property that the object actually has is inaccessible to the subject, and hidden from her, given her circumstances. So

(b) the object perceived is not *impersonally* visually indiscriminable from a red object, for *sight* can discern that the object is not red, even if the subject who is misperceiving is not in a position to do so.

The naïve realist should want to avoid parallel claims in the case of a causally matching hallucination that seems, and merely seems, to have the phenomenal character of a veridical perception of an F, otherwise she would commit to the following two claims:

(a)* In the case of a causally matching hallucination, the experience actually has some phenomenal properties that are distinct from the ones the experience seems to have, and which are hidden from the subject and inaccessible to her, and

(b)* the experience the subject has is *impersonally discriminable* from a veridical perception of an F, for introspection can discern that the experience does not have the phenomenal character of a veridical perception of an F, even though the subject of experience is not in a position to do so.

To commit to (a)* is to commit to a claim that many find implausible and counterintuitive, and in any case if the naïve realist is to appeal to a notion of impersonal introspective indiscriminability in specifying her negative epistemic condition on causally matching hallucination, she cannot accept (b)*.

The lesson the naïve realist will want to draw from this is the following: while we should grant that an experience can introspectively seem to have the phenomenal character of a veridical perception of an F without actually having that phenomenal character, in acknowledging this fact we should avoid pushing too far an analogy with vision, and indeed perception in general. While we think of perception as a mode of coming to be aware of a realm that is independent of that mode of awareness, we should not be led to think of introspection of the phenomenal character of experience in that way. Perception involves the use of a faculty which, when successfully exercised, detects and tracks features and objects in our environment that are independent of our perceptual awareness of them. When that faculty misfires, it may seem to one as though an object possesses a certain feature when in fact it doesn't. And in such circumstances, the feature that the object actually has is hidden from one, where the feature in question is perceivable under optimal conditions, when one's perceptual faculty is working properly. If we were to hold a view of introspection that was modelled on this perceptual paradigm one would be allowing that one could have an experience the real phenomenal character of which was hidden from one, and introspectively inaccessible to one, a phenomenal character that *introspection* could detect under optimal conditions, if one's introspective faculty was working properly.

In light of this we might identify yet a further constraint on a defensible version of the naïve realist's negative epistemic proposal:

Constraint 4: introspection of the phenomenal character of experience is not to be thought of as a mode of coming to be aware of a realm that is independent of that mode of awareness.

Martin advocates a model of our introspection of the phenomenal character of perceptual experience that accords with this constraint: he recommends a view in which your introspective perspective on your phenomenally conscious perceptual experience is not independent of the phenomenally conscious *perceptual* perspective that you have in virtue of the occurrence of that experience. Indeed, he proposes that your introspective perspective on the phenomenal character of your experience *coincides with* that phenomenally conscious *perceptual* perspective. In this view, if it introspectively seems to you as though you are having an experience as of an F, then that constitutes its *perceptually* seeming to you as though there is an F. This proposal about the form of our introspective access to the phenomenal character of experience fits in with the naïve realist claim that it seems to us as though we can only introspectively attend to the phenomenal character of a perceptual experience by perceptually attending to the apparent objects of experience. Moreover, Martin suggests that it accommodates the following idea: in specifying what can and cannot be detected through introspection when a subject has an experience, we are thereby specifying the kind of phenomenally conscious *perceptual* perspective the subject has, i.e. we are thereby specifying how things *perceptually* seem to the subject to be.

If Martin is right about this, then the way in which he accommodates Constraint 4 may enable him to accommodate Constraint 1. Recall that according to Constraint 1, the question of whether a perceptual state satisfies the relevant negative epistemic condition is not simply fixed by the cognitive and behavioural effects of that perceptual state. Now suppose Martin is right to hold that in specifying what can and cannot be detected through introspection when a subject has an experience, we are thereby specifying the kind of *phenomenally conscious perceptual* perspective the subject has. On that supposition the naïve realist can say that when we specify what introspection can and cannot discern in the case of a causally matching hallucination, we thereby ensure that we are specifying the kind of phenomenally conscious perceptual perspective the subject has. This ensures that the experience is phenomenally conscious, and so avoids the concern that satisfaction of the negative epistemic condition is simply determined by the cognitive and behavioural effects of the subject's perceptual state; which in turn avoids the phenomenal zombie objection.

At this point scepticism might be raised about whether the naïve realist really has done enough to specify a phenomenally conscious condition of the subject: the negative epistemic condition merely tells us what *cannot* be known by introspection, rather than specifying what *can* be known by introspection. And it is only by specifying what can be known by introspection that we can ensure that there is a phenomenally conscious perceptual perspective there at all.[10] And, moreover, it might be said that we need to accommodate the idea that something can be known by introspection in the case of a causally matching hallucination, if we are to accommodate the plausible assumption that such an experience can put its subject in a position to know what it's like to have a corresponding veridical perception.

Here it may be open to the naïve realist to say the following: there is, after all, something that is discernible by introspection in the case of a causally matching hallucination. One thing that is introspectively discernible is the truth of the following disjunctive claim: either (a) the experience has the phenomenal character of a veridical perception of an F, or (b) it merely seems as if that is so. In taking this stance, the naïve realist will need to ensure that Constraint 3 is met. That is to say, she will have to say that the fact that the truth of the disjunctive claim is introspectively discernible is not to be explained by appeal to the idea that introspection discerns phenomenal properties that are common to veridical perception and causally matching hallucination. In the case of a causally matching hallucination, the naïve realist will have to deny that the introspective discernibility of the truth of the disjunctive claim is to be explained by appeal to the claim that one can introspectively discern the truth of disjunct (a). For according to the naïve realist, a causally matching hallucination doesn't have the phenomenal character of a veridical perception. So she must adopt the Hintonesque strategy of saying that in the case of causally matching hallucination, the experience introspectively seems, but *merely seems*, to have the phenomenal character of the veridical perception. And this is where the satisfaction of Constraint 4 can help, for if the naïve realist can satisfy Constraint 4 in the way that Martin suggests, then when she says that the experience introspectively seems, but merely seems, to have the phenomenal character of a veridical perception of an F, she doesn't leave open the possibility that the experience has a hidden phenomenal character, a phenomenal character that is inaccessible to the subject of experience, and which is *impersonally discriminable* from a veridical perception of an F.

Now let's reconsider the dog objection. How is the satisfaction of Constraint 4 supposed to help with that? With Constraint 4 satisfied, the naïve realist can say the following: we can make introspective judgements about our experiences, and the dog can't. But this isn't because we have some faculty of inner perception that the dog lacks, a faculty of inner perception that allows us to become aware of, detect, and track phenomenal properties that are independent of our introspective access to them. So a claim about what introspection can and cannot discern that is understood in an impersonal way (Constraint 2) does not commit to any claim about the capacities for judgement that the subject of experience does and doesn't have, and, moreover, it doesn't involve any claim about what a faculty of inner observation would or would not be able to discern if it encountered that experience. Rather, it specifies the kind of phenomenally conscious *perceptual* perspective the subject has, and thereby specifies how things perceptually seem to her. And this is what is needed to accommodate the case of the dog.

As we have seen, Martin's defense of naïve realism in response to the objections raised by the argument from causally matching hallucination is intricate and has a number of moving parts. This is because the tenability of the naïve realist view, in the face of that argument, depends on making coherent a position that adequately accommodates a number of different constraints. Key elements of Martin's attempt to offer such a coherent position, are the proposals he makes about how we should understand the modal notion of indiscriminability that's in play in naïve realist's talk of 'introspective indiscriminability', and the proposals he makes about the model of introspection we should adopt when our concern is with the way in which we introspect our phenomenally conscious experiences. Making further progress on assessing Martin's account will depend on settling whether those proposals are defensible.

An important point to note, however, is that the naïve realist may not need to apply to *all* cases of hallucination, whatever account she proposes to endorse in the case of causally matching hallucination. The intricate negative epistemic account of causally matching hallucination that Martin proposes is supposed to offer the naïve realist a defensible response to the screening-off objection. The screening-off objection is pressing once it is conceded that the kind of psychological effect that occurs in the case of causally matching hallucination also occurs in the case of the corresponding veridical perception. And it is the claim that causally matching hallucination has the same kind proximate cause as veridical perception that makes persuasive that assertion. So the same screening-off objection won't apply to all cases of hallucination, unless it is assumed that the only way in which one can have a hallucination of an F is by undergoing an experience that involves the same proximate cause, or brain state, as a veridical perception of an F.

Specifying conditions that are together necessary and sufficient for an experience to count as a hallucination is far from straightforward. But it's not clear that we're warranted in assuming that an experience only counts as a hallucination if it involves exactly the same kind of proximate cause, or brain state, as a veridical perception. Indeed it's not clear that we're warranted in assuming that an experience only counts as a case of hallucination if it has a phenomenal character that is *impersonally* introspectively indiscriminable from a veridical perception. A subject may think she is a perceiving an F when she isn't, and she may think this because she is having an experience that she isn't able to discriminate from a veridical perception of an F. We might reasonably categorise that experience as a hallucination. But in doing so, we need not assume that the subject's experience is *impersonally* introspectively indiscriminable from a veridical perception. There may be invariably many different factors that could potentially interfere with a subject's ability to discriminate her experience from a veridical perception of an F on a particular occasion. And the presence of such factors may be consistent with its being the case that her experience has a phenomenal character that is *impersonally* introspectively discriminable from a veridical perception.

So the naïve realist, and more generally the disjunctivist, may say she is not obliged to provide a positive metaphysical, or psychological, account of the kind of experience that's common to all cases of hallucination; we should not assume that there is any such uniform account to be given. It is possible that phenomenal/psychological episodes of quite different kinds may be involved in different cases of hallucination, and there may be different factors at work in explaining why any such given episode is taken, or may potentially be taken, to be a veridical perception when it isn't. A similar point was made by Austin, who remarked,

> there is no neat and simple dichotomy between things going right and things going wrong; things may go wrong, as we all know quite well, in lots of *different* ways – which don't have to be, and must not be assumed to be, classifiable in any general fashion.
>
> (1962: 13)

As I have been emphasising, disjunctivism can be thought of as a negative thesis that is adopted in defense of a positive view of veridical perception. Endorsement of the negative thesis involves denying that the sort of conscious perceptual experience that you have when you successfully perceive your environment is one you could be having if you were hallucinating. So from the point of view of the disjunctivist, what is important is that her account of veridical perception should be consistent with the existence of hallucination, and so consistent with the various ways in which 'things may go wrong'. And adopting this stance need not commit the disjunctivist to thinking that there is any uniform account to be given of all the ways in which things may go wrong. There may be no positive, fully general, account to be given of the 'bad' disjunct. And indeed one finds no commitment to there being any such positive account to be given in Hinton's original formulation of the disjunctive claim. A typical formulation of the disjunctive claim that one finds in Hinton's work is the following: Either I am seeing a flash of light or I am having an illusion of a flash of light. And a remark he makes about the latter disjunct is that 'the illusion of seeing a flash of light is the *disjunction* of cases that are not, but to the subject are like, seeing a flash of light' (1967: 218–19, my emphasis). He comments that if one says that one is having an illusion of seeing a flash of light, one does not give a definite answer to the question of what is happening, 'as distinct from an implicitly disjunctive answer' (219). This point will be relevant to our discussion of what a disjunctivist can and should say about illusion, as opposed to hallucination, and it is to that issue that we now turn.

6.3 Perceptual illusion

The distinction between illusion and hallucination is commonly presented as turning on the question of whether perceptual contact is made with some aspect of the environment. According to this way of drawing the distinction, in the case of a hallucination the subject isn't perceptually aware of an item in her environment, even though it seems to her as though she is. In the case of illusion, meanwhile, the subject succeeds in perceiving some item in her environment, but the item she perceives isn't the way that it perceptually appears to her to be. However, not all instances of hallucination will be marked by a *complete* failure to make perceptual contact with the environment. In some cases a subject may succeed in perceiving certain aspects of her environment even though there are hallucinatory elements to the experience she is having, for example a subject may succeed in perceiving the table in front of her, while she is hallucinating a pink rat sitting on top of it. We might categorise such experiences as 'partial' hallucinations, or 'superimposed' hallucinations,[11] and the legitimacy of this category might lead one to question whether certain putative cases of illusion are best treated as superimposed hallucinations. That is to say, the legitimacy of the category of superimposed hallucination might lead one to question whether certain cases of putative illusion are best treated as cases in which the subject is having a superimposed hallucination of the feature that the item she perceives seems to have and lacks.

Martin (2004) offers a sketch of how a naïve realist might develop an account of partial hallucination. He suggests that rather than focusing on experiences *per se*, we can focus on the various *aspects* of an experience: 'the different entities that one can experience and the ways in which they can appear to one' (2004: 81). We can then explain those aspects of a partial hallucination that are not genuinely perceptual in terms of 'that aspect of experience's indiscriminability from the corresponding aspect of a perceptual awareness of that element' (2004: 81). So, one option that may be open to a disjunctivist is to take up this suggestion about partial hallucination and apply it to certain putative cases of illusion.

However, this isn't to suggest that the disjunctivist is obliged to treat all putative cases of perceptual illusion as instances of partial/superimposed hallucination. As I remarked earlier, although it is crucially important to the disjunctivist that her account of veridical perception should be consistent with the existence of hallucination and illusion, this need not commit her to thinking that there is any uniform account to be given of all the ways in which things may 'go wrong'. And she might hold that the use of the single umbrella term 'illusion' masks various different ways in which things can go wrong, and that there are very different accounts to be given of each.

In a discussion of some of the significant differences that can be identified between different examples of illusion, Fish (2009) marks distinctions between the following three broad categories: 'physical illusion', 'optical illusion', and 'cognitive illusion'. In the case of those experiences that Fish labels 'physical illusion', the explanation of why things appear as they do is a matter of how things are in the external world.

> For example, to explain why the stick in water appears bent, we need only appeal to the natural physical phenomenon of light being refracted as it passes through materials of different refractive indices. In a sense, then, the explanation of the illusion ... is complete by the time we get to the subject. Even if our perceptual processing of this visual information is unimpeachable, as often it is, we will still suffer from an 'illusion' because of the particular way that things out there in the world affect the patterns of light incident upon our retina.
>
> (2009: 148)

Fish notes that physical illusions of this kind are predictable, intersubjective, and can be photographed. The experiences that he labels 'optical illusions', are also predictable, and intersubjective; but they differ from physical illusions because they cannot be *completely* accounted for by appeal to the way the subject's environment affects the patterns of light incident on her retina. In the explanation of these illusions, some kind of appeal also has to be made to the systematic and predictable way in which the subject's perceptual processing of the information that reaches her retina plays a role in generating a misleading perceptual appearance. Fish cites as examples of such illusions the Mueller-Lyer illusion, the Ponzo illusion, the Ebbinghouse illusion, and Kanisza triangle. Fish's category of 'cognitive illusions', in contrast to optical illusions, covers cases that are not usually intersubjective and predictable.

They involve cases in which a subject responds in an idiosyncratic way to what she perceives. Fish gives as an example a case in which a subject sees a coil of rope, which she takes to be a snake.

It is not obvious that there is some uniform account of illusion to be given that would adequately cover all of these different cases, and there is certainly plenty of scope for disagreement about which, if any, it would be appropriate to treat as instances of superimposed hallucination. Moreover, as the category of 'physical illusion' suggests, there may even be scope for disagreement as to which experiences it is appropriate to regard as 'illusory' at all. For instance, should we regard the perception of things like rainbows, and reflections, and echoes, as cases in which we are being misled by our senses? Is it correct to say that in such cases we perceive some aspect of our environment that isn't the way it perceptually appears to be? One might think that answers to such questions should turn on the following two factors: (a) what there actually is in our environment, and (b) what our senses are telling us about what there is in our environment. However, there is no philosophically neutral way to settle either of these factors.

Consider, for instance, something as ubiquitous as our visual experience of colours. Are such experiences in fact illusory? An answer to that question will depend on what we think colours are, and what we think our visual experiences purport to indicate about their nature. But those are highly contested philosophical issues, and so controversy over those substantive philosophical issues will be inherited by debates about whether such experiences are illusory. And an important point to emphasise here is that while one arena of debate may centre on controversies surrounding the metaphysical status of the manifest (e.g. the metaphysical status of colours, sounds, odours, tastes, rainbows, shadows, reflections), there are also debates to be had about what our perceptual experiences purport to indicate, or tell us, about the items we perceive.

For some, the question of what our perceptual experiences purport to indicate or tell us about what we perceive falls to the question of what the veridicality conditions of our perceptual experiences are. However, there are others who argue that this sort of representational approach is fundamentally mistaken. Particularly notable, in this regard, is the line of objection to the representational approach that has been developed by Charles Travis, who cites Austin's *Sense and Sensibilia* as an important influence.[12] In *Sense and Sensibilia*, Austin writes though the phrase 'deceived by our senses' is a common metaphor, it *is* a metaphor; and this is worth noting, for in what follows the same metaphor is frequently taken up by the expression 'veridical' and taken very seriously. In fact, of course, our senses are dumb – our senses do not *tell* us anything, true or false.

(1962: 11)

Taking up this line of thought, Travis argues that when we perceive our environment, our senses confront us with what is there, and they bring our surroundings into view, but it is a mistake to think that there is anything in a perceptual experience to make it count as having some one representational content as opposed to countless others. It is a mistake to think that we simply read off from our perceptual experience some one set of veridicality conditions that our senses are testifying to. In that sense, they tell us nothing. In making out, or trying to make out what it is that we are confronted with, we may go wrong, and make false judgements, but when we are misled in this way, this is not because our senses non-veridically represent to us that the world is a certain way.

One form of response to this sort of scepticism about the utility of the notion of perceptual representational content, is to argue that a notion of a perceptual representational content with veridicality conditions is legitimised by a crucial role that it plays in the science of perception, as currently practised. In Chapter 2 I outlined the case that Burge makes for this claim. It should be noted, however, in Burge's argument there is no assumption that the veridicality conditions that are to be assigned to any given kind of perceptual state for the purposes of scientific theorising are ones that we should expect the subject of experience to be able to simply read off from the phenomenology of her experience, and within the representationalist camp, the question of what is and isn't represented within the content of perceptual experience remains a contested issue. So even for those who endorse the representationalist approach, it is by no means trivial to determine what our senses may be 'telling us'.

Nonetheless, despite such controversies, it may be said that we should all at least agree that the category of illusory perception is a legitimate one. Our perceptions of the environment can involve 'misleading' perceptual appearances, or perceptual appearances that are at least potentially misleading, and there remains the question of whether a disjunctivist faces any special difficulties in accommodating them. Well, let us consider the position of those who endorse a relational, naïve realist account of the phenomenal character of veridical perception. What options are available to the naïve realist when it comes to accounting for the existence of misleading, illusory conscious perceptions of our environment? As has already been noted, the naïve realist might appeal to the notion of superimposed hallucination when accounting for certain illusions. However, the minimal commitments of a naïve realist, relational view of conscious perception may be consistent with further options.

Although not all naïve realists endorse exactly the same account of conscious perception, the minimal commitments that distinguish their approach are the following:

(i) the phenomenal character of conscious perception is determined, in part, by the obtaining of a conscious perceptual relation – a conscious perceptual relation that obtains between the subject of experience and aspects of her mind-independent environment; and
(ii) the phenomenal character of the obtaining of that conscious perceptual relation is, in turn, constitutively determined, in part, by what the subject is related to.

The use of the qualifier 'in part', in each of these claims potentially leaves open a number of options for the naïve realist when it comes to accounting for cases of perceptual illusion.

Consider first the qualifier in claim (i). If the naïve realist isn't committed to holding that the phenomenal character of conscious perception is *exhaustively* determined by the obtaining of a conscious perceptual relation to aspects of the subject's mind-independent environment, then she may have open to her a variety of different options when it comes to accommodating the respect in which a conscious perception may mislead its subject; such a naïve realist may hold that a subject's mistaken response to what she perceives may be intelligibly influenced by *non*-relational phenomenal aspects of her experience, which contribute, in part, to the overall phenomenal character of her experience.

The qualifier in claim (ii) is also significant. In Chapter 1 I suggested that a relational approach to conscious perception might invite the notion that there is a division of phenomenological labour to be uncovered. According to that approach, while certain aspects of a conscious experience, and what it is like for one to have that experience, are to be explained in terms of the nature of the entities one is consciously related to when one has the experience, other aspects of the conscious experience, and what it is like for one to have the experience, may be explained in terms of the nature of the relation, the manner in which one is related to those entities. If the phenomenal character of the obtaining of such a conscious perceptual relation is regarded as the joint upshot of these two factors, then the naïve realist need not be restricted to citing only the environmental relata of the perceptual relation when accounting for the respect in which a conscious perception may mislead its subject. She may say that what one makes of what one perceives may be influenced by the manner in which one is related to what one perceives, as well as what one is related to. Likewise, the manner in which one is related to what one perceives may be influenced by a variety of factors, including viewing angle and lighting conditions.[13]

In this connection, Bill Brewer is a disjunctivist who has suggested that when there is some abnormality in, damage to, or interference with, the perceptual processes that enable the obtaining of a conscious perceptual relation of acquaintance with mind-independent objects in our environment, then a form of 'degraded acquaintance' may result.[14] Under such circumstances, a conscious perceptual relation obtains between the subject and aspects of her mind-independent environment, and the obtaining of this conscious relation constitutively determines the phenomenal character of the subject's experience. But in its degraded form, what is available for registration by the subject in virtue of the obtaining of that relation, may be significantly reduced. And this may lead the subject to make mistakes in categorising what she perceives.

Brewer doesn't assume that it is appropriate to apply this form of explanation in all cases of perceptual illusion, and he has proposed some further, alternative explanations that a disjunctivist might appeal to. He suggests that while some illusions may be due to degraded acquaintance, others may be due to superimposed hallucination, and yet others may be explained in the following way: the fact that a subject has an experience in which an object looks F when it isn't F, may simply be due to the fact that the subject is acquainted with that object from a point of view, or in circumstances, in which it has visually relevant similarities with paradigm Fs. These visually relevant similarities are:

> similarities by the lights of the various processes enabling and subserving visual acquaintance: similarities in such things as the way in which

light is reflected and transmitted from the objects in question and the way in which stimuli are handled by the visual system given its evolutionary history and our shared training and development.

(2015: 2)

Such visually relevant similarities between the perceived object and paradigm Fs can, according to Brewer, make intelligible the subject's taking that object to be an F, even though it isn't.

Some important points to note about this proposal are the following. Firstly, the explanation of the illusion depends, in part, on an appeal to the obtaining of a conscious perceptual relation of acquaintance, a conscious relation that obtains between the subject and the mind-independent item she perceives. So this much is certainly in keeping with the naïve realist, relational approach to conscious perception. Secondly, according to Brewer's proposal, the fact that a perceived object has visually relevant similarities with Fs, may be due, in part, to facts about the way our perceptual systems work: 'the way in which stimuli are handled by the visual system given its evolutionary history and our shared training and development.' However, this isn't to be understood as equivalent to the claim that in such circumstances our perceptual systems generate perceptual states that *represent* the object as being a way that it isn't. In Brewer's explanation of such illusions, there is no commitment to the sort of representational approach that Travis opposes, i.e. the approach that assumes that it is possible to identify one set of veridicality conditions that our senses are testifying to. So a disjunctivist endorsing Brewer's account of illusion might say the following: one can mistake an object for an F because it looks like an F, and the fact that the object looks like an F may be due, in part, to facts about our psychology (e.g. how our visual systems operate). But from this it doesn't follow that our visual systems *represent* that object *to be* an F.

The question of whether perceptual illusion is best handled by appeal to perceptual states with representational contents that are specified in terms of their veridicality conditions may turn on settling disagreements about the function of perception; for example, whether Burge is right to assert that perceptual systems have the function of yielding *veridical representations*.[15] They may also turn on disagreements as to whether an appeal to such representational contents can exhaustively account for the phenomenal character of conscious perceptual experience. If they cannot, then when we are misled by our perceptual experiences, it may be that we are being misled by aspects of the phenomenal character of experience that cannot be explained in representationalist terms.

In any case, debates about the phenomenal character of conscious perception are certainly at the heart of these disputes about perception, illusion, and hallucination. What some might regard as the naivety in the naïve realist view is the assumption it makes about the contribution made to the phenomenal character of conscious perception by the *worldly* items we perceive. For example, the assumption that the phenomenal character of a perception of a red object is to be explained, at least in part, by the *mind-independent* sensory quality of redness that we are consciously acquainted with when we have such an experience.[16] The tenability of that naïve realist stance will depend on whether a disjunctivist response to the problem of illusion and hallucination is defensible. But it will also depend on whether it is possible to defend a 'naïve' view of what the world contains in the face of arguments that purport to establish that perceptual illusion is far more prevalent than we naively assume. And at that point, debates about the naïve realist disjunctivist view of perception become inextricably bound up with more familiar, traditional philosophical debates about the status of our manifest view of the world.

6.4 Chapter summary

In this chapter we considered what disjunctivists can and should say about hallucination and illusion. We discussed the difficulties faced by the naïve realist in providing an adequate account of so-called 'causally matching' hallucination, i.e. a hallucination that involves the same kind of proximate cause and brain state as a veridical perception. We also discussed whether it is right to assume that there is a uniform account to be given of the experiences that are involved in all cases of illusion and hallucination; we considered debates and disagreements over which experiences it is appropriate to count as 'illusory'; and we considered how such debates impact on the options that are open to disjunctivists when it comes to providing accounts of the kinds of experiences that are involved in different cases of illusion and hallucination.

First, we critically examined a causal argument that purports to establish that the sort of psychological effect that is produced in the case of a 'causally matching' hallucination is also produced in the case of veridical perception.

We considered how this line of argument can lead to a 'screening-off' objection to naïve realism. According to this line of objection, if we don't need to appeal to anything more than this common psychological effect when it comes to providing an account of causally matching hallucination, this must mean that this common psychological effect suffices to account for the *phenomenal character* of causally matching hallucination. But if the psychological effect that is common to veridical perception and causally matching hallucination suffices to account for the phenomenal character of causally matching hallucination, then that common psychological effect will also suffice to account for the phenomenal character of veridical perception, in which case the psychological effect common to veridical perception and causally matching hallucination will screen off and make explanatorily redundant the naïve realist's account of the phenomenal character of veridical perception.

We discussed Fish's response to this argument, that of denying that the psychological effect that is common to cases of hallucination and veridical perception is sufficient to produce a phenomenally conscious perceptual experience. We also discussed Martin's response to the argument, which involves denying that it is possible to give a *positive, non-derivative* account of the kind of phenomenal event that occurs when one hallucinates. We critically examined Martin's proposal that the naïve realist should affirm that in the case of a causally matching hallucination, the phenomenal character of the experience one has is exhausted by its possession of the following negative epistemic property, that of being introspectively indiscriminable from a veridical perception. We considered various objections to Martin's proposal, and we saw that the tenability of Martin's proposal about causally matching hallucination depends on making coherent a position that adequately accommodates a number of different constraints. We saw that key elements of Martin's attempt to offer such a coherent position, are proposals he makes about how we should understand the 'impersonal' modal notion of indiscriminability that's in play in naïve realist's talk of 'introspective indiscriminability', and the proposals he makes about the model of introspection we should adopt when our concern is with the way in which we introspect our phenomenally conscious experiences. We also discussed the suggestion that the naïve realist may not need to apply to *all* cases of hallucination whatever account she proposes to endorse in the case of causally matching hallucination.

We then considered what disjunctivists can say about different cases of illusion. We discussed the distinctions that Fish draws between the following categories of illusion: 'physical illusion', 'optical illusion', and 'cognitive illusion'. We discussed the idea that disjunctivists may wish to provide different accounts of different sorts of illusion, for example by holding that some examples of illusion involve cases of 'superimposed' hallucination, whereas others involve cases of 'degraded acquaintance'. We also discussed Brewer's proposal that some cases of illusion are to be explained and accounted for in the following terms: the fact that a subject has an experience in which an object looks F when it isn't F, may simply be due to the fact that the subject is acquainted with that object from a point of view, or in circumstances, in which it has visually relevant similarities with paradigm Fs.

In our discussion of disagreements over the question of which experiences it is appropriate to count as illusory, we noted that while one arena of debate centres on controversies surrounding the metaphysical status of the manifest (e.g. the metaphysical status of colours, sounds, odours, tastes, rainbows, shadows, reflections), there are also debates to be had about what our perceptual experiences purport to indicate, or tell us, about the items we perceive. And we noted that there are those, such as Travis, who deny that the question of what our perceptual experiences purport to indicate or tell us about what we perceive falls to the question of what the veridicality conditions of our perceptual experiences are.

Notes

1 This version of the causal argument is a modified version of a causal argument that M. G. F. Martin introduces and considers in his 2004.
2 These are some of the features that Sturgeon (1998) appeals to in arguing that our default view should be the thesis that there is a common factor to veridical perceptions, illusions and hallucinations, the thesis that they all involve perceptual states of the same basic kind.
3 See Fish 2009, Chs. 4 and 5. See also Fish 2008.
4 We will be discussing the position of those who endorse this set of claims in Chapter 7.
5 For critical discussion of this screening-off objection, see Hellie 2013.
6 This is to oppose the suggestion made by Dancy (1995) that the disjunctivist can and should supply a positive account of hallucination.

7 See Siegel 2004 and 2008, Hawthorne and Kovakovich 2006, Johnston 2004, Pautz 2010 and 2011, Smith 2008, Sturgeon 2006 and 2008.
8 See Siegel 2004.
9 For discussion of this point, see Martin 2013.
10 For this line of objection to Martin's account, see Siegel 2008.
11 I take the terminology of 'superimposed' hallucination from Brewer 2011 and 2015.
12 See Travis 2004, and the papers collected in Travis 2013. Important too are Brewer's arguments against a representationalist approach in his 2011.
13 So in this view, what one makes of what one perceives may be influenced by what John Campbell labels the 'standpoint' of the subject. See 4.3 for the earlier discussion of this notion.
14 See Brewer 2015.
15 This is a claim for which Burge argues in his 2010.
16 For objections to this aspect of naïve realism, see Pautz 2006, 2011, 2013.

Further reading

Martin's discussion of, and response to, the causal argument from hallucination are to be found in his 2004, 2006, and 2013. For useful discussion of Martin's position on causally matching hallucination, see Nudds 2009. For detailed discussion of the screening-off objection, see Hellie 2013. For objections to Martin's negative epistemic account of hallucination, see Siegel 2004 and 2008, Hawthorne and Kovakovich 2006, Johnston 2004, Pautz 2010 and 2011, Smith 2008, Sturgeon 2006 and 2008.

For Fish's account of hallucination, see Fish 2008 and 2009, Chs. 4 and 5, and for Johnston's account of hallucination, see Johnston 2004.

For an argument for the claim that our default view should be the thesis that there is a common factor to veridical perceptions, illusions and hallucinations, see Sturgeon 2008. See also Millar 1996.

For Fish's account of illusions, see Fish 2009, Ch. 6. For Brewer's account of illusions, see Brewer 2008, 2011, and 2015. For an excellent discussion of colour illusion, see Kalderon 2011. For an argument for the claim that accommodating certain illusions poses significant difficulties for the disjunctivist, see Smith 2010.

For Travis' arguments against a representationalist approach see Travis 2004 and 2013. For further arguments against the representationalist approach, see Brewer 2011.

References

Austin, J. L., 1962, *Sense and Sensibilia*. Oxford: Oxford University Press.
Brewer, Bill, 2008, 'How to account for illusion', in Fiona Macpherson and Adrian Haddock (eds), *Disjunctivism: perception, action, knowledge*. Oxford: Oxford University Press, pp. 168–180.
——, 2011, *Perception and Its Objects*. Oxford: Oxford University Press.
——, 2015, 'The object view of perception', in *Topoi: an international review of philosophy*, 34: 1–13.
Burge, Tyler, 2010, *Origins of Objectivity*. Oxford: Oxford University Press.
Dancy, Jonathan, 1995, 'Arguments from illusion', *The Philosophical Quarterly*, 45: 421–438.
Fish, William C., 2008, 'Disjunctivism, indistinguishability, and the nature of hallucination', in Fiona Macpherson and Adrian Haddock (eds), *Disjunctivism: perception, action, knowledge*. Oxford: Oxford University Press, pp. 144–167.
——, 2009, *Perception, Hallucination, and Illusion*. Oxford: Oxford University Press.
Hawthorne, John and Kovakovich, Karson, 2006, 'Disjunctivism', *Proceedings of the Aristotelian Society, Supplementary Volumes*, 80: 145–183.
Hellie, Benj, 2013, 'The multidisjunctive conception of hallucination', in F. MacPherson and D. Platchias (eds), *Hallucination: philosophy and psychology*. Cambridge, MA: MIT Press.
Hinton, J. M., 1967, 'Visual experiences', *Mind*, 76 (April): 217–227.
Johnston, M., 2004, 'The obscure object of hallucination', *Philosophical Studies*, 103: 113–183.
Kalderon, M., 2011, 'Colour illusion', *Nous* 45 (4): 751–775.
Martin, M. G. F., 2004, 'The limits of self-awareness', *Philosophical Studies*, 120: 37–89.
——, 2006, 'On being alienated', in Tamar S. Gendler and John Hawthorne (eds), *Perceptual Experience*. Oxford: Oxford University Press, pp. 354–410.
——, 2013, 'Shibboleth: some comments on William Fish's Perception, Hallucination and Illusion', *Philosophical Studies* 163 (1): 37–48.
Millar, Alan, 1996, 'The idea of experience', *Proceedings of the Aristotelian Society*, New Series, 97: 75–90.

Nudds, M., 2009, 'Recent work in perception: naïve realism and its opponents', *Analysis*, 69: 334–346.
Siegel, S., 2004, 'Indiscriminability and the phenomenal', *Philosophical Studies*, 120: 90–112.
——, 2008, 'The epistemic conception of hallucination', in Fiona Macpherson and Adrian Haddock (eds), *Disjunctivism: perception, action, knowledge*. Oxford: Oxford University Press, pp. 205–224.
Smith, A. D., 2008, 'Disjunctivism and discriminability', in Fiona Macpherson and Adrian Haddock (eds), *Disjunctivism: perception, action, knowledge*. Oxford: Oxford University Press, pp. 181–204.
——, 2010, 'Disjunctivism and illusion', *Philosophy and Phenomenological Research*, 80 (2): 384–410.
Sturgeon, Scott, 1998, 'Visual experience', *Proceedings of the Aristotelian Society*, New Series, 98: 179–200.
——, 2006, 'Reflective disjunctivism', *Supplement to the Proceedings of the Aristotelian Society*, 80: 185–216.
——, 2008, 'Disjunctivism about visual experience', in Fiona Macpherson and Adrian Haddock (eds), *Disjunctivism: perception, action, knowledge*. Oxford: Oxford University Press, pp. 112–143.
Travis, Charles, 2004, 'The silence of the senses', *Mind*, 113 (449): 57–94.
——, 2013, *Perception: essays after Frege*. Oxford: Oxford University Press.

7

VARIETIES OF DISJUNCTIVISM

In the literature on disjunctivism, a variety of different forms of disjunctivism have been distinguished, and one finds disagreements about how best to formulate a central disjunctivist commitment that is common to them all. For those approaching the topic of disjunctivism for the first time, these disagreements about how to formulate disjunctivism, and the proliferation of labels attached to different varieties of disjunctivism, can sometimes appear to be a hindrance, rather than a help, when it comes to attaining a clear understanding of what is really in dispute between disjunctivists and their opponents. However, it is important to be aware that that there can be significant differences between some of the views of perception that fall under the disjunctivist label.

As I have been emphasising throughout, disjunctivism is best thought of as a defensive strategy that is adopted in defence of some positive view of perception in the face of considerations that are invoked to challenge and undermine that positive view of perception. The considerations in question centre on claims about what is common to cases of veridical perception, illusion, and hallucination. The disjunctivist is concerned to resist any assumptions about what is common to all three cases that would render as untenable their favoured view of veridical perception. However, not all disjunctivists share exactly the same positive account of veridical perception, and where there is variation in the positive accounts of veridical perception that are endorsed by those who fall under the disjunctivist label, this can be due to differences in the factors motivating whatever positive account of perception they recommend. For example, as we have seen, those who adopt disjunctivism in defence of their positive view of perception might be motivated to adopt their favoured view of perception by any one or more of the following considerations: the concern to provide an account of the phenomenal character of conscious perception, a concern with the role played by perception in enabling, grounding and explaining our distinctive capacity for perceptually based thought about the items we perceive, the role played by conscious perception in grounding our concepts of the objects and features in the environment that we perceive, opposition to a representationalist account of perceptual experience, and a concern with the warranting role played by perception in grounding our acquisition of propositional knowledge about our surroundings. Such variation in motivating factors can lead to variation in the commitments that are incurred by any given disjunctivist, which in turn can introduce variation in the constraints they are under when it comes to addressing the question of what veridical perception, illusion, and hallucination have in common.

Now that we have considered some of the central concerns and arguments of some of the main protagonists in debates about disjunctivism, we are well placed to review and note some of the differences between the views of perception that fall under the disjunctivist label, and consider the discussions about different varieties, and formulations of, disjunctivism that one finds in the literature. That is the topic of this final chapter.

7.1 Fundamental kinds and psychological difference

Common to all disjunctivists is a commitment to the proposal that the sort of conscious perceptual experience that you have when you successfully perceive your environment isn't one you could be having if you were hallucinating. This leaves open a number of different options when it comes to further specifying what the difference between a veridical perception and hallucination might consist in. Some disjunctivists express their commitment to disjunctivism by invoking the notion of a *fundamental* kind. They deny that veridical perceptions and hallucinations are mental phenomena of the same *fundamental* kind.[1]

The assumption here is that in the case of the sort of conscious perceptual experience that's involved when one veridically perceives the world, there is a most specific answer to the question 'What is it?' that tells us what *essentially* that mental phenomenon is, and thereby specifies its *fundamental* kind. Those who express their commitment to disjunctivism in this way may allow that there is a kind K that veridical perceptions and hallucinations can both instantiate. However, what they deny is that such a kind K is the *fundamental* kind of mental phenomenon that's involved when a subject veridically perceives the world. For example, they might assert that the conscious perceptual experience that's involved when one veridically perceives the world is, essentially, a relational phenomenon, and/or a phenomenon that has the sort of conscious phenomenal character that the naïve realist claims is distinctive of successful perception.

A question we might pose about this particular way of formulating a commitment to disjunctivism is the following. Would the adoption of this sort of disjunctivist stance be inconsistent with the science of perception if, as Burge proposes, 'the science of perceptual psychology produces *fundamental* explanatory classifications that attribute a *common* kind or factor' to cases of veridical perception, illusion, and hallucination?[2] So, for example, could it be open to one to consistently endorse the following two assertions:

(a) the sort of conscious perceptual experience that's involved when one veridically perceives the world is, essentially and fundamentally, a relational phenomenon, and/or a phenomenon that has the sort of conscious phenomenal character that the naïve realist claims is distinctive of successful perception; and

(b) there are representational perceptual state-kinds that are common to veridical perception and hallucination and that are *fundamental* to the explanatory classification of perceptual states in the science of perceptual psychology?

Endorsement of claims (a) and (b) will result in inconsistency if an account of the representational perceptual state-kinds that are common to veridical perception and hallucination, and which are fundamental to the explanatory classifications offered by the science of perception, is taken to establish for us what conscious veridical perception most fundamentally, and essentially, is. And at this point a disjunctivist might question whether the science of perception really does establish this for us. Some of the questions one would need to address in order to make further progress on settling such disputes are the following. Is the nature of conscious perceptual experience *exhaustively* accounted for, and explained by, the relevant common representational perceptual state-kinds postulated by the science of perception? For example, does the postulation of these representational perceptual state-kinds adequately account for the phenomenal character of conscious perception? And is this something that the science of perception has itself established? And if not, is the phenomenal character of a conscious perception inessential to it? Has the science of perceptual psychology established that there is no fundamental explanatory role to be assigned to the phenomenal character of conscious perception, for example of the sort that Campbell proposes?[3]

It isn't obvious that appropriate answers to these questions will inevitably end up showing that those who formulate their disjunctivism in terms of the notion of a 'fundamental kind' are adopting a stance that is inconsistent with the science of perceptual psychology as it currently stands. But some have suggested that those who adopt disjunctivism in defence of a positive view of perception (such as naïve realism) do not, in any case, need to commit to any controversial claim about fundamental kinds. For example, Byrne and Logue (2008) suggest that one may hold a naïve realist view according to which mind-independent objects, such as tables and trees, are constituents of the experience one has when one veridically perceives the world, without being committed to a further claim about what the *essence* of such episodes consists in. They also note that naïve realism is often motivated by phenomenological considerations, and they question whether introspective reflection on the phenomenology of the experience one has when one veridically perceives the world puts one in a position to learn anything about the *essence* of the experience one is having.

However, one might question whether a naïve realist who holds that the conscious perceptual experience involved in veridical perception is a *relational* phenomenon, and who appeals to introspective reflection in support of that claim, really should shy away from anything short of a commitment to the claim that such an experience is *essentially* and *fundamentally* relational:

as we discussed in Chapter 2, although those adopting a relational view of conscious perception may agree that when one successfully perceives one's environment, psychological events do occur and perceptual states do obtain, what is denied by the relationalist is that the conscious perceptual experience that one has when one veridically perceives one's environment *just is* some psychological event or state, or some combination of both, that can occur and obtain whether or not the relevant relation of conscious perceptual awareness obtains.

Having said that, some disjunctivists may be happy to express their disjunctivism without invoking the notion of a fundamental kind, and by instead simply emphasising the idea that there are significant *psychological differences* between cases of veridical perception and hallucination. According to this alternative way of formulating disjunctivism, the disjunctivist holds that veridical perceptions and hallucinations differ mentally in some significant respect, i.e. there are certain mental features that veridical perceptions have that hallucinations cannot have. So the disjunctivist rejects the claim that the differences between a case of veridical perception and a case of hallucination can simply be due to differences in the extra-mental states of affairs that obtain in those situations.

Where there is variation in the positive accounts of veridical perception offered by different disjunctivists, we can expect to find variation in their accounts of what these psychological differences and commonalities consist in. For example, some disjunctivists – i.e. those concerned to defend a naïve realist account of veridical perception – will deny that veridical perceptions and hallucinations have the same phenomenal character. But others may be happy to grant that veridical perceptions and hallucinations can have the same phenomenal character, for their concern may be to defend alternative proposals about the psychological differences between veridical perceptions and hallucinations.

So, for example, the disjunctivist who favours a representationalist approach to perceptual experience may hold that a veridical perception has a representational content that a hallucination cannot have. This sort of disjunctivist may hold that the representational content of a veridical perception is constitutively dependent on mind-independent objects, while the representational content of a hallucination is not. One route to this view proceeds through the claims that a veridical perception of the world is a perceptual state with a representational content containing *demonstrative* elements that refer to the mind-independent items in the environment that are perceived,[4] and that truth-evaluable representational contents with demonstrative elements that successfully refer are *object-dependent*. In this view, a particular experience E that is a veridical perception of a particular mind-independent object O will have a representational content with a demonstrative element that successfully refers to O, and a distinct particular experience E* will have a representational content with the same veridicality conditions only if its representational content contains a demonstrative element that also refers to O. If E* is a hallucination it will not have a representational content with a demonstrative element that successfully refers to O, so it will not have an representational content with the same veridicality conditions as E. Suppose we now add the following assumption: (A) If two experiences have representational contents which differ in their veridicality conditions, then this is not just a respect in which these mental events differ, it is also amounts to a difference in their mental kinds.[5] We can now derive the conclusion that veridical perceptions and hallucinations are experiences of different mental kinds. Assumption (A) needs to be made explicit, as it is controversial and not agreed upon by all.[6] But without entering into that controversy here, the general point to highlight for our purposes is the following: someone adopting the sort of representationalist view that I've just outlined may claim that it is possible for a veridical perception and a hallucination to have the same phenomenal character, for they may claim that it is possible for experiences to have the same phenomenal character despite the fact that they do not have the same representational content.

Those adopting this approach might claim that hallucinations have an existentially quantified representational content and they might hold that veridical perceptions also have a layer of content that is existential. They might then propose that this layer of existential content, which is present in experience whether or not one is veridically perceiving the world, provides a common mental factor for veridical and hallucinatory experiences. However, Tye (2007) recommends a somewhat different approach. He maintains that veridical perceptions have object-dependent singular representational contents that hallucinations cannot have, and he also holds that veridical perceptions and hallucinations can have the same phenomenal character. However, he rejects the claim that there is a layer of existential content that provides a common mental factor for veridical and hallucinatory experiences. According to Tye, veridical perceptions and hallucinations have representational contents that represent clusters of properties. In the case of veridical perception the cluster of properties is represented within a content that is singular and object-dependent, whereas in the case of hallucination the cluster of properties is represented within a content that is 'gappy'.[7] Tye's suggestion is that veridical perceptions and hallucinations have contents with a common structure, and this structure may be conceived as having a slot in it for an object. In the case of veridical perception the slot is filled by the object perceived, and in the case of hallucination the slot is empty, and hence the content is 'gappy'. Tye claims that the phenomenal character of a given visual experience is the cluster of properties represented by that experience, and he claims that this is why veridical perceptions and hallucinations can have the same phenomenal character.

Clearly, Tye's claim is one that the naïve realist will reject, for the naïve realist insists that a veridical perception has a phenomenal character that a hallucination cannot have. Whether the naïve realist can accept that both veridical perceptions and hallucinations involve perceptual states with representational contents that have a common structure is another matter. Some naïve realists are opposed to the postulation of perceptual representational content, and will deny this.[8] But others may take their naïve realist account of the phenomenal character of veridical perception to be consistent with the proposal that there obtain representational perceptual states that are common to cases of veridical perception and hallucination.[9]

7.2 Disjunctivism and common element claims

Some of the debates on how to formulate disjunctivism focus on the question of whether a disjunctivist can and should allow that there is a psychological element that is common to cases of veridical perception, illusion and hallucination. Byrne and Logue (2008 and 2009) apply the label *moderate* to a view that accepts the claim that veridical perception and hallucination are different in significant mental respects, despite having a common mental element, and they suggest that a commitment to this sort of claim is too weak to capture a distinctively disjunctivist stance on perceptual experience. Byrne and Logue (2008) propose that the label *metaphysical disjunctivism* should be reserved for an account of perceptual experience that commits to the claim there is *no* common mental element to veridical perception and hallucination. On this formulation a *moderate* view, such as Tye's, will not count as a disjunctivist one. Moreover, according to Byrne and Logue, those who deny that veridical perceptions and hallucinations are mental events of the same *fundamental* kind are not *thereby* committed to *metaphysical disjunctivism*, as Byrne and Logue use this label. For as they point out, those who reject the claim that veridical perceptions and hallucinations are mental events of the same fundamental kind need not deny that there is a common mental element to veridical perception and hallucination.

One concern with this way of formulating the disjunctivist commitment is that it may be too strong to accommodate the views of the majority of those who regard themselves as disjunctivists. So let us now review the commitments of some of the main protagonists in the these debates about disjunctivism – the naïve realists – and consider what they can and can't concede about a psychological element that is common to cases of veridical perception and hallucination, and consider whether any concession of the existence of such a common element would make inapposite the 'disjunctivist' label.

In Chapter 2, I suggested that someone endorsing Hinton's disjunctivism need not deny that there is some common effect that occurs both in cases of veridical perception and causally matching hallucination. According to Hinton, we may be justified in asserting that there is some common effect that occurs both when one genuinely perceives an O, and when one hallucinates an O. He says, 'It would be absurd not to posit that happening' (1967: 220). In Chapter 2 I also suggested that Hinton, and those naïve realists who adopt Hinton's disjunctivist defensive strategy, are not obliged to insist that the common effect that occurs in cases of veridical perception and causally matching hallucination is merely some brain state or neural condition: in adopting Hinton's disjunctivist stance one doesn't thereby rule out the possibility that there is a common *psychological* effect that occurs in cases of veridical perception and cases of causally matching hallucination. Moreover one doesn't thereby rule out that there may be a common psychological effect that plays an important explanatory role in the science of perception. In adopting Hinton's disjunctive strategy, what one rejects is a particular stance on what that common psychological effect will be.

According to Hinton, although we may be justified in asserting that there is something that happens both when one genuinely perceives an O, and when one hallucinates an O, the 'chimera' with which one has no reason to identify that common effect is some conscious experiential event that occurs both when one genuinely perceives an O, and when one hallucinates an O, and which has exactly the same introspectible, 'worn-on-the-sleeve', phenomenal properties in each case. So, those adopting Hinton's disjunctivist strategy can allow that there is a psychological effect common to veridical perception and hallucination, as long as they deny that this common psychological effect is a conscious experiential event the phenomenal properties of which account for the phenomenal character of the experience one has in the case of veridical perception.

As we saw in Chapter 6, consideration of the argument from causally matching hallucination reveals significant constraints on what a naïve realist can say about the phenomenal character of causally matching hallucination if they are to avoid the objection that an account of the phenomenal character of causally matching hallucination will 'screen off', and make redundant, any explanatory role that they might wish to assign to the phenomenal character that is distinctive of veridical perception. Given such constraints, the naïve realist will have to maintain one or both of the following claims:

(i) we can provide a positive account of a perceptual state that is common to cases of veridical perception and hallucination, but the obtaining of this perceptual state won't suffice to account for the phenomenal character of a causally matching hallucination.
(ii) There is no positive, non-derivative account to be given of the phenomenal character of a causally matching hallucination, for the phenomenal character of a causally matching hallucination is to be exhaustively accounted for in negative epistemic terms, in terms of its possession of the negative epistemic property of being introspectively indiscriminable from a certain veridical perception.

A naïve realist like Fish may accept claim (i) and withhold assent from claim (ii) on the grounds that we have no good reason to assume that a causally matching hallucination would involve a perceptual experience that has a phenomenal character.[10] But those naïve realists who are willing to grant the assumption that a causally matching hallucination would involve a perceptual experience that has phenomenal character, will need to endorse claim (ii) if they are to avoid the screening-off objection. In what respects, if any, are these naïve realists committed to a view that it would be appropriate to label 'disjunctive'? Here it might be said that there is no need to express in disjunctive form any psychological element that these naïve realists can allow is common to cases of veridical perception and causally matching hallucination. That common element may be some perceptual state, which we can give some positive account of, but which doesn't suffice to account for the phenomenal character of causally matching hallucination, as in claim (i). Or that common element may be something we can express in negative epistemic terms, as in claim (ii). So such common psychological effects needn't be expressed in disjunctive form.

However, it might be argued that the naïve realist will need to appeal to the sort of disjunctive 'neutral experience reports' that Hinton appealed to when it comes to responding to a certain line of objection to her account of the phenomenal character of causally matching hallucination. Recall that in Chapter 6 we considered a concern that one might have as to whether the naïve realist really does succeed in specifying a phenomenally conscious condition of the subject if she restricts herself to characterising the phenomenal character of causally matching hallucination in purely *negative* epistemic terms. The concern is that the negative epistemic condition merely tells us what *cannot* be known by introspection; it doesn't specify what *can* be known by introspection, and it is only by specifying what can be known by introspection that we can ensure that there is a phenomenally conscious perceptual perspective there at all. I suggested that it may be open to the naïve realist to say the following in response. There is, after all, something positive that is discernible by introspection about the phenomenal character of a causally matching hallucination. For one thing that is introspectively discernible is the truth of the following *disjunctive* claim: either (a) the experience has the phenomenal character of a veridical perception of an F, or (b) it merely seems as if that is so. So arguably, the naïve realist will find that in the end she does need to appeal to disjunctive claims (or claims that are equivalent to, and no more committal than, such disjunctive claims), when it comes to specifying what *positive*, yet neutral, experience reports are warranted by introspective reflection on the phenomenal character of conscious perceptual experience. And for that reason alone, one might hold that 'disjunctivism' is an appropriate label for the view they commit to.

7.3 Epistemological disjunctivism and its metaphysical commitments

A further distinction between forms of disjunctivism that one finds discussed in the literature is the distinction between *epistemological* disjunctivism and *metaphysical* disjunctivism.[11] In Chapter 5, we touched on the question of whether those disjunctivists who are motivated by epistemological concerns (and in particular those like McDowell who are motivated by a concern with the role played by perception in warranting *propositional* knowledge) need commit to a form of metaphysical disjunctivism at all. As we have seen, not everyone agrees on how we should characterise the commitments of those who endorse a 'metaphysical disjunctivism'. And such disagreement is likely to impact on an assessment of whether epistemological disjunctivists can and should commit to a form of metaphysical disjunctivism. However, as I noted in Chapter 5, our assessment of whether an epistemological disjunctivist needs to commit to a form of metaphysical disjunctivism is also complicated by the fact that there are different strands to the sort of epistemic proposal that McDowell recommends, some of which appear to involve a commitment to some form of metaphysical disjunctivism, and others of which don't. And some may be willing to accept only those aspects of McDowell's proposal that don't commit one to a form of metaphysical disjunctivism.[12] And for such philosophers, there will remain the question of whether they are endorsing a form of disjunctivism, an epistemological disjunctivism that doesn't commit to any metaphysical disjunctivist thesis.

Consider, for instance, McDowell's suggestion that if we give an *epistemic* characterisation of our fallible perceptual capacity in terms of the notions of *conclusive* warrant and *knowledge* of our environment, then we make room for the idea that a successful, non-defective exercise of that capacity does not yield anything less than conclusive warrant.[13] Here it might be said that in making room for that idea we thereby show that the following 'highest common factor' claim is not obligatory: when you successfully perceive your environment, the warrant that you have for making judgements about your environment is no better than, no stronger than, the warrant that you would have for making such judgements if you were having a subjectively indistinguishable hallucination. As I noted in Chapter 5, it is not clear that someone making this sort of defensive move against this *epistemically* expressed highest common factor claim need commit to a form of metaphysical disjunctivism: it is not clear why we should assume that defective and non-defective exercises of an epistemically characterised capacity cannot involve psychological states of the same metaphysical kind. In which case, it may be open to an advocate of this particular aspect of McDowell's epistemic proposal to disavow any association with any further claims that might commit her to a form of metaphysical disjunctivism.

I shan't at this point rehearse again why one might think that there are further strands to McDowell's overall epistemic proposal that appear to commit him to some form of metaphysical disjunctivism; those details can be found in Chapter 5. The general point I want to highlight here is simply this. When approaching the question of the metaphysical commitments of any of those who endorse a form of epistemological disjunctivism, we can't simply depend on hasty generalisations. Our assessment of that question in any given instance will have to depend on a careful consideration of the particular claims, concerns, and arguments that are being advanced.

7.4 Disjunctivism in Snowdon's argument against the causal theory of perception

A further important consideration to keep in mind when assessing the metaphysical commitments of those who appeal to a disjunctive conception of perceptual experience, is the particular *dialectical* use that they make of that appeal. For some philosophers associated with the disjunctive theory of perception are simply concerned to argue that certain common element claims lack adequate justification, thereby leaving us free to resist arguments about perception that depend upon such claims in their premises. For example, Paul Snowdon, one of the philosophers most associated with the disjunctivism, appeals to the *possibility* of a disjunctive approach to perceptual experience in order to undermine an argument for a thesis about our *concept* of perception.[14]

According to the thesis that Snowdon aims to challenge it is a conceptual requirement that, necessarily, if S (a subject) sees O (an object) then O is causally responsible for an experience undergone by (or had by) S. This thesis has been labeled the Causal Theory of Perception (henceforth it will be referred to as the CTP). There are a few points to note about this way of stating the CTP:

(i) what is distinctive of this way of stating the CTP is the idea that it is a *conceptual* requirement that the causal condition hold if the subject is to see objects in the world. So someone who accepts that it is a general empirical truth that when we perceive the world our experiences are usually caused by the objects we perceive need not be committed to this conceptual thesis;

(ii) the thesis makes a claim about what is required for seeing *objects*, and does not specify what is required for seeing properties of objects;
(iii) the thesis involves a claim about what is *necessary* for seeing an object, and does not commit to the claim that the obtaining of this condition is *sufficient* for seeing an object;
(iv) the necessary requirement for seeing an object that is specified is not simply that the object must causally affect the percipient of the object, but that the object must cause the subject's experience.

H. P. Grice (1961) originally propounded the main argument for the CTP.[15] Grice's argument takes the following general form. We are asked to consider cases in which a subject is having an experience appropriate for seeing an object of a certain kind, for example, the subject is having an experience such that it seems to her as if there is a clock in front of her. There is in fact a clock in front of the subject; however, the subject fails to see the clock, for the subject's experience is a hallucination, perhaps induced by a neuroscientist stimulating her visual cortex. It is argued that such cases are indeed conceivable, and that in such cases the best explanation of the subject's failure to see the object before her is the absence of an appropriate *causal* connection between the object and her experience. Hence the CTP is justified.

According to Snowdon, the plausibility of this argument rests on a conception of perceptual experience that is wedded to a common element assumption, in particular, the assumption that the kind of experience one has when one genuinely perceives the world is one whose intrinsic nature is independent of the kinds of objects perceived. On this conception of experience, experiences are amongst the events, the intrinsic natures of which are independent of anything outside the subject. According to this view, the 'looks' sentences that are true in cases of hallucination and in veridical perception (e.g. 'It looks to S as if there is an F') are made true by (or are true in virtue of) exactly the same kind of occurrence in both cases. Once this conception of perceptual experience is in play, we might then ask after the extra-mental conditions required for seeing objects in our environment. The Gricean thought experiments suggest that simply having an experience that matches your surrounding environment will not, in itself, be sufficient for seeing objects in your environment. So the temptation then is to think that an appropriate causal connection between your experience and those objects is necessary for you to see them. The motivation for the CTP is therefore undermined, according to Snowdon, unless it can be shown that it is part of our *concept* of perception that the common element claim assumed in the argument is correct.

Following Hinton's lead, Snowdon argues that from the fact that 'looks' sentences are true in cases of hallucination and in veridical perception, and are not ambiguous, it does not follow that they are made true by (or are true in virtue of) exactly the same kind of occurrence in both cases, for they may instead have disjunctive fulfillment conditions. According to the disjunctive theory Snowdon considers, the claim that 'It looks to S as if there is an F' should be treated as being true in virtue of two distinct sorts of states of affairs: *either* (there is something which looks to S to be F) *or* (it is to S as if there is something which looks to S to be F). This disjunctive theory allows that the two cases (perception and hallucination), which are described in the same way, might be of a quite different nature. In particular it allows that the kind of experience a subject has when she genuinely perceives the world is such that its nature is not independent of the kinds of objects perceived.

Snowdon remarks 'in general, with concepts that will be acknowledged to be causal, there is a manifest effect end involved in their instantiation' (1990: 137). However:

> when we see an item there is nothing in the occurrence which is both manifest to us and can count as an effect induced by, and hence separate from, the item seen ... In perception there is nothing to latch on to other than the world; in particular, there is no such thing as a state produced in us, and which is manifestly distinct from the world, to which we can attend.
>
> (1990: 136)

Snowdon accepts that this line of thought against the causal theory is not decisive, but he suggests, it does highlight the burdens on its proponents. And for Snowdon, the important point is that the availability of the disjunctive approach to perceptual experience undermines the argument for the CTP, unless proponents of the argument can say something which is legitimately *conceptual* and which shows that this disjunctive approach must be wrong. So it's worth noting that according to Snowdon, an assertion of the disjunctive theory is not actually needed for a rejection of the Gricean argument for the CTP.

7.5 Conclusion

Given the range of different positions, concerns, and arguments advocated by those who have been labelled 'disjunctivists', one might be sceptical of the very idea that there is a *theory of perception* – a *disjunctive theory of perception* – that is common to them all. And if such scepticism is warranted, then who should we say has genuine propriety over the disjunctivist label?

In a way, these debates about labels are of secondary importance. Of more central concern are the substantive philosophical positions and arguments that these disjunctivists have advanced. As we have seen, their arguments, and the concerns that motivate them, are relevant to a number of key debates in the philosophy of perception, epistemology, and the philosophy of mind: debates about the metaphysics and phenomenology of perceptual consciousness; the relation – and differences – between thought and sensory experience; the epistemological role of perceptual experience; self-knowledge; our concept of perception. As I noted at the end of the previous chapter, some of these debates are also inextricably bound up with familiar, traditional philosophical debates about the metaphysical status of our manifest view of the world. Regardless of how we may choose to label the various positions that these disjunctivists defend, the substantive philosophical debates they have inspired seem set to continue.

7.6 Chapter summary

In this chapter we reviewed some of the differences between the views of perception that fall under the disjunctivist label, and we considered and clarified some of the discussions about different varieties, and formulations of, disjunctivism that one finds in the literature.

We discussed the way in which some disjunctivists express their commitment to disjunctivism by invoking the notion of a *fundamental* kind: they deny that veridical perceptions and hallucinations are mental phenomena of the same *fundamental* kind. We saw that some disjunctivists may be happy to express their disjunctivism without invoking the notion of a fundamental kind, and by instead simply emphasizing the idea that there are significant *psychological differences* between cases of veridical perception and hallucination. We noted that while some disjunctivists – i.e. those concerned to defend a naïve realist account of veridical perception – will deny that veridical perceptions and hallucinations have the same phenomenal character, others may be happy to grant that veridical perceptions and hallucinations can have the same phenomenal character, for their concern may be to defend alternative proposals about the psychological differences between veridical perceptions and hallucinations. Here, we outlined a view on which veridical perceptions and hallucinations are thought to be experiences of different mental kinds, because veridical perceptions have representational contents that hallucinations cannot have.

We then considered debates about how to formulate disjunctivism that focus on the question of whether a disjunctivist can and should allow that there is a psychological element that is common to cases of veridical perception, illusion and hallucination. We discussed the way in which Byrne and Logue (2008 and 2009) apply the label *moderate* to a view that accepts the claim that veridical perception and hallucination are different in significant mental respects, despite having a common mental element, and we discussed their proposal that the label *metaphysical disjunctivism* should be reserved for an account of perceptual experience that commits to the claim there is *no* common mental element to veridical perception and hallucination. Here, we reviewed the commitments of some of the main protagonists in the these debates about disjunctivism – the naïve realists – and considered what they can and can't concede about a psychological element that is common to cases of veridical perception and hallucination. We also considered whether any concession of the existence of such a common element would make inapposite the 'disjunctivist' label.

We then discussed the distinction between *epistemological* disjunctivism and *metaphysical* disjunctivism and considered whether those disjunctivists who are motivated by epistemological concerns need commit to a form of metaphysical disjunctivism at all.

Finally, we outlined the dialectical use that Paul Snowdon makes of his appeal to a disjunctive conception of perceptual experience. We discussed how Snowdon argues that the availability of the disjunctive approach to perceptual experience undermines the argument for the Causal Theory Perception, unless proponents of the argument can say something which is legitimately *conceptual* and which shows that this disjunctive approach must be wrong.

Notes

1 This formulation is principally due to Martin 2004 and 2006, but see also Snowdon 2005: 136.
2 Burge 2011: 48 (my emphasis).
3 See Chapter 4 for discussion of Campbell's proposal.
4 See Brewer 1999, Burge 1993, and Tye 2007. For objections to this idea see Davies 1992 and McGinn 1982.
5 See Brewer 1999.
6 For example Burge 1993, 2005, and 2010. For critical discussion of the assumption, see also Martin 2002.
7 For the proposal that hallucination has a 'gappy' content, see also Schellenberg 2010.
8 For example Travis 2004.
9 For discussion of the proposal that naïve realist/relational views are consistent with the postulation of perceptual states/events with representational content, see Siegel 2010, Schellenberg 2011 and 2014, Logue 2014, and Nanay 2014.
10 See Fish 2009.
11 See Byrne and Logue 2008 and Snowdon 2005.
12 For example see Millar 2007 and 2008. For a discussion of epistemological disjunctivism that is presented as being neutral on the question of metaphysical disjunctivism, see Pritchard 2012.
13 See McDowell 2010 and 2013.
14 See Snowdon 1980–1981, 1990, and 2011.
15 Other advocates of the theory include Pears 1976 and Strawson 1974.

Further reading

For discussions varieties of disjunctivism, and how to formulate disjunctivism, see Byrne and Logue 2008, the introduction to Byrne and Logue 2009, the introduction to Haddock and MacPherson 2008, and Snowdon 2005.

For the claim that veridical perceptions are perceptual states with representational contents containing *demonstrative* elements that refer to the mind-independent items in the environment that are perceived, see Burge 1993. For an appeal to such a claim in an argument for a disjunctivist view of perception, see Brewer 1999. See also Tye 2007. For a rejection of the idea that this claim should lead to a disjunctivist view, see Burge 1987,

2005, and 2011. For critical discussion of this issue, see also Martin 2002. Defence of the claim that perceptual experience has an existentially quantified content can be found in McGinn 1982 and Davies 1992.

For Snowdon's appeal to a disjunctive conception of experience in arguments against the CTP, see Snowdon 1980, 1990, 1998, and 2011. For the original arguments for the CTP, see Grice 1961, Strawson 1974, and Pears 1976. For a defence of the causalist approach against disjunctivism, see Lowe 2008. For a defence of the claim that disjunctivism is compatible with the CTP see Child 1992, 1994, and 2011.

References

Brewer, Bill, 1999, *Perception and Reason*. Oxford: Oxford University Press.

Burge, Tyler, 1983, 'Russell's problem and intentional identity', in James E. Tomberlin (ed.), *Agent, Language, and the Structure of the World*. Indianapolis: Hackett Publishing Company, pp. 79–110.

——, 1993, 'Vision and intentional content', in E. LePore and R. Van Gulick (eds), *John Searle and his Critics*. Oxford: Blackwell, pp. 195–213.

——, 2005, 'Disjunctivism and perceptual psychology', *Philosophical Topics*, 33: 1–78.

——, 2010, *Origins of Objectivity*. Oxford: Oxford University Press.

——, 2011, 'Disjunctivism again', *Philosophical Explorations*, 14 (1): 43–80.

Byrne, Alex and Logue, Heather, 2008, 'Either/or', in Adrian Haddock and Fiona Macpherson (eds), *Disjunctivism: perception, action, knowledge*. Oxford: Oxford University Press, pp. 57–94.

Child, William, 1992, 'Vision and experience: the causal theory and the disjunctive conception', *Philosophical Quarterly*, 42 (168): 297–316.

——, 1994, *Causality, Interpretation and the Mind*. Oxford: Oxford University Press.

——, 2011, 'Vision and causal understanding', in N. Eilan, H. Lerman, and J. Roessler (eds), *Understanding Perception, Causation and Objectivity*. Oxford: Oxford University Press.

Davies, M., 1992, 'Perceptual content and local supervenience', *Proceedings of the Aristotelian Society*, New Series, 92: 21–45.

Fish, William C., 2009, *Perception, Hallucination, and Illusion*. Oxford: Oxford University Press.

Grice, H. P., 1961, 'The causal theory of perception', *Proceedings of the Aristotelian Society, Supplementary Volumes*, 35: 121–152.

Haddock, Adrian and Macpherson, Fiona, 2008, *Disjunctivism: perception, action, knowledge*. Oxford: Oxford University Press.

Logue, Heather, 2014, 'Experiential content and naïve realism: a reconciliation', in Berit Brogaard (ed.), *Does Perception Have Content?* Oxford University Press, pp. 220–239.

Lowe, E. J., 2008, 'Against disjunctivism', in Adrian Haddock and Fiona Macpherson (eds), *Disjunctivism: perception, action, knowledge*. Oxford: Oxford University Press, pp. 95–111.

Martin, M. G. F., 2002, 'Particular thoughts and singular thought', in A. O'Hear (ed.), *Logic, Thought and Language*. Cambridge: Cambridge University Press, pp. 173–214.

——, 2004, 'The limits of self-awareness', *Philosophical Studies*, 120: 37–89.

——, 2006, 'On being alienated', in Tamar S. Gendler and John Hawthorne (eds), *Perceptual Experience*. Oxford: Oxford University Press, pp. 354–410.

McDowell, John, 2010, 'Tyler Burge on disjunctivism', *Philosophical Explorations*, 13 (3): 243–255.

——, 2013, 'Tyler Burge on disjunctivism (II)', *Philosophical Explorations*, 16 (3): 259–279.

McGinn, Colin, 1982, *The Character of Mind*. Oxford: Oxford University Press.

Nanay, B, 2014, 'The representationalism versus relationalism debate: explanatory contextualism about perception', *European Journal of Philosophy*, 23: 321–336.

Pears, David F., 1976, 'The causal conditions of perception', *Synthese*, 33 (June): 25–40.

Schellenberg, S., 2010, 'The particularity and phenomenology of perceptual experience', *Philosophical Studies*, 149 (1), pp. 19–48.

——, 2011, 'Perceptual content defended', *Nous*, 45 (4): 714–750.

——, 2014, 'The relational and representational character of perceptual experience', in Berit Brogaard (ed.), *Does Perception Have Content?* Oxford: Oxford University Press, pp. 119–219.

Siegel, Susanna, 2010, *The Contents of Visual Experience*. Oxford: Oxford University Press.

Snowdon, P. F., 1980–81, 'Perception, vision and causation', *Proceedings of the Aristotelian Society*, New Series, 81: 175–192.

——, 1990, 'The objects of perceptual experience', *Proceedings of the Aristotelian Society Supplementary Volumes*, 64: 121–150.

——, 1998, 'Strawson on the concept of perception', in L. Hahn (ed.), *The Philosophy of P. F. Strawson*. Chicago and Lasalle: Open Court, pp. 293–310.

——, 2005, 'The formulation of disjunctivism: a response to Fish', *Proceedings of the Aristotelian Society*, New Series, 105: 129–141.

——, 2011, 'Perceptual concepts as non-causal concepts', in N. Eilan, H. Lerman, and J. Roessler (eds), *Understanding Perception, Causation and Objectivity*. Oxford: Oxford University Press.

Strawson, P. F., 1974, 'Causation in perception', in *Freedom and Resentment*. London: Methuen, pp. 73–93.

Travis, Charles, 2004, 'The silence of the senses', *Mind*, 113 (449): 57–94.

——, 2007, 'Intentionalism and the argument from no common content', *Philosophical Perspectives*, 21 (1): 589–613.

GLOSSARY

Categorical: Categorical properties of an object are the underlying intrinsic, non-dispositional properties of an object that ground and explain the object's dispositions.

Causal theory of perception: According to the causal theory of perception it is a conceptual requirement that, necessarily, if a subject, S, perceives an object, O, then O is causally responsible for the perceptual experience undergone by (or had by) S.

Causally matching hallucination: A causally matching hallucination is a hallucination that is subjectively indistinguishable from a veridical perception and which involves the same kind of proximate cause and brain state as that involved in the corresponding veridical perception.

Conclusive warrant: Warrant for a belief is conclusive if and only if the believer's having that warrant is incompatible with the falsity of that belief.

Conscious character: In this book, the term 'conscious character' is used interchangeably with the term 'phenomenal character'. See **Phenomenal character**.

Credence: Credence is the degree of confidence in the truth of a proposition. The more confident you are in the truth of p, the higher your degree of credence in p.

Criterion of identity: A criterion of identity is a standard by which identity is to be judged, for example a standard for judging whether a concrete object

O that exists at time T is numerically identical with a concrete object O* that exists at a distinct time Tn.

Dependency thesis: The dependency thesis holds that to perceptually imagine an F is to imagine a perceptual experience of an F. Applied to the case of visualising, the thesis holds that to visualise an F is to imagine a visual experience of an F.

Distal cause: In a causal chain of events leading to an event E, an event D will be a distal cause of E, relative to some other event P in that causal chain of events, if D occurs earlier than P.

Entitlement: Epistemic entitlement is often characterised as a type of epistemic warrant that need not be fully accessible to the warranted subject. Those who acknowledge the existence of such entitlements maintain that a subject can be warranted in holding a belief by being epistemically entitled to that belief and that the subject can be so warranted without having the conceptual repertoire needed to understand their entitlement.

Empiricism about concept possession: To hold an empiricist account of a range of concepts is to hold that our grasp of those concepts depends on, and is ultimately grounded in, perceptual experience.

Epistemological disjunctivism: Epistemological disjunctivism is distinguished by its commitment to the following set of claims:

(a) there is a significant epistemic difference between the case in which you successfully perceive your environment and the case in which you have a subjectively indistinguishable hallucination;

(b) this epistemic difference is to be explained, at least in part, by appeal to a difference in the epistemic grounds for judgement that you have access to in each case;

(c) when all goes well and you successfully perceive your environment, you have access to conclusive grounds for judgements about your environment, i.e. epistemic grounds for judgement that don't leave open the possibility that those judgements are false.

Epistemological internalism/externalism: The epistemological internalist holds that a subject knows that p (or is justified in believing that p) only if that subject has, or can have, a form of access to the epistemic grounds that warrant their belief that p. The epistemological externalist, by contrast, denies that such access is necessary for knowledge/justified belief. According to one prominent version of internalism, which has been labelled 'mentalism', a subject's beliefs are justified only by that subject's mental states. The epistemological externalist, by contrast, allows that things other than that subject's mental states can operate as justifiers.

Functional role: The functional role of a mental state is the causal role that the state characteristically plays in the cognitive system of which it is a part. This causal role is often specified in terms of the state's causal relations to sensory stimulations, other mental states, and behaviour.

Fundamental kind: One formulation of disjunctivism invokes the notion of a fundamental kind. According to this formulation, the disjunctivist is committed to denying that veridical perceptions, illusions and hallucinations are conscious events of the same fundamental kind. The assumption here is that for mental events, there is a most specific answer to the question, 'What is it?' that tells us what essentially the mental event is, and thereby specifies its fundamental kind. On this formulation, the disjunctivist is committed to denying that whatever fundamental kind of conscious event occurs when one is veridically perceiving the world, that kind of event can occur whether or not one is veridically perceiving.

Gappy content: The notion of a 'gappy' content has been invoked by some as a way of accommodating the following two claims:

(a) Veridical perceptions, and only veridical perceptions, have representational contents that are singular and object-dependent;

(b) veridical perceptions and hallucinations have contents with a common structure.

In one such view, veridical perceptions and hallucinations have representational contents that represent clusters of properties, and in the case of veridical perception the cluster of properties is represented within a content that is singular and object-dependent, whereas in the case of hallucination the cluster of properties is represented within a content that has a 'gap', or slot in it, to be filled by a concrete object. In the case of veridical perception the slot is filled by the object perceived, and in the case of hallucination the slot is empty, and hence the content is 'gappy'.

Highest common factor claim: The claim that when you successfully perceive your environment, the warrant that you have for making judgements about your environment is no better than, no stronger than, the warrant that you would have for making such judgements if you were having a subjectively indistinguishable hallucination.

Intentionalism: Intentionalism about perceptual experience is that view that

  (a) our perceptual experiences are directed on the environment in a representational manner (i.e. in virtue of having a representational content that can be veridical/non-veridical);
  (b) that the phenomenal character of experience is determined by its representational properties.

Introspection/Introspective reflection: In this book the terms 'introspection' and 'introspective reflection' refer to the distinctive mode of access that one has to one's own mental states/events in virtue of being the subject of those mental states/events. On this understanding, one cannot introspect the mental states of others, and the knowledge that you acquire about your own mental states/events by introspection/introspective reflection does not depend on the testimony of others.

Introspectively indistinguishable/indiscriminable: An experience is said to be introspectively indistinguishable/indiscriminable from a veridical perception of an F if its subject cannot come to know via introspection alone that it is not a veridical perception of an F. In this book the terms 'introspectively indistinguishable/indiscriminable' and 'subjectively indistinguishable' are used interchangeably.

Mental event and mental state: A mental event is an aspect of mind that occurs, happens, and/or unfolds over time. A mental state, by contrast, occupies an interval of time by obtaining over that interval. Some hold that a subject's mental state is to be thought of as a psychological property of that subject, and on this conception one can think of the contrast between a mental state and a mental event as the contrast between a psychological property of a subject (state), and a psychological episode that the subject undergoes (event).

Metaphysical disjunctivism: In its broadest use, the term 'metaphysical disjunctivism' refers to a family of views that commit to the claim that veridical perception and hallucination differ in significant mental respects. Naïve realism is a prominent example of a metaphysical disjunctivist view. Unless explicitly stated otherwise, the use of the term should be understood in that broad way in this book. Byrne and Logue deploy the term 'metaphysical disjunctivism' in a more restrictive way, reserving it for accounts of perceptual experience that commit to the claim that there is no common mental element to veridical perception and hallucination.

Moderate views: 'Moderate' is a label that Byrne and Logue have applied to any view that accepts the claim that veridical perception and hallucination are different in significant mental respects, despite having a common mental element.

Naïve realism: According to naïve realism, when one veridically perceives the world, the mind-independent items perceived, such as tables and trees and the properties they manifest to one when perceived, partly constitute one's conscious experience, and hence determine its phenomenal character.

Negative epistemic condition: A negative epistemic condition is a condition that is specified in terms of what cannot be known when one is in that condition. For example, M. G. F. Martin's negative epistemic characterisation of the phenomenal character of causally matching hallucination appeals to a claim about what cannot be known about the phenomenal character of the experience via introspection.

Neutral experience report: 'Neutral experience report' is a term used by Hinton to refer to the kind of report we make about an experience we are undergoing when we are remaining neutral on the question of whether that experience is a veridical perception, an illusion, or a hallucination. For example, when making a report about one's experience in this neutral way one might say 'I seem to see an F', which can be true whether or not one is actually seeing an F, or one might make a claim about what appears to one to be the case.

Non-conceptual content: The content of a mental state/event is said to be non-conceptual if the subject of that mental state/event need not possess any of the concepts that we, as theorists, exercise when we state the veridicality conditions for that content.

Object-dependent representational content: Those who hold that the representational content of successful perception is object-dependent endorse the following claim. When a subject perceives an object in her environment, the conditions required for the content of the subject's experience to be veridical depends on the identity of the particular object being perceived. That is to say, the subject could not be having an experience with the same veridicality conditions if she were not perceiving that particular object (e.g. if she were instead perceiving a qualitatively indistinguishable, but numerically distinct, object).

Perceptual warrant: Perceptual warrant is the epistemic ground for judgement/belief that is made available to a subject in virtue of having a perceptual experience.

Phenomenal character: If there is something it is like for a subject to be in a given mental state, or undergo a given mental event, then that mental state/event is said to have a phenomenal character. The phenomenal character of the mental state/event is what it is like for its subject to be in that mental state, or undergo that mental event. In this book the term 'phenomenal character' is used interchangeably with the term 'conscious character'.

Phenomenal concept: Phenomenal concepts are concepts of phenomenal properties/phenomenal character that a subject can acquire and possess only if she has or has had experiences of the relevant phenomenal kind.

Phenomenal properties: Phenomenal properties of an experience are those properties that determine the phenomenal character of the experience, i.e. that determine what it is like for its subject to have that experience.

Phenomenal zombie: Phenomenal zombies are imaginary creatures that feature in various thought experiments designed to illustrate problems about phenomenal consciousness. They are creatures exactly like us in all physical respects, who behave like us, but who lack experiences that are phenomenally conscious.

Proximate cause: In a causal chain of events leading to an event E, an event P will be a proximate cause of E, relative to some other event D in that causal chain of events, if P occurs later than D.

Proximality principle: According to the proximality principle, on any occasion, given the total antecedent psychological state of the individual and system, the total proximal input into the system suffices to produce a given type of perceptual state, assuming no malfunction or interference. This is a principle that Tyler Burge has suggested is implicit in the causal explanations offered by the science of perception.

Qualia: Qualia (singular, quale) are phenomenal properties of mental states or events, those properties of mental states or events that determine 'what it is like' to have them. In its broadest use, the term 'qualia' is used to refer to any phenomenal properties of mental states/events. In its more restrictive use (which is how the term is deployed in this book), the term refers specifically to intrinsic, non-representational phenomenal properties of experience that contribute to determining what it is like for one to have that experience.

Relational view of experience: According to those who hold a relational view of experience, the conscious character of perceptual experience is constitutively determined, at least in part, by the objects (and the properties of those objects) that one is perceptually aware of in having that experience.

The term is often used to refer specifically to naïve realist views of perception. In its broadest use, it can also be used to refer to sense-datum theories of perception, as sense-datum theorists hold that the phenomenal character of experience is constitutively determined, at least in part, by the sense-data (and their properties) that one is directly aware of in having that experience, and so they too advocate the idea that the phenomenal character of perceptual experience is to be explained, at least in part, by appeal to its relational structure.

Representational content (of perceptual experience): The notion of the representational content of experience is appealed to by those who hold that a subject's perceptual states represent to her how her environment is. The representational content of experience is how the world is represented to the subject to be. Such experiences are said to be veridical if the representational content is correct and the world is as represented.

Sense-datum theory of perception: According to the sense-datum theory, whenever one has a conscious perceptual experience one is perceptually aware of entities – sense-data – that are not the mind-independent material objects that we ordinarily take ourselves to perceive. Many sense-datum theorists regard these entities as mind-dependent, existing only when sensed, whereas others hold they are mind-independent, albeit distinct from the sorts of mind-independent material objects, such as rocks, tables and chairs, that we ordinarily take ourselves to perceive.

Separatism: Separatism is the view that all phenomenal and intentional aspects of mind are mutually independent and entirely separable. Phenomenal aspects of mind are those for which there is something it is like for one to undergo them or be in them. Intentional aspects of mind are those aspects of mind in virtue of which our mental states are about, or directed upon, other things.

Standpoint: According to John Campbell we are to think perceptual consciousness of an object as a three-place relation between a person, a standpoint, and an object. He suggests that we need to factor in the notion of a 'standpoint' as our experience of objects is always, in some sense, partial. You always experience an object from a standpoint, and you can experience one and the same object from different standpoints. The notion of standpoint encompasses the position of the perceiver, the modality of perception, and in the case of vision such factors as the relative orientations of the perceiver and the entities she perceives, and whether there is anything obstructing the light between them.

Subjectively indistinguishable: See **Introspectively indistinguishable/ indiscriminable**.

Veridicality conditions: Those who hold that perceptual experiences have representational contents (i.e. contents that represent the experiencing subject's environment as being a certain way), often specify the representational content of an experience in terms of its veridicality conditions. The veridicality conditions of an experience are the states of affairs that have to obtain if the environment is to be the way the subject's experience represents it to be.

INDEX

Austin, J. L. 17–18, 27, 44, 53, 183, 186–187

Brewer, B. 113, 114, 189–190, 193, 194, 213
Brogaard, B. 153, 154
Burge, T. 35–38, 46, 76–78, 84, 91, 153, 187, 190, 199, 222
Byrne, A. 28, 53, 54, 113, 114, 153, 200, 203–204, 212, 220, 221

Campbell, J. 3, 53, 111–113, 117, 200, 223; objections to Campbell's view 101–111; on colour 107–108; on the explanatory role of conscious perception 93–101
Cassam, Q. 113, 114
categorical quality/object 99–100, 104, 107–108, 217
causal argument against naïve realism 158–169
causal argument for sense-datum theory 19–26

causally matching hallucination 22–24, 41–45, 48–51, 158, 160–169, 217; *see also* negative epistemic account of hallucination
causal theory of perception 208–211, 213
Chalmers, D. 54
Child, W. 213
Cohen, J. 113, 114
conclusive warrant 128–129, 135, 140–146, 152, 207, 217
Conee, E. 153, 154
Crane, T. 28
Crowther, T. 81
Currie, G. 81
Cussins, A. 81

Dancy, J. 194
Davies, M. 213
demonstrative reference 86, 99, 100, 104, 114, 201–202
dependency thesis 67–68, 70–73, 75–78, 81, 110, 218

Dickie. I. 114
Dorsch, F. 81
Dretske, F. 53, 81, 153, 154

entitlement 138, 153, 154, 218
epistemological disjunctivism *see* McDowell and epistemological disjunctivism
epistemological externalism/internalism 145, 147–148, 153, 218
Evans, G. 53, 54, 81

Fish, W. 28, 166, 185–186, 192–193, 194, 205, 214
fundamental kind 198–203, 204, 211, 219

gappy content 203, 213, 219
Goldman, A. 154
Grice, P. 209–210, 213

Haddock, A. 153, 213
Hardin, C. L. 113, 114
Harman, G. 53, 54
Heck, R. 81
Hellie, B. 193, 194
highest common factor 118–119, 136–137, 140, 145–147, 151–152, 207, 219
Hilbert, D. 113, 114
Hinton, J. M. 44–53, 54, 176–177, 183, 204–206, 221
Horgan, T. 113

illusion: disjunctivist accounts of 184–191; vs. hallucination 184; and partial hallucination 184–185; varieties of 185–186
impersonal indiscriminability 174–176, 178, 181–183, 192

introspection 10, 220; and sense-datum theories 14–15; and the science of perception 34–35, 47; Hinton's discussion of 49

Jackson, F. 90, 113, 114
Johnston, M. 14, 113, 114, 168, 193

Kriegel, U. 113
Kalderon, M. 113, 114, 153, 154, 194

Langsam. H. 113, 114
Logue, H. 28, 53, 54, 153, 200, 203–204, 212, 220, 221
Lowe, E. J. 213

Macpherson, F. 153, 213
Martin, M. G. F. 28, 54, 80–81; objections to Martin's argument for naïve realism 74–80; on causally matching hallucination 167, 169–182, 192; on partial hallucination 184; phenomenological argument for naïve realism 65–74
McDowell, J. 4, 114, 118–120, 151–153, 207–208; and epistemological disjunctivism 127–136; objections to McDowell's epistemological disjunctivism 136–145; on scepticism 145–151
McGinn, C. 213
metaphysical disjunctivism 4, 120, 146–149, 153, 203–204, 207–208, 212, 220
Millar, A. 153, 154, 193
moderate views 203, 212, 221
Moore, G.E. 10–12, 14, 26, 28

Nanay, B. 213
negative epistemic account of hallucination 169–178, 180, 182, 192, 205–206
Neta, R. 153
neutral experience report 206, 221
Nida-Rümelin, M. 114
non-conceptual content *see* representational content and non-conceptual content
Noordhof, P. 81
Nudds. M. 193

object-dependent content *see* representational content and object-dependent content

Palmer, S. 53
Pautz, A. 54, 108, 113, 114, 194
Peacocke, C. 53, 54, 81, 153, 154
Pears, D. F. 213, 214
Price, H. H. 15
Pritchard, D. 153, 154, 214
proximality principle 36, 41, 46–48, 52–53, 222

qualia 38–39, 60, 85, 88–93, 96–98, 105, 165–167, 222

Ravenscroft, I. 81
representational content (of perceptual experience) 223: and conscious character 37, 60–65, 85, 220; and non-conceptual content 60, 102–103; and object-dependent content 201–202, 221; and perceptually based thought 85–86, 106–107; in the science of perception 32–35, 187
Robinson, H. 28

scepticism 122, 144, 145–154
Schellenberg, S. 213
screening-off objection to naive realism 167, 169–170, 176–177, 182, 192–193, 194
Searle, J. 53, 54
Sedivy, S. 114, 153
sense-data 15–17, 21–27, 38, 109, 223
sensory imagination *see* visualising
separatism 87, 92, 98, 104–105, 113, 223
Siegel, S. 53, 54, 173, 193, 194, 213
Smith, A. D. 28, 193, 194
Snowdon, P. 54, 153, 208–211, 212, 213, 214
standpoint 94, 194, 223
Strawson. P. F. 213, 214
Sturgeon, S. 193, 194

Thau, M. 153
Tienson, J. 113
Travis, C. 53, 186–187, 190, 193, 194, 213
Tye, M. 53, 54, 81, 113, 114, 202–204, 213

Vendler, Z. 81
visualising 67–77, 81; *see also* dependency thesis

Williams, B. 81, 121, 153
Wright, C. 145, 153
Williamson, T. 153, 154

eBooks
from Taylor & Francis

Helping you to choose the right eBooks for your Library

Add to your library's digital collection today with Taylor & Francis eBooks. We have over 50,000 eBooks in the Humanities, Social Sciences, Behavioural Sciences, Built Environment and Law, from leading imprints, including Routledge, Focal Press and Psychology Press.

Choose from a range of subject packages or create your own!

Benefits for you
- Free MARC records
- COUNTER-compliant usage statistics
- Flexible purchase and pricing options
- All titles DRM-free.

Benefits for your user
- Off-site, anytime access via Athens or referring URL
- Print or copy pages or chapters
- Full content search
- Bookmark, highlight and annotate text
- Access to thousands of pages of quality research at the click of a button.

REQUEST YOUR FREE INSTITUTIONAL TRIAL TODAY

Free Trials Available
We offer free trials to qualifying academic, corporate and government customers.

eCollections

Choose from over 30 subject eCollections, including:

Archaeology	Language Learning
Architecture	Law
Asian Studies	Literature
Business & Management	Media & Communication
Classical Studies	Middle East Studies
Construction	Music
Creative & Media Arts	Philosophy
Criminology & Criminal Justice	Planning
Economics	Politics
Education	Psychology & Mental Health
Energy	Religion
Engineering	Security
English Language & Linguistics	Social Work
Environment & Sustainability	Sociology
Geography	Sport
Health Studies	Theatre & Performance
History	Tourism, Hospitality & Events

For more information, pricing enquiries or to order a free trial, please contact your local sales team: www.tandfebooks.com/page/sales

www.tandfebooks.com